Praise for Untangled

"Lisa Damour's *Untangled* is the best description of the female adolescent journey that I have ever read. Empathetic and wise, every page is filled with a deep understanding of girls and their parents. If you read this book you will know what your daughter is experiencing, and with Damour's advice, you will know how and when (and when not) to talk to her about it."

—MICHAEL THOMPSON, PH.D., co-author of *Raising Cain*

"This is the book parents have been waiting, hoping, and praying for, because it's far more than a book. It's a map, flashlight, and GPS device for navigating the landscape of adolescent girlhood. Lisa Damour proves to be the perfect guide and companion: wise, whip-smart, and relentlessly practical on every page. As the father of three teenage girls, I wish I had this book years ago—and I hope that it is read by every parent, teacher, coach, administrator, and human being who wants to help girls grow and thrive in today's world."　　　　　　　—DANIEL COYLE, author of *The Talent Code*

"There are books about teenagers that are smart. And there are books about teenagers that are practical. Lisa Damour thankfully provides us with one that is both. With palpable empathy and understanding for adolescent girls and the families they reside in, Damour equips parents with a flexible blueprint for anticipating challenge and encouraging growth in their daughters. If you have a daughter (or were a daughter!) *Untangled* is mandatory reading."　—MADELINE LEVINE, PH.D., author of *The Price of Privilege*

"In exceptionally clear prose, Damour—a clinical psychologist—skillfully blends research analysis, psychological insight, and stories of girls and their families into a compelling narrative about what's right about our daughters. She illuminates the seven transitions that girls must untangle to become fully themselves, with each offering a corresponding opportunity for parents to stretch and transform themselves. Throughout, Damour offers unstintingly practical advice to parents about how to talk with their daughters about what matters most and in ways that they are likely to be heard."

—KIMBERLYN LEARY, PH.D., associate professor, Harvard Medical School;
chief psychologist, Cambridge Health Alliance;
Robert Wood Johnson Health Policy Fellow

UNTANGLED

untangled

Guiding teenage girls through the
seven transitions into adulthood

Lisa Damour, Ph.D.

Atlantic Books
London

First published in the United States of America in 2016 by Ballantine Books,
an imprint of Random House, a division of Penguin Random House LLC, New York.

This edition published in Great Britain in 2017
by Atlantic Books, an imprint of Atlantic Books Ltd.

Grateful acknowledgment is made to Hal Leonard Corporation for permission to reprint
an excerpt from "Sexual Healing," words and music by Marvin Gaye, Odell Brown, and
David Ritz, copyright © 1982 by EMI April Music Inc., EMI Blackwood Music Inc., and
Ritz Writes. All rights administered by Sony/ATV Music Publishing LLC, 424 Church
Street, Suite 1200, Nashville, TN, 37219. International Copyright Secured. All rights
reserved. Reprinted by permission of Hal Leonard Corporation.

10 9

A CIP catalogue record for this book is available from the British Library.

Paperback ISBN: 978 178 2395560
E-book ISBN: 978 178 2395553

Printed and bound in Great Britain by Clays Ltd, Elcograf S.p.A.

Atlantic Books
An Imprint of Atlantic Books Ltd
Ormond House
26–27 Boswell Street
London
WC1N 3JZ

www.atlantic-books.co.uk

In loving memory of Jim Hansell,
whose brilliant mind was guided by the kindest heart

While an adolescent remains inconsistent and unpredictable in her behavior, she may suffer, but she does not seem to me to be in need of treatment. I think that she should be given time and scope to work out her own solution. Rather, it may be her parents who need help and guidance so as to be able to bear with her. There are few situations in life which are more difficult to cope with than an adolescent son or daughter during the attempt to liberate themselves.

—ANNA FREUD (1958), "Adolescence"*

* Here and elsewhere, I've taken the liberty of revising the 1958-style default to male pronouns by placing "her" and "she" where Ms. Freud had "his" and "he."

Contents

Contents

Introduction

WE NEED A NEW WAY TO TALK ABOUT TEENAGE GIRLS, BECAUSE the way people do it now isn't fair to girls or helpful to their parents. If you're reading this book, someone has probably already remarked about your daughter, "Oh, just *wait* till she's a teenager!" (And parents who say this never mean it in a good way.) If you've read other books about teenage girls, you may have noticed that they tilt toward the dark side of adolescence—how girls suffer or cause suffering in their parents and peers. It's certainly true that girls can be hard on themselves and others, and even when they are at their best, they're often unpredictable and intense. But too often we talk about adolescence as if it's bound to be a harrowing, turbulent time for teenagers and their parents. We make raising a teenage girl sound like a roller-coaster ride: the whole family hops on, white-knuckles their way through, and the parents hope that after all the ups and downs their daughter steps off at the end as a healthy, happy adult.

I'm here to tell you that life with your teenage daughter doesn't have to feel like a tangled mess. There is a *predictable* pattern to teenage development, a blueprint for how girls grow. When you understand what makes your daughter tick, she suddenly makes a lot more sense. When you have a map of adolescent development, it's a lot easier to guide your daughter toward becoming the grounded young woman you want her to be.

To give us a new and helpful way to talk about teenage girls, I've taken the journey through adolescence and organized it into seven distinct developmental strands that I introduce, one per chapter, in this book. These developmental strands make plain the specific achievements that transform girls into thriving adults and help parents appreciate that much of their daughter's behavior—however strange or challenging it may seem—is not only normal but evidence of her excellent forward progress.

The early chapters in this book describe the developmental strands that tend to be most salient in Years 7 to 9 (ages eleven to thirteen for most girls) and the later chapters address the strands that usually become prominent as girls move through Years 10 to 13. Normally developing teenagers move along each of these strands at different rates, and girls are always growing on several fronts at once, a fact that helps us appreciate why the teenage years can be so stressful for girls and the adults who love them.

I'm one of those adults who care deeply about teenage girls and I have built my professional life around them. Every week I meet with girls and their parents in my private psychotherapy practice, instruct graduate students in the Department of Psychological Sciences at Case Western Reserve University as they learn to work with teenagers, and advise students in my office at Laurel School, an independent all-girls school that runs from a toddler program to Year 13, where I work as a consulting psychologist and direct the school's Center for Research on Girls. And, as the proud mother of two daughters,

I'm lucky enough to have girls at the heart of my personal life, too.

Seeing girls through so many different lenses inspired me to appreciate that the work of becoming an adult sorted itself into meaningful categories and I realized that we could use those categories—those strands—to measure how girls were coming along in their growth. The concept of developmental strands isn't new; it was first proposed in 1965 by Anna Freud, Sigmund's daughter and an esteemed psychoanalyst in her own right, as a way to organize the normal turmoil of childhood development. She pointed out that children advance on multiple fronts—from dependency to self-reliance, from play to work, from egocentricity to companionship—and noted that we can accurately assess a child's development in terms of maturation along these and other strands.

Anna Freud was one of many thinkers to propose a framework for healthy psychological growth. In 1950, Erik Erikson articulated a developmental model spanning from infancy to old age, marked by existential challenges to be mastered at each step along the way. Modern psychologists maintain the tradition of studying development in terms of its component parts. Today, we typically consider aging in terms of its physical, emotional, cognitive, and social facets. In other words, scholarly approaches to human growth broken down into discernible phases now constitute a rich theoretical tradition and a robust body of research; I stand on the shoulders of intellectual giants in proposing a concrete and comprehensive model of what, *exactly,* girls must accomplish to move through their teenage years successfully.

Once I had this model in mind and found that it illuminated so much of what I observed, I introduced it to my graduate students to help them shed light on the complex adolescent cases that come their way. Normally developing teenagers can be impulsive and oppositional and can even seem downright odd by adult standards, so these budding clinicians needed a framework for evaluating the mental health of teenagers seeking psychotherapy. When we asked, "Along which strands is the teen progressing, struggling, or stalled?" we could make order out of what looked like chaos and orient novice clinicians to the work they were learning to do.

Thinking about girls in terms of the strands of teenage development is practical for professionals, but much more important, it allows parents to pinpoint the specific achievements that turn girls into grown-ups and makes sense of familiar, but confusing, teenage behavior. Last year your daughter may have happily participated in the children's games at your street party, but this year, she insists on hanging out with the adults while complaining that she's bored. What accounts for the shift? It might be that she has begun the work of parting with childhood (chapter 1). And how do you understand the girl who is equally excited to buy a copy of *The Economist* for her Model UN research paper and three copies of an *Us Weekly* magazine featuring her favorite boy band? Well, you're likely looking at her foray into entering the romantic world (chapter 6). When you understand the important developmental work your daughter is doing, you'll fret less about some of her puzzling behaviors.

Thinking in terms of developmental strands helps us to focus our energy where it's needed most. For example, your daughter may enjoy a loyal group of friends and have succeeded in happily joining a new tribe (chapter 2), but she might neglect her schoolwork and need help planning for the future (chapter 5). Perhaps she's aiming to play softball in college but ignores the advice of her coaches. She may be committed to her goal, but that doesn't cancel out her trouble contending with adult authority (chapter 4). Attending to the many domains of your daughter's development will keep you from letting her success in some areas distract you from her difficulty in others.

And thinking in terms of strands allows us to weigh any one moment in a girl's life against her overall progress on the relevant developmental strand. Should you be worried about your daughter's meltdown when she loses a student council race? That will depend on whether she's usually pretty resilient or instead she's having a lot of trouble harnessing emotions (chapter 3). Should you ignore her decision to go without a coat on a cold day, or is her disregard for her well-being part of an alarming pattern of difficulties with caring for herself (chapter 7)? Given that teenage girls routinely do things their parents don't understand, it's helpful to have a way to know when it's okay to hang back and when you should step in.

But if teenagers typically do things that would be considered abnormal at any other time of life, how do you know when something's really wrong? To clarify the difference between normal teenage behavior and that which is truly concerning, every chapter ends with a "When to Worry" section that will help you know if your daughter has moved to a level where a dramatic shift in approach or a professional consultation might be in order. In other words, we'll consider both the garden-variety challenges that come with raising teenagers and gain new insight into why some teenage girls collapse in on themselves or act out in destructive ways.

There's a universal quality to the developmental strands introduced in this book: they capture the timeless aspects of adolescence for girls and boys, and for teenagers from many backgrounds. Though you and I developed along these strands, growing up today differs from what we remember now that we're raising children in a high-speed culture of intense competitive pressure and 24/7 digital connection. We'll address the enduring aspects of adolescence *and* how our current culture shapes the realities of being a teenager—and the parent of one—today.

Fundamentally, girls and boys are more alike than they are different, so don't be surprised to discover that some of the stories and advice that follow speak to your experience of knowing or raising a teenage boy. But girls face unique challenges as teenagers and this book takes a deep dive into the cutting-edge research that parents raising daughters need to know. The developmental strands presented here apply across racial and economic lines, and those contextual factors with regard to teenagers will also be addressed. That said, the internal, psychological nuances of adolescent development will be our central focus.

I'll share stories to illustrate the strands of teenage development, but they aren't the specific details of any one girl or family. Rather, they are amalgams of the many, many interactions I've had over the years with teenagers and their parents. At times, the particular events of an interaction are so critical to its telling that I've removed any identifying information while maintaining the emotional integrity and educational value of what occurred.

This book aims to be more descriptive than prescriptive—to offer you a new way to *understand* your daughter, not tell you how to raise her. Throughout, I offer suggestions for how you might respond to the many normal but perplexing challenges you will face as her parent, but don't feel bound by my advice. I believe that when it comes to parenting, there are many ways to get it right. What works for one family won't work for another. You know your daughter and the dynamic within your family best. My hope is that you'll marry that knowledge to the framework offered here and use the examples I provide to consider your daughter's teenage behavior in terms of the growth she's trying (or should be trying) to achieve.

By providing you with a blueprint for the work of adolescence, this book will help you to understand your daughter better, worry about her less, offer her useful assistance on her journey through adolescence, and recognize—in fact, stand in awe of—just how much developmental ground she will cover as a teenager. This book won't, and couldn't, address every challenge you will face as your daughter grows, and in trying to describe teenage girls in general, I will certainly fail to describe anyone's daughter perfectly. But girls act in patterns, and their guides (I'm looking at you) benefit from knowing what those patterns are. I admire the parents of teenagers at least as much as I admire their daughters, and I have written this book to support you so that you can do an even better job of supporting your girl.

UNTANGLED

ONE

· · · · · · · · · · · ·

Parting with Childhood

IN THE WAITING ROOM OF MY PRIVATE PRACTICE, I MET MAYA FOR the first time. With an easy air, long limbs, and dark hair showing the beginnings of gray, she stood to greet me, then gracefully pivoted to return the magazine she'd been reading to its place on a low table, next to a lamp. She followed me to my office and took the far end of my couch. It's not the closest spot to the armchair where I sit, but not so far away as a chair preferred by clients who want more distance. She kept her light jacket on—we were meeting on a crisp, sunny day in late October—and crossed her legs, clasped her hands, and leaned forward as we talked.

Over the phone, Maya told me that she was worried about the sudden change in her relationship with her twelve-year-old daughter, Camille. In my office, she told a familiar story—one that we'll consider in a totally new light.

Maya explained that until two months ago, Camille had been her funny, joyful companion who was almost always up for a trip to the library, grocery store, or mall. Yet at the start of Year 8, Camille abruptly transformed. She came home from school and headed straight to her bedroom, where she closed the door and held marathon texting sessions with friends until required to join the family for dinner. Bewildered, Maya described how Camille sat sullenly at the dinner table and gave one-word answers to questions about her day. Even while saying so little, Camille managed to express that her parents were asking the dumbest questions she had ever heard and that sitting with them was the last thing she wanted to do.

Occasionally, the old Camille made a brief appearance; Maya's eyes brimmed with tears as she described these savored moments. Most of the time, though, Maya felt angry with Camille for being so prickly, missed her warm relationship with her beloved girl, or experienced a wearying mix of both feelings at once. Maya's friends reassured her that Camille was "normal" and that "girls break up with their parents when they become teenagers," but Maya had called me anyway. She worried that something just wasn't right.

Maya's friends weren't wrong, but their scope was too narrow and their viewpoint far too personal. They were missing the bigger picture. Girls don't dump their parents just for the heck of it. They pull away to start their journey along one of the seven developmental strands of adolescence: parting with childhood. By age twelve most tweens feel a sudden, internal pressure to separate themselves from almost everything that seems childlike and, as Maya was learning the hard way, a girl's pleasant relationship with her family is usually one of the first casualties. Parting with childhood isn't always the first developmental strand that girls tackle during adolescence, but it's a strand that parents can't miss. When girls distance themselves from their mom and dad they all but announce, "In case you guys hadn't noticed, I'm a teenager now!"

If we step back from what feels like a highly personal rejection, we can appreciate that, when it comes to parting with childhood, our daughters have a lot of developmental ground to cover in a short time. They have to get from point A, where they happily hold our hands and act like total morons in public, to point B, where they claim the independence and self-determination that come with being young women and trade their goofiness for relatively mature behavior (at least when strangers are around). To progress along this strand, girls stop telling us their secrets, bristle when we use pet names, and make it clear that they're doing us a favor by agreeing to join the family holiday picture. But a girl's journey away from childhood isn't all about her relationship with her parents. She might also experiment with makeup, suddenly insist that riding the school bus is for babies, and curse when with her friends.

Girls' efforts to part with childhood are both conscious and not. Young teens admire older teens and fervently wish to be like them. I have my own Year 10 flashbulb memory of watching a group of Year 13 girls, dressed in Madonna's mid-'80s style, as they danced and lip-synced to "Borderline" during a talent show. They were beyond cool, and I remember resolving, in that moment, to close the gap between their lace-gloved sophistication and my newly realized dorkiness. But a lot goes on behind the scenes in the unconscious mind, too. Even though they might not be aware of it, twelve-year-olds do the math and realize that, if all goes according to plan, they will be leaving home in five or six years. They suddenly feel pressed to prepare for adult independence by ridding themselves of the marks of childhood.

Maya had come to my office because she was worried that something was really wrong, and it's my job to take parents' concerns seriously. So I began to ask the questions that help me to know what was normal about Camille's behavior, and what wasn't: Was she rude to all adults, or just to her mom and dad? How were things at school and with her friends? Did she have interests, sleep well, and talk about what she wanted to do over the summer or next year?

Maya filled in the picture.

Teachers went out of their way to comment on Camille's kind and conscientious nature. Camille dog-sat for the neighbors, and Maya heard the same about her from them. Maya explained that her daughter did well in school, had solid friendships, and spent hours each weekend on the family's unfinished third floor, which she had turned into an elaborate apartment for her dolls. And though Maya suspected that she sometimes sneaked her phone into her room for nighttime use, Camille usually slept well. She looked forward to going to camp each summer and also talked about her faraway goals to become a teacher or a scientist.

I reassured Maya that her friends were probably right—that her daughter's prickly behavior *was* normal. Then I encouraged her to see the change in Camille from a new perspective: there were seven transitions she would be making as she journeyed toward adulthood, and parting with childhood was one of them. Camille was doing exactly what we expect—even want—teenagers to do. And she was doing what they have done at least since 1958, when Anna Freud noted that the typical teenager lives "in the home in the attitude of a boarder, usually a very inconsiderate one so far as the older and younger family members are concerned." Despite the fact that it has long been normal for teenagers to hold their parents at arm's length, most of us feel rocked by the seismic shift in our relationship with our daughter.

You'll notice that Anna Freud's wisdom appears throughout this book; there are two reasons for this. First, she holds a special place in the history of psychology for being among the first to articulate, and *normalize,* many of the predictable challenges that unfold during adolescence. Needless to say, this book aims to build upon that fine tradition. Second, she holds a special place in my heart because she played a small role in my decision to become a psychologist.

When I was six years old, my father's work for an American bank transferred us from Denver to London for a few years and, by coincidence, a family friend made the same move in the same week. Carla, a reedy graduate student with a mane of wavy red hair, was headed to London to study with Anna Freud. My parents essentially adopted Carla, and she looked after me, their only child, over long weekends when they traveled together. Carla lived in north London, near Anna Freud's training clinic, in a tiny flat consisting of a living room, a miniature mid-1970s British kitchen, a cramped bathroom, and a bedroom that was overwhelmed by the queen-sized bed we shared when I stayed over. The radiator in the kitchen ran on coins, and it soon became part of our weekend routine. Carla would save up pence between my visits and let me drop them into the radiator's slot when I arrived. Then we'd sit in her kitchen and I'd start with my questions: "What brings the children to therapy? What do you say to them? What do they say to you? How does all that talking help them get better?" Carla was incredibly patient and generous with me. Replaying our conversations in my mind, I can hear how fully she addressed my curiosity about her work, even as she pitched her answers to a six-year-old.

I was hooked. Shortly after I turned seven, I walked into our London flat and announced to my mother, "I want to do what Carla does." Nearly forty years later, Carla remains a close friend and mentor, and I remain grateful that she introduced me to a career that I have found deeply gratifying, both professionally and personally.

The Cold Shoulder

From your perspective, five or six years gives your daughter plenty of time to ease into being an independent young adult. But from her perspective, an abrupt withdrawal (like Camille's) provides a perfect solution: she gets to practice leaving her childhood relationship with you behind for several years before she actually has to strike out on her own. She can pretend to live alone, or in her bedroom turned practice dormitory, while still enjoying the comfort of your home and the safety net you provide. It's the psychological equivalent of putting training wheels on a bike. She learns how to ride on two wheels while knowing that they are there to catch her if she loses her balance.

That said, don't assume that your daughter fully understands why she's pulling away from you. The urge to hold you at a distance is largely an unconscious one. This means that her feelings about you change for reasons she can't explain. What she knows is that you *used* to be pleasant company but you have suddenly become inexplicably annoying. You *used* to have a wry sense of humor but suddenly your same old jokes are corny and embarrassing, especially if you crack them in front of her friends. You *used* to be a source of helpful advice, but now your suggestions seem totally irrelevant. Parents on the receiving end of their daughter's new attitude feel like they *used* to be a jelly bean but now they've turned into a Brussels sprout. You might be good for her, but you are to be avoided when possible.

I sympathize. Though the comparison is a silly one, it's actually deeply painful to become a Brussels sprout.

I had been working as a psychologist for several years before I appreciated the similarity between scorned vegetables and parents of teenagers because, like many clinicians, I started helping parents before I had children myself. There are certain advantages to this (you don't compare your kids to those of your clients) and some distinct disadvantages (no one can tell you what it's like to wake to a vomiting child at 2:00 A.M.— you've just got to live it).

At the time when my older daughter was three, I was having my last session of the day with the parents of Erin, a charismatic sixteen-year-old girl. I connected easily with her father around our shared perspective—we both enjoyed his daughter and were worried about her brittle relationship with her mother. I had a harder time feeling empathy for Erin's mom; she was harshly critical of her daughter's appearance and affronted by her daughter's "ingratitude" for her years of personal sacrifice.

As Erin's mother detailed her disappointment in her daughter, an image popped into my head: that of my darling pigtailed girl who would be flinging herself at me when I got home. I thought, "Hold on! *This* is what parents of teenagers are talking about when they stop me in the grocery store, look wistfully at my toddler, and tell me to 'enjoy this time.' They don't mean that I should get a kick out of cleaning applesauce off the ceiling. They mean that I'm really going to miss it when my daughter no longer thinks I'm awesome and wants as much of me as she can get."

With some overdue empathy on board, I said to Erin's parents, "I'm sure it's not easy to be rejected by someone you love so much. Especially when you used to be so close and have such a good time together." Therapists hope for some outward sign that we've hit the mark with our comments, and my sign was suddenly right there, flowing down the mother's cheeks. The father put his arm around his tearful wife, and together, the three of us could see that as long as Erin's mother focused on feeling angry with her daughter, she didn't have to do the work of mourning the affectionate, happy relationship they used to share. Once we could talk about how much both parents missed the past, we could find new ways for them to feel connected to their daughter in the present.

Well-meaning reassurances from friends (or psychologists!) that it's all normal don't take the sting out of losing the friendly bond that many parents had with their preteen girl. Even if your daughter enjoys your company much of the time, it still feels awful when she freezes you out or halts conversations with her friends until you walk away. On top of that, girls distance themselves from their parents just when they are facing new risks and making decisions of greater consequence than ever before. It's bad enough to be rebuffed by your daughter—it's worse that it happens right when you feel that she needs you most.

So what should you do when your daughter retreats to her room and comes out only when summoned? How do you connect with her when she's annoyed even by the way you breathe?

You should start by allowing your daughter more privacy than she had as a child. Interestingly, findings from a research study that examined how much parents seek to know about their teenagers—and how much teenagers choose to share— suggest that we grant greater privacy to our sons than to our daughters. We are more likely to ask girls what they're up to behind closed doors, and our daughters, more than our sons, answer our questions. This research finding certainly fits with the conversations I have with parents who expect their teenage sons to be sphinxlike (as in, "You know, he's a boy—he just doesn't talk to us") but express grave concern when teenage daughters withdraw. In the name of blocking double standards at our doorsteps, it's helpful to remember that teenage girls, like teenage boys, often want privacy for its own sake. Some parents wrongly suspect that if their daughter is closing her door, she must be up to something, but most teenage girls close their doors to do the exact same things they used to do with the door wide open.

Here I'm reminded of fourteen-year-old Ashley, whose parents came to me concerned about their daughter's "sneaky" behavior. When I asked about the evidence of Ashley's alleged sneakiness, I learned that her dad became instantly suspicious when she started closing her bedroom door at age twelve. Ashley had never closed her door as a child, so her father figured that she was hiding something—illicit behavior or drugs—in her room. Based on his suspicions, he insisted that Ashley keep her door open, at least partially, at all times. When Ashley was away on a sleepover, he made a sweep of her bedroom and discovered a small, locked safe—clearly a secret purchase—in the back of his daughter's closet. When she returned from her sleepover, he demanded that she open the safe, which she refused to do. That's when they called me.

Ashley's father could only imagine the contraband hidden in his daughter's safe and was now convinced that he had a full-blown delinquent on his hands. It turned out that the safe contained nothing but a diary where Ashley kept an intensely personal, but PG-rated, record of her first year of high school. Ashley knew that her father would not respect her privacy and that she needed to go to extreme measures to secure it. In failing to grant his daughter even the refuge of her bedroom, Ashley's father managed to alienate and insult his well-meaning girl.

If you allow your teenage daughter the sanctuary of her bedroom—assuming, of course, that she is lucky enough to have a room to herself—you may wonder if she will only be seen again when she needs money, food, or a ride to a friend's house. For this reason, some families establish a family time one evening a week, or as often as logistically feasible for everyone in the family. This might be a game night, movie night, dinner-out-as-a-family night, or any other "night" that fits your tastes. Needless to say, it is easier to enforce attendance at the designated night if this tradition begins before your daughter is a teenager and isn't sprung on her as some sort of punishment when you haven't seen her for more than five consecutive minutes in three weeks. You can enhance the appeal of the family night by having everyone take turns selecting the evening's game, movie, or restaurant and by scheduling the evening to end with plenty of time for an older teenager to head out for a night with her friends.

If your daughter complains about your compulsory family get-togethers, or if you didn't put a family night in place before she became a teenager, you've still got options. Older adolescent girls can be surprisingly amenable to having one-on-one time with their parents. A meal or outing with just one parent can have an air of sophistication that's missing from family-wide events, especially if the family includes rowdy younger siblings. And being with only one parent can tweak tricky family dynamics. As one girl explained to me, "When I'm with both of my parents, my dad asks a bunch of annoying questions and I look to my mom to tell him to back off. But when it's just me and my dad, somehow we get along better."

Whether or not you've designated a family night, aim to eat meals with your daughter throughout the week. You've probably heard about research showing that family meals contribute to girls' health, academic achievement, and overall sense of well-being. While those results are important, my favorite study on family dinners found a way to address a critical "Yeah, but ..." question: What if teens benefit from family dinner *not* because of what happens at the table, but because they have a strong relationship with their parents that happens to include lots of family meals?

To tackle this question, psychologists Suniya Luthar and Shawn Latendresse measured relationship variables, such as how close teens felt to their parents and how much teens felt their parents criticized them (in addition to asking how often the family ate dinner together). Surprisingly, when the research team stripped the relationship data from the family dinner equation, they *still* found that eating together as a family improved teens' grades and psychological health. In other words, teens benefited from having family dinner, even when they reported that they weren't getting along with their parents. Further, the same study counted eating dinner with only one parent as a family dinner and found that the advantages hold up so long as teens eat with at least one parent, more nights a week than not.

There's a lot of research out there about family dinners, but this study stands out to me for two reasons, one professional, one personal. As a psychologist, I welcome evidence that girls should join the family dinner even if they feel disconnected from their folks. Any parent whose daughter brings hostile silence to the table is bound to question the value of making family dinner happen—Maya certainly felt that way when eating with Camille. To me, the results of this study suggest that girls who feel remote from their families may be the ones who *most* need for their parents to prioritize time with them— whether it's over dinner, breakfast, or a weekend lunch—even if the time together feels strained.

As a mother, I am grateful that the researchers were flexible in their definition of a family dinner. Given the busy schedules that many parents and kids maintain, I know I'm not the only one for whom a nightly, full-family dinner seems nearly impossible. This study heartens me on evenings when my husband or I eat alone with our daughters and makes me feel as if I've won the lottery when we're all there. (Here are some questions I'm hoping future research will address: Must the meal be hot? Must it last more than ten minutes to achieve its magical benefits? And how often can I freak out about table manners and still have a positive influence on my daughters? Obviously, important work waits to be done.)

If you really want to connect with your daughter, car time can be your most valuable ally. The conditions of riding in a car—not having to look directly at the parent who is driving, the assurance that the conversation will end when the ride ends—are just what some girls need to open up. This effect can be multiplied by the number of girls in the car. The next time a parent asks you to share a lift to or from a social event, say yes, and—if you want a real snapshot of what's happening in your daughter's life—offer to be the one who picks the girls up at the end of the night. Girls and their friends seem to forget that the chauffeur is actually someone's mom or dad and will chatter quite openly with one another when being transported in groups. Offering to share a lift will come at the cost of your time, petrol, and likely your sleep, but you will learn more about what is going on in your daughter's personal life in the time it takes to drop off her friends and get back to your home than you will in three weeks of asking about how things are going. Wise chauffeurs know it's best to really play the part; trying to join the conversation or ask questions usually breaks the spell and ends the chatter or—even worse—gets the girls to take the conversation to their phones.

As a final option, be willing to exchange some of your favorite traditions for more grown-up ways to connect with your daughter. You may long to recapture a tender moment from your daughter's childhood—decorating the Christmas tree while singing Bing Crosby songs together—but your daughter might sprain her eye-rolling muscles at the suggestion. If you want to have some quality time with your girl, consider making some popcorn and joining her on the couch to rewatch your fourth-choice holiday movie.

Allergic to Questions

In the middle of a family night, over dinner at home, or even in the car, you've likely discovered that your teenage daughter has developed an allergy—intermittent or chronic—to being asked questions. Last year she might have welcomed your curiosity, but now that she's parting with childhood, she may be downright offended by it. You don't always have to play the role of the furtive chauffeur; there are times when you *should* step forward with questions. But when I invite teenage girls to explain to me why they are so bothered by their parents' questions, the girls invariably shake their heads, exhale heavily, and say, "Ugh, their questions are *so* annoying!"

So I ask: What makes them annoying? Can parents pose questions that aren't annoying? If your parents want to start a conversation with you, how should they go about it? When asked honest questions, I always find that girls produce honest answers.

Here's what they tell me.

A girl will bristle when her parents ask questions at the wrong time—when she's deeply engaged in her work, already halfway out the door, or closing her eyes to catch a little extra rest on the couch on a quiet afternoon. A girl will reject a question if she suspects the parent doesn't really care about the answer and has asked just to try to connect. And girls don't like questions designed to pry. You can ask about how the party went, but not if you're pursuing an angle. And the worst? When a parent doggedly follows a preplanned line of questioning and won't allow the course of the conversation to be shaped by the girl's answers.

So what works?

Girls want questions driven by genuine interest. Consider ditching the ones we usually grab as handy conversation starters ("So, how was your day?") and ask about something specific that you really want to know. If she mentioned last week that further math was giving her fits ask (in a tone that makes it clear that you don't have an agenda), "How's it going in math? I know that you weren't loving it last week." Again, honest questions get honest answers. Girls tell me that they want their parents to pick up the conversational topics they put on the table, so shelve your carefully crafted, genuine question if your daughter offers a topic of her own. Should she volunteer that her music teacher seems to have gotten crankier try, "Really? What kind of cranky?" or "Huh, any idea what's going on?" And girls appreciate not being asked questions at all. More than a few girls have told me that they'd enjoy spending time in the car with any parent who would drop the chitchat and turn over the control of the sound system.

What if you're playing by the rules—picking your moments, asking genuine questions, following her lead—and still getting a withering stare in response to your friendly inquiries? What if your daughter doesn't even respond to you or gives answers that are curt at best? Go ahead and be clear with your daughter that you are *not* expecting her to write you daily love letters, but that she does need to conduct herself in a way that is, at minimum, polite.

I've given a lot of thought to what it means to encourage girls to be polite. On the one hand, the word smacks of a saccharine nicey-nice quality that I'm loath to encourage in girls. On the other, it works well because it's concrete. Girls know what it means to be polite or impolite. So, I've come to prefer "be polite" over injunctions, such as "be respectful," that are too abstract to be readily enforced and, to my mind, set an unfairly high bar. Put another way, I can be polite to people who don't earn my respect, and I think this is as much as we should ask girls to do. If your daughter gets grumpy when you pose a reasonable question, feel free to say, "You may not like my questions, but you need to find a polite way of responding." Of course, this request can only be made if you model the kind of decency you are asking of her.

As a general rule, I don't think parents should allow their daughters to treat them in any way that is objectively disrespectful. You may be reluctant to do anything that might push away an already distant girl—especially one who seems to be a talkative delight with every adult *except* you—but teenagers know when they are misbehaving, and they feel uncomfortable when they get away with it. When your daughter is being rude, find a way to call her on it.

Bear in mind that you have the right to make the many optional good deeds you do for your daughter contingent on her decent treatment of you. She should not expect you to take her to the mall on a moment's notice if her day-to-day interactions with you are consistently unpleasant. Is this emotional blackmail? Absolutely not. It's how the world works. People don't do nice things for people who are mean to them. Better for your daughter to learn this lesson before she leaves your home than after she is out on her own. If, after a stretch of treating you like a nosy landlord or a meddling chauffeur, your daughter asks you to run an errand on her behalf, invite her to address the difficulty she's created. You might say, "I feel really torn. I love you and want to help you out in any way I can, but you've been snarky for days and I don't want to give you the impression that you can treat people poorly and expect them to go out of their way for you. Got any suggestions for how we can make this right?" Alternatively, and depending on the mood of the moment, you could say, "No way, sister! Not with how you've been acting. Warm it up several degrees and try again later."

Surprisingly Mean

Cathy was early to our appointment, so we chatted while waiting for her husband to join us. We were meeting to talk about Kirsten, her fifteen-year-old daughter who had been struggling with anxiety. "Kirsten really got to me this week," said Cathy, who went on to explain that she had spent the last month carefully preparing for a major presentation at work. On the day of the presentation, Cathy—a good-looking woman who kept herself physically fit—put on her favorite knit dress and was about to leave for the office when Kirsten came downstairs. Cathy reminded Kirsten that it was the big day and asked if she looked all right. Cathy then imitated Kirsten's response for me. She tilted her head, cocked an eyebrow, and said, "Yeah, you look okay . . . if you don't mind looking like a lumpy librarian." Cathy laughed, and so did I, but it was clear that she had been really hurt by the comment.

In the words of my wise colleague, psychologist Renée Spencer, girls are "exquisitely attuned" to the adults they know well. And at times, they use their insider's knowledge to be surprisingly mean. Your daughter may already give you the cold shoulder as part of moving on from her generally pleasant but, as far as she's concerned, childish relationship with you. Being mean allows your daughter to take her departure from childhood a step further; she's not just shutting you out, she's actively pushing you away.

Like Kirsten's comment, a girl's meanness toward her parents usually has two impressive qualities. First, it's carefully aimed at their vulnerabilities; a girl knows how to be mean in just the way that will hurt or reject *her* parents. One girl I know insisted that only her father, a lawyer and former athlete, could examine her sprained ankle, not her mother—an esteemed radiologist. Another declared that her mother's Thanksgiving food was "weird" (her mother was a dedicated and talented cook) and made herself some packaged macaroni cheese to eat at the Thanksgiving table. Girls often aim their most severe meanness at their mothers—especially if they have had a particularly close relationship in the past—but dads can be targets too. I think here of a girl who mused aloud that her intensely devoted father "was sort of like a robot . . . just some TV-watching machine who lives with us" as he made himself late to work so that he could drive her to school.

Second, girls' meanness can be astonishingly unpunishable because most adolescent girls avoid pedestrian tactics like name-calling. Instead, they operate in a retaliation-proof margin that's aggressive but hard to prevent, pin down, or penalize. Like Kirsten, they make observations about their parents that are as witty as they are wounding. While maintaining an air of innocence—or even offering what she considers to be helpful feedback about your haircut, tastes, or deeply held values—your daughter might casually toss off a comment that ruins your whole day, especially if, like Cathy, you were feeling vulnerable to start.

And not all of their meanness is straight-up mean. Sometimes girls tease their parents in order to pull them close and push them away at the same time. I watched this dynamic unfold between Andy, a dear friend from high school, and his sixteen-year-old daughter, Grace, during a summer visit to my hometown of Denver. Andy, his wife, Sharon, and I were catching up in their backyard when Grace, a talented violinist, joined us. Grace sat silently, legs folded beneath her on the outdoor furniture, and followed the conversation.

We were discussing the fact that Andy's work took him to Indonesia and Ghana when I asked if his family ever had the chance to join him on his adventures. He explained that the travel occurred on short notice, making a family trip impossible, but that his accrued flight miles were put toward their family vacations. Grace chimed in, "Wow, Dad, you're a lot more useful to us when you're gone than when you're here. And the house smells better too." Andy, chuckled, said, "Gee, thanks, Grace," and the conversation carried on. Andy wasn't hurt. I think he knew that Grace was making it clear that she was no longer Daddy's little girl, but that they were still close. (Truly, it takes a certain amount of intimacy to tease someone about how he smells.) At another moment, in a different mood, or with a testier tone, Grace's teasing might have crossed a line. But that night I got to watch Andy's amusement at Grace's clever jab and the playful way she claimed her connection with him.

Should your daughter cross a line with you, or catch you feeling vulnerable and unable to take her teasing in stride, you don't just have to sit back and take it. If you can gather your wits in the moment, you might respond with "Ouch" or "Wow, that's mean" or "That's not how we talk to one another in this family." If she gets defensive, looks at you blankly, or stomps off in a huff, commend yourself for doing your job. What job is this? The one where you remind your daughter that no self-respecting person will enjoy her company when she treats people the way she just treated you.

You may need a while to absorb a given blow and let some time pass to cool off before you say your piece. Ultimately, you might share with your daughter something along the lines of, "I need to let you know that I was really hurt by what you said. You may have been joking around, but that was hard to hear." Other times, you might jump in to defend your partner if he or she is the one under attack. Words such as, "Your mom made us a terrific Thanksgiving dinner and you are being rude—put away the macaroni cheese" will do. Believe me, girls know when they're stepping over a boundary and find it strange when adults seem not to notice.

So far, here's the picture I've painted of adolescent girls: aloof, withdrawn, and, sometimes, surprisingly mean. There's truth to this picture, but for parents it's not the whole story. Being pushed away is only the half of it. Raising a teenage girl becomes that much more stressful when she interrupts days of distance with moments of intense warmth and intimacy.

The Swimming Pool

Let me explain. Consider the metaphor in which your teenage daughter is a swimmer, you are the pool in which she swims, and the water is the broader world. Like any good swimmer, your daughter wants to be out playing, diving, or splashing around in the water. And, like any swimmer, she holds on to the edge of the pool to catch her breath after a rough lap or getting dunked too many times.

In real life, it looks like this: your daughter has been so busy spending time with her friends, activities, or schoolwork that you feel as though you might need to reintroduce yourself the next time you see her. Then something goes wrong in her world and she is suddenly seeking your advice, sharing the details of her latest misfortunes, and perhaps (gasp!) wanting you to hug or cuddle her. In other words, she's had a hard time in the water and has come to the edge of the pool to recover.

You're in heaven—she's back. To mix metaphors, you're a jelly bean again! She wants to be with you, to hear your wisdom, to be comforted by your physical presence. Paul Simon's "Mother and Child Reunion" plays in your head as you start to imagine the many fantastic adventures you'll share with your new best friend.

Then she pushes you away. Hard. What just happened? Well, like a swimmer who gets her breath back, your daughter wants to return to the water, and she gets there by pushing off the side of the pool. This often takes the form of picking the dumbest fight ever or being nasty in a way that is both petty and painful ("Please tell me you didn't actually wear *those shoes* with *that skirt* today"). While you could have hummed Paul Simon all day long, your daughter needs to hurry back to the depths as soon as she feels restored. Why can't she linger? Because, to her, lingering feels babyish, which is just about the last thing that any normal teenager who is parting with childhood wants to feel. Clinging to you quickly becomes as uncomfortable for your daughter as it is pleasantly nostalgic for you. She rushes back to the work of parting with childhood with an abrupt—sometimes painful—shove.

It hurts when warm moments with your daughter so quickly turn cold. There is no way to prevent these stinging interactions altogether, and there are many real benefits for your daughter in having them. That said, there are some things that you can do to lessen the pain of a rejection that comes on the heels of overdue closeness. To begin, anticipate the push-off. When your daughter swims to you, enjoy it, but don't get your hopes up that she has rediscovered the value of your wisdom and affection and will never again forget it. When she shoves off, don't allow your daughter to mistreat you. If her push-off is rude, tell her so. She may or may not apologize, but you need to say—and she needs to hear you say—"That's hurtful."

Next, stand strong. Your daughter needs a wall to swim to, and she needs you to be a wall that can withstand her comings and goings. Some parents feel too hurt by their swimmers, take too personally their daughter's rejections, and choose to make themselves unavailable to avoid going through it again. Of course, in some ways it *does* feel better to avoid certain emotional whiplash. But being unavailable comes at a cost. Unavailable parents miss out on some wonderful, if brief, moments with their daughters. Worse, their daughters are left without a wall to swim to and must navigate choppy—and sometimes dangerous—waters all on their own.

Finally, rally your supports. In the opening pages of this book I included one of my favorite quotes from Anna Freud and it is as true today as it was when she wrote it in 1958: "There are few situations in life which are more difficult to cope with than an adolescent son or daughter during the attempt to liberate themselves." Raising teenagers is not for the fragile, and that's true even when everything is going just as it should. Parents of teenagers need supportive partners and friends to prop them up when they feel that they just can't take one more push-off. Knowing that you can serve as a reliable, safe base allows your daughter to venture out into the world; having the strength to stay in place when your daughter clings to and rejects you in short order usually requires the loving support of adult allies.

I've used my swimming pool metaphor for years. It's a more elaborate metaphor than I typically go for, but too many parents have sought me out over the years to say, "That swimming pool bit really got us through our daughter's teenage years" for me to give it up. Once, at a school leaving party, a mother told me she had been swimming-pooled that very afternoon. She went on to explain that her daughter—whom I knew to be particularly reserved, especially at home—had returned from the leaving ceremony brimming with tearful nostalgia for her school years. The girl hurried to show her mother her yearbook and sat close on the couch as she shared her favorite pictures and told funny stories that her mother had never heard before. The mother, still basking in the glow of the yearbook tour, waited on the couch while her daughter went to her room to change out of her formal clothes. Only twenty minutes later did the mother realize that the girl had left for a friend's party without so much as a good-bye.

Anyone raising a teenage daughter can attest to the unevenness of her development. Like the school leaver, she can range from clinging to rejecting, and many parents find that their daughters are incredibly competent in some areas but not so much in others.

Totally Competent, Except for When She's Not

Over lunch a friend said to me, "Here's one for you. Tracy refuses to put in her own contacts." Tracy is her thirteen-year-old daughter, a terrific girl who gamely navigates public transportation to get to school, afternoon art classes, and friends' houses on the weekend. She writes catchy songs for her guitar and is auditioning drummers and singers to help her round out an all-girl band. When her parents work late, Tracy finishes her homework, makes sure that her younger brother gets started on his, and sets the table for dinner. In other words, she is a very competent girl.

My friend went on, "We've gotten into this horrible morning routine where I tell her to try to put them in, she insists she can't, we haggle back and forth for a while, and then I finally give in because she's getting upset about running late for school. She's decided that she's too cool for glasses, which I understand, but I never expected that managing her contacts would turn out to be so hard."

My friend isn't alone. Many parents of a teenage girl are as awed by their daughter's incredible capabilities as they are stunned by the things that she claims she cannot do. The same girl who organizes a fundraiser for a classmate with a rare disease will refuse to return overdue books to the local library because she doesn't want to face the librarian. The girl who uses power tools to build elaborate wooden models will also insist that she cannot start dinner because she's scared of the stove. In most families, the parents' certainty that their daughter can manage the task at hand meets its match in their daughter's steadfast belief that she absolutely cannot.

Girls don't part with childhood in one fell swoop. They don't need you one minute and become completely independent the next. Instead, their skills—or, really, their confidence in their skills—develop at an uneven pace. Looked at logically, it seems that any girl who can develop a computer simulation of how proteins fold can figure out how to wrap a present. But try telling that to the girl. In my experience, I've only been able to identify one clear pattern when it comes to the areas where girls seem much less capable than we'd expect: they can be especially wary of tasks that involve dealing with adults outside the family. For example, some girls become paralyzed when they are expected to manage payment at a salon or call to reschedule an orthodontic appointment. Other girls freeze up if they need to confront or disappoint an adult and will turn themselves inside out to avoid talking to a teacher about a grading mistake or telling the neighbors that they're not available to babysit.

There are lots of ways to support your daughter, and there's one way to respond that's not helpful at all: becoming exasperated when your reasoning fails to convince your daughter that if she can work a table saw she can work a stove. Instead, you might recall your daughter's toddler years, the other phase of her life that, like adolescence, involved rapid but uneven development. Back then, you never would have thrown your hands in the air and cried, "If you can figure out how to work the remote control you can certainly tie your shoes!" So you don't want to do the equivalent now. Instead, consider the advice we psychologists give to parents of toddlers and break the work of handing tasks over to your daughter into stages. Specifically, think in terms of helping your daughter move from having you do the task *for* her, to doing it *with* her, to *standing by to admire* her as she does it, and finally, to *letting her do it alone*.

I suggested that my friend could set aside time on the weekend to move from putting Tracy's contacts in *for* her to putting the contacts in *with* her. She could narrate her technique, then have Tracy attempt one step of the process while she does the others. They might proceed slowly or speed along to the subsequent steps, but they will only make progress if Tracy's mom withholds judgment and accepts that handing the job off to her daughter will be a gradual process.

If your teenager refuses to call her pediatrician to make an appointment, have her stand nearby while you make an appointment for a far-off physical, then offer to stand by while she makes hers. Again, leave the judgment out of it. I have found that girls can be surprisingly reluctant to speak to adults on the phone. Unlike those of us who spent hours holding the handset to our ear when we were teenagers, many of our daughters rarely use the phone these days for actually speaking, and they may have few opportunities to learn phone etiquette by overhearing adults, since so many parents have also come to prefer texting or emailing to making calls.

Don't assume that your daughter's insistence that you're the only one who can make her a proper sandwich means that she will be living with you until she's forty. If she's independent, if she's rejecting your help in other areas, don't worry. Chances are that she'll be moving out on time. Accept that girls part with childhood gradually and embrace opportunities to do things *for* her, *with* her, and to *stand by to admire* her when she's doing more and more for herself.

Blooming, Reluctantly

Laurel, the all-girls school where I consult for part of each week, is an amazing place, but I've decided that it would not be fair to anyone to send my own girls there. My daughters deserve a school where their mother doesn't know as much as they do about the daily happenings, and the girls at Laurel should be able to check in with a psychologist who isn't a classmate's mom. Instead, my girls are students in Shaker Heights's terrific public school system, which means that at the end of Year 5, my daughter and I walk to our neighborhood primary school to attend the Ladies Night Out for the rising Year 6 girls and an accompanying adult female relative. The evening, led by a friendly local pediatrician, introduces the facts of puberty. The mood in the room could not be more divided. While I exchange cheerful, "Wow! Are we here already?" greetings with the other moms, the girls slump into the beige metal folding chairs arranged in careful rows in the gymnasium. As the pediatrician begins her spiel, the girls slide even lower in their seats. They look at the floor, shoot "Can you *believe* this?" glances at one another, and broadcast that they want, more than anything, to go home.

While adults may be convinced by our own sales talk— we often introduce puberty as a joyous blossoming of womanhood—most tween girls don't buy it. And why should they? However we choose to describe the facts of puberty, many girls *actually* hear: "Get ready, ladies, because that body of yours that has hardly given you any trouble up till now is about to gain smelly armpits that you'll need to deodorize, sprout hair that you may choose to shave, erupt pimples right on your face, and develop breasts that will inevitably be compared to those of your female classmates. Oh, and did we mention that your vagina will bleed?" In fact, it's surprising to me that adults routinely put such a cheerful gloss on the facts of puberty. Have you ever, in all your life, heard a woman say, "Puberty? I feel that it came at the exact right moment and the whole thing was wonderful!"

Many girls experience the physical changes of puberty as simply gross. On top of that, girls' bodies part with childhood at a moment girls don't select and may not like. To make matters even worse, puberty advances at a speed girls can't control. Given that girls are striving to part with childhood, you'd think that they'd all welcome the biological shift to womanhood. But they often don't. Here's why: girls like to part with childhood on their own schedule. You may have noticed that one minute your daughter lobbies to download songs with raunchy lyrics, and the next, she curls up on the couch in the exact same position she adopted at age six to read a book she enjoyed at age eight. Her seemingly paradoxical behavior is actually brilliant. She's parting with childhood while regulating the process. She's sending developmental troops forward to conquer new ground (such as flirting, or considering philosophical questions) and then letting her troops fall back to safe, established base camps (playing with dolls, reading childhood books) when they need to rest and regroup. But then here come the physical realities of puberty! These troops disregard their leader and march ahead on their own. What adults advertise as a joyous blossoming feels to some girls like an all-too-public mutiny.

Shortly before Thanksgiving, Maya called me to set up another appointment. She had found it useful to regard Camille's cold shoulder as part of the developmental strand of leaving childhood behind and, though Maya agreed that her daughter was on track developmentally, she wanted to keep meeting because she was a fairly private person who was glad to have a place to talk frankly about Camille's path through adolescence. Actually, some of my favorite work in my practice involves serving as a confidential sounding board for parents of girls who, in many ways, are thriving. When our kids are little, we stand around on the playground and discuss who's moving out of diapers, but when they're teenagers, we don't always feel that we can ask our friends how their daughters are coming along with managing their periods, getting along with their friends, or navigating the college process. Personal discretion, respect for our daughters' privacy, or even competitive feelings within tight communities make it hard for parents to talk with one another about the garden-variety challenges that come with raising teenagers.

When we next met, Maya shared that puberty was now well under way for her daughter, but that Camille would quickly change the subject if she broached the topics of menstruation, wearing deodorant, and so on. Clearly, Camille was one of those girls who felt that her troops were defying their leader, and her solution was to try to avoid the issue altogether. Maya knew that puberty was addressed in health class at school but doubted that Camille ever spoke up, even if she had a pressing question. Maya didn't want Camille to feel awkward or embarrassed and didn't want her to harbor unanswered questions, but she could not find a way to have a successful conversation with Camille about her changing body.

Not all girls feel uncomfortable about the onset of puberty. Some are excited about it and are happy to seek or accept advice on how to manage their new self-care demands. But if, like Camille, your daughter seems to feel awkward discussing her new personal hygiene routines, consider giving her an age-appropriate book about puberty (several good options are listed in the Recommended Resources). Don't make a big deal about the book and don't ask her to report back to you about whether she's read it; just know that you've given her a way to educate herself about the facts of life on her own schedule. At my suggestion, Maya bought some books for Camille, put them in her room with a note reading, "Found these while browsing at the bookstore. Love, Mom," and left it at that. Even if your daughter readily seeks or takes your advice about managing puberty, she may enjoy having books that allow her to read up on the topics she's interested in and that she can use to initiate conversations with you when she wants further details.

Shortly after leaving the books for Camille, Maya was surprised (and heartened!) one evening when Camille asked Maya how old she was when she got her period and when she had started using tampons. Maya answered the questions in a matter-of-fact way and did not try to strike up a broader conversation on the subject. By this point Maya had aptly intuited something I've come to learn over my years of practice, which is that having a delicate conversation with a teenager is like trying to talk with someone on the other side of a door. Camille opened the door a little bit and Maya wisely worked within the small space she'd been given. Had Maya barged through with all sorts of uninvited information, Camille would have slammed the door, locked it tight, and hesitated to ever open it again.

You will hear from many girls and their parents throughout this book, but in almost every chapter, we'll be checking back in with Maya and Camille (whose names, like all of the others in this book, have been changed). The more I got to know Maya, the more I admired her wisdom and appreciated her openness to collaborating with me as we thought about her daughter. And, as much as any girl, Camille's path through her teenage years highlights how different developmental strands become salient at different points on the journey through adolescence.

Girls who feel uncomfortable opening the door to get help from their mothers about the physical changes that come with puberty may welcome the support of a neutral third party. I know an enterprising mom who made a reconnaissance mission to the lingerie department of our local department store where she learned the hours of a friendly, professional bra fitter. With her daughter's agreement, they returned to the store and the mother did her own shopping while the saleswoman sized her daughter for a bra. Along similar lines, if your daughter rejects your advice about how to manage her acne, consider making an advance call to her pediatrician or family doctor before her next routine visit and ask her doctor to address skin care as part of that appointment. In other words, if your daughter wants to have privacy from you around her changing body, respect her wishes while connecting her with the information and resources she needs to take good care of herself.

Occasionally, girls will feel so overwhelmed by the onset of puberty that they pretend it isn't happening. They minimize or deny their need for a bra, deodorant, regular showers, acne control, or even supplies for managing menstruation. If your daughter hopes that by ignoring puberty it will go away, you'll need to address her denial while honoring the signals she's sending that she's not looking for a long conversation on the topic. Try something such as, "It used to be my job to help you take care of your body, but it's now time for you to take over that work. Clearly, you're not happy that things just got a lot more complicated. I know that it's a hassle to deal with pimples, your period, and stuff like that, but I think you'll feel better about the whole thing when you address it head-on and take better care of yourself."

Looking around the gym at my daughter's primary school, it's clear that the puberty talk is overdue for many of the nine- and ten-year-old girls in the room. New results from a massive study conducted by experts from around the USA show that the first signs of puberty, usually the beginnings of breast development, now arrive earlier than ever. By age seven, breast buds appear in 24 percent of African-American girls, 15 percent of Hispanic girls, 10 percent of Caucasian girls, and 2 percent of Asian girls, and those numbers jump to 43 percent, 31 percent, 18 percent, and 13 percent, respectively, by age eight. The age at which girls first start menstruating is also dropping, but not as precipitously: one hundred years ago, periods arrived around age fourteen, not twelve as is now common.

In their fascinating book *The New Puberty,* physician Louise Greenspan and psychologist Julianna Deardorff summarize the known factors that, alone or in combination, may be triggering early puberty: childhood obesity, exposure to hormone-disrupting chemicals, and social and psychological stressors. They note that these risk factors are especially common in impoverished communities, which largely accounts for the high rates of early puberty in minority American girls.

The schools in Shaker Heights are well integrated, but the district's racial and economic lines overlap and the minority students are disproportionately among the poorest. Though it's impossible to know what accounts for the timing of puberty in any one girl, the broad demographic trends hit me over the head at every lower secondary program I attend. A striking percentage of fully developed African-American *Year 6* girls perform for the audience of parents and relatives alongside Caucasian classmates who, for the most part, still look like children. Watching the programs I always find myself worrying and wondering, "What must it feel like to have the body of an eighteen-year-old when you're only eleven?"

Here's what I know: for girls whose physical development rushes far ahead of their psychological development, it feels pretty weird. At best. If you suspect that your daughter sees the changes in her body as too much, too soon, help her keep things in perspective. You can say, "Your body has decided that it's time to start acting older, but that doesn't mean that the rest of you needs to be on the same schedule. Feel free to keep doing kid stuff for as long as you'd like. It will all even out eventually."

Smoke Without Fire

In Year 10 of secondary school, my best friend and I became obsessed with Marvin Gaye's now classic song "Sexual Healing." For weeks on end swimming, we listened to nothing else during our fifteen-minute ride to and from practice. While Nancy drove, I manned the tape deck—whirring the tape backward when the song ended and hoping to release the rewind button somewhere near the song's beginning. In Nancy's white Volkswagen Beetle with its maroon leather interior, we grooved and sang along: "If you don't know the thing you're dealing, oh I can tell you, darling, that it's sexual healing." And I can tell you that there was no correlation between our passion for the song and our interest in actually pursuing sex. The only steam in our loveless lives was coming off our wet hair as we drove home from practice in the Denver winter. But thanks to Marvin, we were dabbling in sexual (and melodic) sophistication and getting on with the work of parting with childhood.

Girls who are eager to leave their childhood behind often equate being older with taking an interest in sex and, like Nancy and me, they can do an alarmingly good job of mimicking adult sexuality. If they aren't singing provocative songs, they may be trying out risqué outfits, heavy makeup, or seductive dance moves. It's not uncommon for parents to complain to me about the racy dresses their daughters want to wear to school dances and even parents who succeed in sending their daughter off to the dance in an age-appropriate outfit often suspect that she hiked up her skirt, ditched her tasteful top, and changed into hobbling stilettos as soon as she was out of their sight. But when teenage girls succeed in looking like sexy adults (a distinctly female form of parting with childhood), I don't think that grown-ups should assume that the girls fully comprehend the messages they are sending. In my experience, girls often don't get it. They fail to draw a connection between *looking sexy* and *being sexual*. Just as little girls who try on lipstick to look grown-up have no interest in actually acting like an adult, the teenager dressed in revealing clothes may have no intention of backing up her appearance with action. The terms have changed, but the aim is the same: both the child and the teen are *playing at* looking older.

You might feel shocked, or even angry, if your daughter presents a vulgar or sexualized persona, but hold off on a strong response until you've asked yourself, "Is this all smoke, or might there be fire?" If you've got reason to worry that something's on fire, know that this book contains plenty of advice on handling risky behavior. If you think it's all smoke remember Ashley, the door closer, and her father, the overreactor, when planning your next move. Ashley's dad hurt their relationship by investing her door closing with much more meaning than it actually had, and if your daughter does a world-class job of looking trashy, you might feel a powerful impulse to make the same mistake by telling her that she looks cheap or like a tramp.

While you may mean these comments to provide helpful feedback, most girls won't hear them this way. Your daughter may have assembled an outfit that she believes projects an air of adult sophistication, perhaps even successfully copying a look that she saw in a magazine or online. However tacky or tawdry her styling might be, when you call it cheap, she hears, "Your carefully crafted attempt to appear more mature has failed and you actually look ridiculous." If you say that she looks like a tramp, your daughter will *not* hear you saying, "You are presenting yourself in a way that our culture often associates with promiscuity." She'll hear, "I think you're a tramp." Instead, consider something such as: "Honey, you have captured a look meant for adults—it's not appropriate at thirteen." Should you run into (all but guaranteed) resistance, you might need to follow up with, "That outfit will draw sexual attention your way that, frankly, *no one* in this family is ready for."

Girls also use online environments to try on personas that don't really match their actual personalities. By posting risqué comments or images that suggest sophistication, girls sometimes conduct digital experiments in parting with childhood. I'm most likely to hear about a girl's online behavior when parents come across content that has nothing in common with the girl they know. It sometimes happens that utterly charming girls post digital language that would put a foul-mouthed truck driver to shame. And I've helped parents try to make sense of a girl's online claims—that she has been getting drunk or running around with older boys—that they know cannot be true.

If your daughter's posts don't accord with the girl you know, don't assume that she's doing every wild-child thing she boasts about, but don't be naïve either. Have a conversation with her about what you've found online and ask her to explain what's going on. If you sense, or know, that your daughter's engaging in false advertising, try to figure out what she was *hoping* to accomplish with her inappropriate postings and have a conversation about that.

Smoke and fire aside, girls often present themselves online in ways their parents would not approve of in person. If this happens with your daughter, take the opportunity to invoke or create an agreement about what's acceptable for digital posting. Teens have a hard time appreciating the potential impact of what they post and often need rules spelling out what they can and can't do online, as well as effective consequences for breaking them. Consider the "Grandma" rule: if your daughter wouldn't feel comfortable with Grandma seeing it, she shouldn't post it. If she goes ahead and posts it anyway, your daughter should be prepared to live without her phone, or at least the internet, for a while.

Even if your daughter doesn't push the boundaries of adult behavior in her appearance or digital postings, some of her peers will. Capitalize on these prime opportunities to weigh in about when and where the outward signs of adulthood should kick in. If you pick your daughter up from a dance and see girls wearing high heels, ovarian-length skirts, and spilling out of their tops, feel free to say, "Man, those girls are looking pretty sexy. You and your friends will have decades to be adults and dress like that if you want. Now's your big chance to go to these dances and have fun wearing comfortable clothes that look good."

If you happen to notice that one of your daughter's friends seems to be engaged in an online marketing campaign to seem twenty-five when she's really fifteen, go ahead and comment: "If Megan is hooking up with lots of boys—and I doubt that she really is—I wonder if she's okay. And I worry about her impulse to announce that online." Don't expect that your daughter will want to have a long conversation about what's going on with Megan, but don't miss the opportunity to let your daughter know that your position is one of concern, not judgment. Doing so will help keep channels of communication open between you and your daughter about the many conversation-worthy things her peers will do.

Any parent of a teenager knows that digital technology plays a critical role in the lives of adolescents and makes raising teenagers as complex as it has ever been. Not surprisingly, today's technology impacts every developmental strand of adolescence, so we'll continue to address its role in your daughter's life, and the part you play as her parent, as we consider the six remaining strands.

Parting with Childhood: When to Worry

Given how unusual *normal* behavior can be in teenagers, it's sometimes hard for parents to know when something's truly wrong. If an adult were to suddenly become very private, cling to loved ones then reject them, refuse to acknowledge the need for personal hygiene, or constantly experiment with new looks or identities, we'd have grounds for concern. Yet I've offered all of these behaviors as typical examples of how teenage girls go about the crucial work of parting with childhood.

So how do we know when it's time to worry?

Paradoxically, it's often time to worry when a teenager's behavior *isn't* all over the map—when she hangs out at one extreme or the other. In terms of parting with childhood, I worry about teenagers who seem overly reluctant to grow up and about teenagers who want nothing to do with being a kid.

The Female Peter Pan

Some girls seem to be committed to a never-ending childhood. They are sweet and forthcoming, embedded in the bosom of their family, and quite easy on their parents. In my private practice, they use euphemisms like "Sugar!" instead of actually swearing, or they say that they tell their mothers everything, leading me to think, "Really? You do? Why?" The answer to that "Why?" comes in many forms. Some live with troubled parents who cannot withstand rejection. Some serve as the chief confidante for a single or unhappily married parent, and loyalty to that parent trumps the impulse to give him or her a developmentally appropriate cold shoulder. At the furthest extreme are girls whose parents cannot stand the idea of their daughter growing up. These parents actively cultivate dependence and insist on caring for their daughter as if she were a child even well into her teenage years. I've seen parents in this category go so far as to generously redecorate their daughter's childhood bedroom to better suit her tastes as a college graduation gift.

These girls come to my practice for at least one of three reasons: they are anxious, depressed, or lonely. If they're anxious, it's usually because unconsciously, they're furious. They are being robbed of their adolescence and they know it. These girls appear to be frightened of the outside world, but it soon becomes clear that they are frightened of their inner worlds. They are terrified of their own impulses to be rude and rejecting because they can't act on those impulses and maintain their parents' love. If they are depressed, it's usually because they have directed their anger inward. Not having the latitude to be unpleasant with their parents, they become unpleasant with themselves. "My parents are struggling" morphs into "I am struggling," a depressive distortion that is safer than reality.

And they are sad because they know that they are missing out. Girls engaged in a perpetual childhood often have few friends during adolescence because they strike peers as being both too babyish and too mature. Age-mates who are eagerly parting with childhood want nothing to do with girls who seem childlike. Further, I have found that girls who are too closely allied with their parents tend to take a rigid view of their peers' behavior and can come across as dull and aloof. They look down on drinking and are totally freaked out by any form of teenage sexuality. Needless to say, the party invites don't come rolling in.

If you recognize your daughter as you read this, step back to consider why she may be clinging to her childhood. Healthy adolescent development requires certain conditions—one being parents who can handle rejection. You don't have to be as tough as a concrete pool, but it's best if you can be durable; you may need to build your adult support network in order to give your daughter permission to *really* grow up. If you are relying on your daughter for emotional support, look for adults you can count on, including, perhaps, a good psychotherapist. Given how tuned in girls are to their parents, your daughter will likely sense that you've found yourself some needed reinforcement and start to lean away.

If you suspect that your daughter thinks you *need* her to depend on you, take steps to change her mind. Celebrate any move she makes toward independence or ask why she's not branching out. You may have to acknowledge that you've had a hard time with the fact that she's growing up but that you don't expect her to sacrifice herself to take care of you. If your daughter won't loosen her grip on you, find a seasoned psychotherapist to help her learn to let go.

Throughout this book you'll notice that the "When to Worry" section at the end of each chapter offers a few explanations to consider and some suggestions for addressing concerning behavior, then often directs you to seek further resources (in addition to those suggested in the Recommended Resources at the back of this book). In the spirit of Tolstoy's apt line that "happy families are all alike, every unhappy family is unhappy in its own way," girls who are truly struggling usually need, and certainly deserve, guidance tailored to their specific circumstances. Indeed, every troubled girl I have ever worked with has a complex story that, once known, explains her difficulties. But those stories are as unique as the girls who live them, and their telling goes beyond the scope of what this book aims to offer. There are shelves of books about girls whose adolescence has taken an alarming or dark turn; this book centers on the normal developmental challenges navigated by the majority of teenage girls and their families.

Rushing into Adulthood

We should also worry about girls who race too far ahead. I'm not talking about girls who are mature in the real sense of the word—running babysitting businesses and becoming impressively self-sufficient. I'm talking about thirteen- and fourteen-year-olds having sex or experimenting with drinking or drugs. Unfortunately, some social cachet comes with dabbling in what experts call "pseudomature" behavior because teens focused on leaving childhood behind can be dazzled by peers on the fast track. But research finds that teens who push the limits early tend not to fare well down the line. Over time, they are more likely to have trouble with relationships, substances, and the law than their slow-lane peers.

Who is most likely to experiment with sex, drugs, or drinking at an early age? Psychological science consistently points to two factors: disproportionately, girls on the fast track come from disrupted families or lack a close relationship with at least one parent. The link between having a difficult family life and early risky behavior often comes down to low levels of supervision. Parents contending with poverty, personal difficulties, or other major stressors can't always fill their daughter's time with structured extracurricular activities or be around after school. Left alone (and often becoming lonesome), girls sometimes go looking for trouble.

Ava, a Year 9 student, was the epitome of a disconnected, pseudomature girl. Her mom and dad hauled her into my office shortly after they came home late one weeknight to find her vomiting into the toilet while her friend lay passed out on the bathroom floor. Ava had taken advantage of her parents' long hours at work to mix samples from every bottle in their liquor cabinet before inviting a friend over to share the concoction.

In our first meeting, Ava sat apart from her parents in the extra chair at my private practice while her parents, wordless with fury, shared my couch. They glared at their daughter, a beautiful girl with carefully tweezed, arched eyebrows. Ava removed the designer sunglasses that served as her headband and chewed indifferently on the end of one arm of the glasses while glaring right back.

Ava's father broke the silence by describing the incident that triggered their visit. Before he finished, he indignantly added, "Ava just doesn't get it. Her friend could have *died.*"

Her mother finally spoke. "We work so hard to give her a good life—and this is how she acts."

Adopting the brand of irrational, egocentric logic that tarnishes the name of teenage girls everywhere, Ava retorted, "If you actually cared about me, you'd let me do what I want."

With a mixture of anger and incredulity, her father turned to me. "She wants us to drive her to high school parties!"

Saying nothing, Ava's mother gave her daughter a look that told the whole story: both parents worked demanding jobs with long hours to keep the family afloat and it pained her to watch Ava ruin sunglasses that almost certainly cost more than what her parents could comfortably afford. Ava gnawed away while seeming to relish the knowledge that her mother wouldn't bark at her to get the glasses out of her mouth while they were still in my company.

Watching the scene that played out before me, I strongly suspected that the fury burning in my office was actually kindled by the pain of Ava's lonesome isolation and her parents' fears for her safety. I hoped that if I could get the family to work with me in therapy, they would come to see this too.

Even in families that are intact, or provide supervision, girls are more likely to find trouble if their relationships at home are corroded by parental stress. There's ample evidence showing that the parent-child relationship can be strained by the hardships of poverty, but, until recently, affluent families were relatively neglected by psychological research. As Suniya Luthar, the prolific psychologist who led my favorite family dinner study, notes, "If a lack of income implies poor parenting, the logical corollary would be that ample income will imply generally good parenting." But that's not what the research shows. Recent studies find that wealth can isolate girls, both physically and emotionally, from their parents. Affluent parents may trade time at home for lucrative jobs and exercise the option of hiring a brigade of nannies, tutors, or housekeepers to help raise their daughters. In these cases, parental absence seems to contribute to a girl's emotional distress and drug use. Put another way, compared to wealthy teens, lower- and middle-class teenagers are, to their benefit, more likely to spend more time hanging around the house with their parents.

Lacking a close parental relationship, girls shop elsewhere for connection. They gravitate to older teens or other unsupervised peers. Or they turn to the media for cues about how to grow up. Psychologist Monique Ward, a leading researcher on how popular media shapes what adolescents believe, has found that teens who watch television for the purpose of companionship are more likely to see women as sexual objects, and the more time teens spend watching sexualized television, the more likely they are to engage in sexual behavior themselves. In sum, if parents aren't present to raise their daughters, our sex-saturated media (which happens to profit from marketing racy content to tweens) will gladly do the job for them.

If what you're reading has you worried, start by asking yourself: Do I usually know where my daughter is and what she's doing? Are we connected? Are we eating dinner together more nights a week than not? If you can't say yes to these questions, take steps to spend more time with your daughter and to deepen your relationship with her. If your daughter has already attached herself in a peer group of much older teens, find ways to connect her with age-mates and wise, supportive adults. Volunteer programs, after-school jobs, or church and synagogue youth programs can be good places to start. If your efforts to reconnect with your daughter fail, or if you can't pry her away from a crowd that is rushing too far ahead, seek help from her pediatrician or your family doctor, the guidance counselor at her school, or a trusted psychotherapist (physicians who work with teens are often a reliable source for suitable mental health referrals).

Should you ban sexualized media? Good luck. Even if you succeed in keeping it out of your house, your daughter will come across it on her own time. Do what you can to keep your daughter from being exposed to highly explicit content, and consider treating the rest as a useful conversation starter. You want your daughter to become a critical consumer of the media, so use what she's watching to help her build those skills. Swing by the couch or lean over her laptop and say, "I'm all for mindless entertainment, but you know that I'm not a big fan of shows that celebrate women for being sexy and stupid." Your daughter may roll her eyes, but do it anyway. Girls can listen and roll their eyes at the same time.

Some parents see development as a race to be won and encourage their girls to adopt the trimmings of adulthood. They promote their daughter's worldly appearance or provide her with items (handbags, jewelry) generally reserved for women, not young girls. But that's not how it works. Normal development is a powerful, internal force that propels girls forward along the strands of adolescence. Most teenage girls don't need to be encouraged to grow up—they push ahead at a healthy pace and sometimes ask for more freedom or privilege than makes sense. When they want to grow up too fast, it's our job as parents to slow them down by pulling back. If you're familiar with this tension, be reassured—it means your daughter is doing *her* job and you are doing *yours* as she undertakes the work of parting with childhood.

TWO

. . . .

Joining a New Tribe

MY OFFICE AT LAUREL SCHOOL, WHICH RESIDES IN A MAJESTIC 1920s Tudor building, is known as the "Harry Potter office" because, like Harry's bedroom at the Dursleys', it's tucked under a staircase. In the deep and narrow space beneath the school's glorious main stairs there's enough room for my desk where the ceiling slopes down, two chairs that face each other, and a small bench for my bag and papers. I cherish my cozy space and would never lobby for a different one. The best thing about my office: it's in the center of the building but almost completely hidden. Not every girl who meets with me wants the whole school to know, and my location allows girls to slip discreetly down the stairs to find me. The second best thing about my office: it sits above a closet that houses the sound system for a gymnasium used by the elementary school and staffed by inventive teachers who occasionally play music during gym class. This means that the throbbing disco beat of "Car Wash" often comes up through my floor and lightens the mood when I'm meeting with students.

I was working at my desk—without a disco beat—when Jo-elle, a spritely, affable Year 10 student, peeked around my door and asked, "Can I talk to you about something?" Adopting the hunched-over stance that lets me get up from my desk without banging my head, I said, "You bet" and moved from be-hind my desk to the chair where I sit when I've got a visitor. Joelle settled in across from me.

"What's up?" I asked, eager to make it clear that she was welcome without an appointment.

"I think that it's time for me to give up soccer, but I really can't decide. I've played since I was five, but I'm not sure there's enough time for it anymore. I'm really getting into speech and debate, and I'm doing okay with the high school workload, but I don't want to fall behind. Practice is harder than it used to be so I'm coming home really tired, and between soccer and speech meets, my weekends are pretty much gone. I'm worrying so much about whether I should quit soccer that it's messing with my sleep."

I said, "It sounds like you're ready to move on. What's get-ting in the way of quitting soccer?"

As only a teenage girl can do, Joelle shot me a look that managed to communicate two things at once: "Are you actu-ally serious that you don't know what the issue is?" and "I can see that you're trying to help, so I'll forgive your ignorance."

She said, "My closest friends are on the team."

Instantly, I understood the "How could you not know?" ele-ment of the look she'd given me. If she quit soccer, she would be all but cut off from her friends, and that was reason enough to stay on the team. Having distanced herself from her close relationship with her parents, Joelle was already making terrific headway on the second developmental strand we'll consider— the work of joining a new tribe. Before adolescence, most girls are happily grounded within their families and have their most intimate relationships with their parents and siblings. By the end of adolescence, we expect that girls will loosen their close ties to their families and strengthen their connections with their peers. Indeed, as girls progress along this developmental strand, they often come to count on their peer relationships as much as, if not more than, their relationships with their parents.

For some teenagers, joining a tribe turns out to be pretty easy. They find a couple of good friends who stay loyal all mthe way through secondary school or, like Joelle, they fall in with a group of girls who share their interests. But for most teens, joining a tribe raises some tough questions. Do I like my tribe? Does my tribe like me? Does my tribe represent who I am or want to be? Should I try to join a better tribe? What are the benefits and costs of belonging to my tribe? And what do I do about the tribe members I dislike?

I can't overstate the significance of a teenager's tribe membership. Teenagers aren't just looking to make friends, they are replacing the family they've withdrawn from (or, at least, might barely acknowledge in public) with a tribe that they can feel proud to call their own. Failing this, they are left with the stomach-turning options of returning to the bosom of their family or navigating the world alone. Further, a girl's membership in a tribe will shape—and be shaped by—her interests, her academic achievement, her social status, her sense of personal worth, and even her bent toward risk-taking behavior. Considered this way, Joelle's dilemma makes sense. If she quits the team, she's distanced from her tribe. On top of that, she'd be moving away from her tribe right at the start of Year 10—a stressful juncture that's often eased by a secure sense of social belonging.

Given the critical importance of joining a new tribe, girls often become extremely upset when they're at odds with their peers. Before considering how you can help your daughter manage social stress, let's define two terms: *conflict* and *bullying*. Most of the friction between teens—and people of all other ages as well—constitutes conflict. Conflict is the common cold of human interaction: we don't like it, we can't cure it, and we just have to live with it. When humans spend time with other humans, we come into conflict with one another (and get colds). And as with the common cold, there are things we can do to relieve conflict and steps we can take to keep conflict from worsening.

Bullying, on the other hand, has more in common with pneumonia. Victims of bullying are exposed, over time, to negative actions by one or more peers and have difficulty defending themselves. Bullying is serious and potentially dangerous, and it needs to be treated aggressively. Just like pneumonia, bullying can cause real, lasting damage if ignored. But our culture's preoccupation with bullying has led to its overdiagnosis. Too many unpleasant interactions among young people are now referred to as bullying, and misdiagnosis leads to improper treatment. Treating conflict as bullying is the equivalent of prescribing a full-blown course of antibiotics for the common cold. The treatment isn't necessary, will not cure the cold, and creates new problems. Of course, treating bullying as if it were everyday conflict is the equivalent of misdiagnosing pneumonia as a common cold—left untreated, the situation can reach critical proportions.

Fortunately, conflict is much more common than bullying. But to adolescent girls, even peer conflict is deeply troubling, so most of this chapter centers on helping your daughter manage the stress and rivalry that often arise while gaining or maintaining membership in a tribe. The "When to Worry" section of this chapter addresses what you can do if your daughter becomes socially isolated, experiences bullying, or bullies others.

The Pull of Popular

Maya and I settled into a rhythm of meeting on Tuesday mornings. It wasn't until February, after she'd been coming to see me for four months, that Maya raised a concern about Camille's social life. Camille's class schedule shifted after the winter break and she no longer shared a lunch period with Sara, who had been one of her closest friends since Year 5. In the past few weeks, Maya heard Camille talk about her new friends, a group of popular girls, several of whom shared Camille's lunch period and who, apparently, had invited her to join their table. Maya was worried about the shift in her daughter's social life. Camille was clearly thrilled to be included by the popular girls, but Maya knew that last year, in Year 7, the group had excluded classmates and invented bitchy nicknames for some of the girls outside their circle.

Exasperated, Maya explained to me that on the Saturday night before our meeting, she and her daughter ended up in a fight because Raina, one of the new friends, sent a last-minute text inviting Camille over. Camille already had plans to go to a movie with her old friend Sara, but she begged Maya to help her make up an excuse to ditch Sara then drive her to Raina's house. Maya refused to do either and insisted that Camille do the right thing by keeping her plans with Sara. Helpless to do otherwise, Camille glumly went to the movie with Sara while refusing to speak to Maya on the drive there or back.

Maya was appalled by her daughter's willingness to ditch Sara. I saw her point but noted that Camille was hardly the first Year 8 girl to be seduced by the power of popularity. If we think about it in tribal terms, girls begin to value what popularity seems to promise: social cachet that guarantees a place in a desirable tribe. It's no coincidence that the concept of popularity gains traction at the exact moment when girls pull away from their own families. The fear of being tribeless—distanced from one's family yet without a peer group—cuts to the quick and leads to the idealization of popularity and the social connections that come with it. In fact, most of the social drama for which girls are known makes a great deal more sense when we appreciate that they are simply trying to secure membership in a tribe.

Researchers who study peer relationships have found that there are actually two different kinds of peer popularity. *Sociometric popularity* is the term used to describe well-liked teens with reputations for being kind and fun, while *perceived popularity* describes teens who hold a lot of social power but are disliked by many classmates. These two distinct groups emerge in studies that employ a simple peer-nomination method to examine social dynamics in school settings. Girls are given lists naming all the girls in their class (and boys are given lists naming all the boys) and asked to circle the names of the three girls they like the most, the three girls they like the least, and the girls who are considered to be popular. With this technique, researchers have found that many well-liked girls aren't considered to be popular, and that many girls who are considered to be popular aren't actually well liked. In fact, the disliked-but-popular girls are described by their classmates as domineering, aggressive, and stuck up, while the liked-but-unpopular girls are described as kind and trustworthy. A third group also emerges: well-liked girls who are identified by peers as being popular. They are amiable and faithful but differ from their liked-but-unpopular peers in that they aren't easy to push around. In other words, the girls in the liked-and-popular group have found the relational sweet spot of being both friendly and assertive—a skill set girls often struggle to master and to which we'll return soon.

So we know from the research that when teens use the term

popular, they're likely to be describing girls with *perceived popularity*—girls who use cruelty to gain social power. Adults would like to think that girls who are mean would be shunned by their peers, but unfortunately, the opposite tends to occur. A girl who allows herself to be mean enjoys many "friends" who are eager to stay on her good side, and she is often feared and indulged by her remaining classmates who have no interest in becoming her target. While meanness between girls sometimes involves name-calling or physical intimidation, girls are more likely to use potent but indirect forms of aggression, such as spreading rumors about another girl, excluding her, or poisoning her relationships with others. In short, mean adolescent girls maintain their power by threatening the tribal memberships their peers hold most dear.

Girls are rarely able to maintain social power indefinitely through meanness. By Year 11, most girls feel secure enough in their friendship groups to ignore or isolate girls who continue to be nasty. Year 8 students, though, having just withdrawn from their home tribe, are particularly vulnerable. They are often willing to be mean—or put up with peers who are mean—in order to secure a new tribe. Not all Year 8 students become preoccupied with securing social ties this way, but meanness generally seems to reach its peak around this time.

What's with Year 8? Though we currently lack the science and technology to prove this, I suspect that, neurologically speaking, the "how to use and abuse social power" switch in the brain turns on some time around Year 8, but the "let me think for a minute about the implications of using and abusing social power" switch doesn't turn on until Year 9 or after. Put another way, the social dynamics of Year 8 are perfectly captured by an old *New Yorker* cartoon featuring two politicians with the Capitol in the background. One says to the other, "But how do you know for sure that you've got power unless you abuse it?"

With these thoughts in mind, I routinely encourage parents to capitalize on opportunities to deconstruct the meaning of the term *popular*. As we know, when teens say that a girl is popular, they're usually saying that she's powerful. And when she's powerful, it's usually because she's willing to be mean and everyone knows it. If your daughter mentions that a girl is popular, ask, "Is she popular or just powerful? Do kids like her, or are they scared of her?" Give your daughter a good reason to take popularity off of its pedestal.

You can also point out that when it comes to friendship, quality trumps quantity. Indeed, research finds that the happiest teens aren't the ones who have the most friendships but the ones who have strong, supportive friendships, even if that means having a single terrific friend. Why? One explanation is that popularity brings hard work, regardless of how girls come by it. Girls who are at the center of large tribes have a lot of social connections to maintain and often run into loyalty conflicts. Consider the popular girl whose family will only let her invite two friends for a sleepover. She must think carefully about whom she'll choose and make a plan to manage the hurt feelings of the friends she doesn't invite. On top of that, heavy social demands can undermine what cultural anthropologists call "sustainable routines," the predictable patterns of daily life that go a long way toward reducing stress. Popular girls have to make complex calculations before they decide whom they'll ask to the movies or call when they're upset. Girls with one or two good friends can lean on their small tribes and skip those calculations.

Maya and I talked it over and decided that she should put her energy behind supporting Camille's ongoing friendship with Sara, even as Camille looked to become closer with the popular crowd. We worried that Camille might drop Sara—a loss that would be unfortunate in its own right and made that much worse if (more likely, when) her new friendships turned sour. As soon as an opportunity presented itself, Maya planned to say, "I can tell that you're psyched about your new friends, but you seem really tense on the weekends while you wait to hear from them. Sara may not be as fun as the girls you're getting to know, but you seemed more relaxed when you were spending time with her. Do you want to ask her to come over?" We didn't bank on Camille dumping the popular girls and rushing back to Sara but trusted that it would be useful for Maya to offer a little values clarification: having one good old friend usually beats having many powerful new friends.

Though Maya was strongly tempted to do so, I counseled her against talking with Camille about her new crowd's bad reputation. It is tempting to pan peers who have been unkind, but it's best to remember that girls change quickly during the teenage years. I know parents who regret having bad-mouthed a girl who went on to develop a close, happy friendship with their daughter, so if you feel you must criticize your daughter's friends—and sometimes you must—use your words and your tone to communicate that the girls are in a tricky situation, not that they are bad people. When we next met, Maya told me that she decided to weigh in on Camille's new friendships while she and Camille were watching a television show in which girls talked behind one another's backs. Without expecting a response, Maya said, "I can still remember the girls at my school who tried to fit in by pointing out who *didn't* fit in. It's not the most mature behavior, and I'm impressed that it's not your style." With her comment, Maya aimed to set a high bar for Camille's behavior without directly criticizing Camille's popular friends.

Tribal Warfare

It didn't take long for Sara to figure out that Camille was neglecting her in order to spend time with her new friends. Hurt and insulted, Sara told several of their classmates that Camille had struggled with bedwetting late into Year 4 (this was true but shared in confidence). Camille found out about the gossip and referred to Sara as a "bitch" while pencil-texting—writing back and forth in a notebook—with one of her new friends during study hall. The study hall monitor saw the slur, confiscated the notebook, and called home to Maya. When Maya confronted Camille about the information from school, Camille defensively admitted what she had done but insisted that Sara had started it by telling everyone about her bedwetting.

Girls can be really punishing when a tribe member has been disloyal. Sara was understandably hurt but acted on her feelings in unacceptable ways and inspired Camille to do the same. There's no excuse for either girl's behavior, but there's an explanation: as a culture, we do a terrible job of helping girls figure out what to do when they are mad. As far as girls know, they can either be a total doormat—think Cinderella—or flat-out cruel like Cinderella's stepsisters. We rarely help girls master assertion—the art of standing up for oneself while respecting the rights of others. We send our daughters the message that "good girls" are nice all the time, and then we're somehow surprised when girls act out in unacceptable ways. Adult women struggle with how to stand up for themselves without being called "pushy," "bossy," or worse. If adults struggle with it, you can bet that girls do, too.

Teaching your daughter to be assertive takes time. The first step involves acknowledging and validating her negative feelings. Maya called me after her unsuccessful effort to get Camille to own her bad behavior. We agreed that Camille's actions were out of line, but I encouraged Maya to help Camille to separate what she was thinking and feeling from how she chose to *act* on her thoughts and feelings. Later that evening, Maya reopened the conversation about what had happened at school by saying, "I know that Sara really upset you—what she did would make anyone feel embarrassed and mad. You have a right to those feelings, but you can't act on them in hurtful ways." Teenagers benefit when adults distinguish thinking and feeling from doing because *everyone* has thoughts and feelings that are unpleasant. They're a fact of life and, as we'll see in chapter 3, "Harnessing Emotions," psychological discomfort can help girls learn and grow. But what we think and feel should inform, not dictate, what we do.

Had Camille sought Maya's help before she had started calling Sara names, they might have worked together to craft a dispassionate, assertive statement that Camille could say (or text) to Sara: "I'm hurt that you shared my personal problems at school. I get that you might be angry with me but you could've let me know in a different way." That sounds fine, but few adults—and fewer teenagers—would actually say something like that. So be aware that even if your daughter doesn't take your advice, or if she asks for it too late to be heeded, girls still benefit when adults suggest measured alternatives to impulsive action. Most parents find themselves building their daughter's assertiveness skills by belated fire-fighting of situations that could have been better handled. (Bear in mind that you'll only have a chance at this kind of coaching if you've shown your daughter that you'll validate her feelings while keeping negative judgment to a minimum.) Talking about examples of mature, assertive behavior can help girls tone down their future reactions or come up with their own options for an appropriate response.

Even if you don't hear from your daughter about her own struggles with aggressive behavior, you're likely to hear about unkindness in her class. These conversations can prove to be fertile ground for helping her build assertiveness skills. If your daughter tells you that a group at school has started to exclude one of its members, you could say, "They may have a reason for not wanting to hang out with her like they used to, but they need to find a nicer way of letting her know that they've got an issue. What would you do if you were in their shoes?"

Be careful about how often you take advantage of these opportunities; girls clam up around adults who try to turn almost every conversation into a teachable moment. Nodding and asking genuine questions about your daughter's view of the situation can also go a long way toward helping her develop her thinking about how she and her peers should treat one another. Long story short, the success of all of your conversations with your teenage daughter will depend as much on what you *don't* say as it does on what you *do* say. The more you bite your tongue, the more she may be willing to share and the more impact your advice will have when you give it.

Securing a friendship group isn't easy for girls who find themselves jockeying for social power and juggling loyalties to old and new friends. And once girls are embedded within their tribes they often face new challenges as they move along this developmental strand. They might find themselves managing the politics of the tribes they ultimately join, engaging in risky behavior to maintain their social ties, or feeling stressed by outsized obligations to care for needy friends. We'll consider these challenges next.

Frenemies

The linguist Michael Adams refers to slang as "the people's poetry," and it's hard to deny the poetry of the slang term *frenemy*. Teens use this word to capture a variety of conflicted relationships, including that with a peer who is lots of fun except when she's being completely rotten. Unfortunately, the teenage social landscape isn't simply comprised of nice girls and mean girls. Those of us who spend time with teenagers know that girls who are sometimes mean can be extremely friendly—sharing intimate secrets or being utterly selfless— when they're *not* being unkind. This creates a dizzying situation for any girl who has a frenemy and can make some girls (and their parents) long for sincere enemies.

If your daughter has a frenemy, you probably won't hear much about the friendship when things are going well. But when your daughter's frenemy turns on her, you might learn about behavior that is surprisingly nasty. For instance, I worked with a family in my practice whose Year 9 daughter got into trouble at school over a cheating incident. She explained to her parents that a classmate had copied answers from her social studies quiz and confirmed that this was the same classmate who had recently caused a lot of drama by taking and then posting an embarrassing photo of the girl. Feeling angry and protective, my clients were ready to call the classmate's parents when their daughter begged them not to. She explained that she and her classmate were actually really good friends and showed her boggled parents weeks of light-hearted texts that had recently passed between them.

You might suspect that your daughter has a frenemy if you find yourself stuck in a repeating cycle where your daughter complains about a peer's antics, you encourage her to avoid that peer, things quiet down for a while, and then you hear new complaints about what the peer has done. Most parents in this situation expect that their daughter will figure out that she should stay away from the source of her suffering and are surprised when she's soon back to being as close with her frenemy as ever. Doing more of what already isn't working—in this case, encouraging a girl to avoid her frenemy—tends to be a failing parenting strategy. If you find yourself in this spot, you can support your daughter by asking more about both the hot and cold currents of the frenemyship. With a fuller sense of the relationship, you are in a position to say useful things such as, "It's really up to you whether you keep hanging out with her. If you do, be careful when she's being nice because you know that it may not last." Or, "We love you and hate seeing you put yourself in a position where you keep getting hurt." Or, "It sounds like she can be fun—I see why you guys hang out so much. But real friends don't do such mean stuff to each other."

Though it might feel as if you're stating the obvious, girls don't always have a way to know that their frenemy's behavior is completely inappropriate, especially if other girls put up with it and the frenemy herself is totally unapologetic. Teens appreciate it when parents confirm that they have a right to expect that their friends will generally be kind. And though there are occasional frenemyships between girls and boys, girls are most likely to have—and to talk with their parents about—female frenemies.

It's unrealistic for parents to try to prevent an adolescent friendship given that they don't actually have the power to monitor and control every aspect of a teenager's social life. And, as tricky as a frenemy can be, it may be even trickier for girls to try to break off the friendship. Adolescent tribes are held together by complex social webs, and a girl who cuts herself off from one peer may lose several friendships, or an entire tribe, in the bargain. Often, girls decide to put up with one difficult peer in order to keep peace in their tribe. It shouldn't be this way, but it is.

You can do a lot to help your daughter navigate a delicate situation by recognizing that she may not have an easy way out of a complicated friendship. Remember, teens don't operate like adults. If we decide that we want to end a friendship, we can stop making lunch dates, hope not to run into our old friend at the grocery store, and apologize for being "so darn busy that it's hard to get together" when we do. Teens see one another at school every day, whether they want to or not. If she'll let you, strategize with your daughter about how she can politely maintain a safe distance from her frenemy, even if they're in the same social circle.

What if you have reason to think that your own daughter mistreats her friends? One option would be to help your daughter understand that her friends won't always go along with her behavior. If your daughter likes to tease her friends (or do other things along those lines) go ahead and say, "Honey, we know you think your teasing is funny, but we're guessing your friends don't think so. They might not make a big deal out of it now, but don't be surprised if they start to pull back."

If necessary, you can also point out that she's having fun at the expense of her friends. When teens have fun by being mean, they are engaging in conduct that's a remnant of early childhood. Three-year-olds specialize in having "mean fun"— gleefully doing things that they know will annoy their parents—but most children grow out of this type of low-grade sadism. Given that teenagers are parting with childhood and driven by the wish to be seen as mature, parents can sometimes change behavior by pointing out its immaturity. For instance, you could say, "We know that you like to tease your friends—it may seem funny now, but it probably won't fly in a year ot two." Be cautious when calling a teenager's behavior immature. Doing so can be an effective way to help girls grow up, but it can also be received as a powerful insult. There's no upside in insulting teens (or anyone else, for that matter), so be sure you're coming from a warm and loving place if you try this approach.

If Your Tribe Jumped Off a Bridge . . .

Teenagers, even really mature and thoughtful ones, sometimes do dumb things. And the chance that your teenager will do something dumb increases when she's with her friends. You may have suspected as much—perhaps you even remember how your own judgment evaporated around your teenage friends—and psychologists Margo Gardner and Laurence Steinberg (a leading expert in all things teenager) came up with a clever way to demonstrate this phenomenon in a research lab. They compared how young teens (ages thirteen to sixteen), young adults (ages eighteen to twenty-two), and adults over the age of twenty-four played a video game that gives points for risky driving and docks points for being overly cautious or having a collision. Everyone in the study played the video game under one of two conditions: some played alone, while others played in front of age-mates.

The study found that, across all ages, the subjects took roughly the same number of risks when they were alone. Here's where things got interesting. With peers watching, older adults played the video game the same way they did when alone, the late teen/young adult group became quite a bit more risky when with peers than when alone, and the young teens were *twice* as risky when their peers watched them play. The bottom line? Compared to adults, teens are highly likely to throw caution to the wind when they are with their friends.

In technical terms, once puberty arrives, the brain's socio-emotional network can readily outmatch its sensible cognitive control system. At the neurological level, teenagers, more than adults or children, experience social acceptance as highly rewarding. Finding themselves in emotionally charged situations with social rewards—such as when a popular peer suggests that it would be fun to smoke pot—can cause teenagers to set aside their good thinking and let their impulses take over. As Laurence Steinberg puts it, "In adolescence, then, more might not only be merrier—more may also be riskier."

If anything keeps parents of teenagers up at night, it's fears about safety. But in the attempt to keep their daughters safe, some parents go to extremes that don't account for the importance of being cool in the eyes of the tribe and may actually place girls in greater danger. At one end, we find parents who think they can scare their daughter safe by threatening terrible punishments. While it may make the parents feel better to tell their daughter she'll be shipped off to military school if she even *thinks* about tasting beer, such threats can backfire when good teenagers find themselves in bad situations. Teens often have fluid weekend plans, and a girl who sets out for a Saturday night thinking she's going to a supervised get-together might find herself at a dicey party. If the party is out of control, or the girl just has a bad feeling about it, she will have to decide which of the following poses the greater threat: riding out the party to see where it goes or asking her parents to come get her. What girl would elect to humiliate herself in front of her tribe by inviting an enraged parent to yank her from the party? Of course, none of us would want our daughter to decide that it's a better bet to stay at the party than call us for help.

At the other extreme, we find parents who aim to keep their daughter safe by becoming her best friend and perhaps even serving alcohol to minors while hosting parties at their home. Though I also disagree with this parenting choice, I understand what usually drives it. Party parents figure that if their daughter is going to do risky things when with her friends, she'll be safer if she and her friends do those risky things right under their noses. But party parents rob their daughter of one of the best protections she has: the ability to blame her good behavior on them.

I think that the safest girls are the ones who can point to their parents' "crazy rules" to avoid risky behavior. If a friend offers marijuana, a girl should be able to say, "I want to smoke with you, but my mom has a nose like a bloodhound. If she smells weed on me when I get home, she'll throw me in rehab." You may not have a bloodhound's nose, you may have never discussed your marijuana policies with your daughter, and you may not even care if she tries it. But if you spent last weekend dancing on the tables with your daughter's friends, she cannot plausibly use this, or any other threatening story, to get out of a bad spot while saving face with her tribe. You may have mixed feelings about a safety strategy that involves fabricated tales of your Draconian policies, but remember that it's better for your daughter to be safe than for her friends to think you're cool. As the video game study shows, teens get riskier, not safer, around their friends. And it's just not realistic to expect a teen who has been offered marijuana to say, "Why thank you, but I'll have to pass. Marijuana isn't legal in our state, and even if it were, I'm a minor."

You can make it possible for your daughter to blame her

good behavior on you by being warm and accessible with her in the privacy of your home and utterly grown-up (even to the point of being remote) when her friends are around. Feel free to be as kind and hospitable as your daughter can stand when her friends are around, but stay firmly in your role of boring middle-aged parent so that she can paint you as the bad guy when needed. Teens sometimes push for their parents to lighten up, but they actually count on us to act like adults. In fact, I've learned that girls find it strange when parents act like teenagers from occasional conversations at my private practice office that go like this:

Girl: "So, Tanya's mom said that she'd buy beer for us this weekend."

Me: "Is that cool, or is it kinda weird?"

Girl: "It's *weird*. My mom isn't as fun as Tanya's, but at least she doesn't do stuff like that."

In addition to being adult enough that your daughter can always blame her good behavior on you, be sure to talk with her about the fact that she might find herself in a bad situation and develop an agreement that you will retrieve her—no questions asked—from any circumstance at any time. She should expect to have a long conversation with you over breakfast about how she found herself at a strange party fifteen miles from home, but make it clear to her that you will never give her a reason to regret asking for your help. Consider this: some parents even arrange a code with their daughter so that if she calls to say "I forgot to turn off my iron" they know that she wants to be rescued and they start yelling into the phone. The girl can hold the phone away from her ear, make faces while her friends listen to the rant, and apologize that she has to go home because her mom has gone berserk. You'll do your best parenting when you recognize your daughter's wish to side with her tribe, even if she's choosing not to join in with what they're doing.

When Tribes Need Elders

For several months I had an after-school appointment in my private practice with Lana, a smart, no-nonsense Year 12 student who came to me for support during her parents' contentious divorce. On a rainy Thursday, she stretched her legs across my couch and used one smooth motion to pull an elastic band from her wrist and whip her curly hair into a topknot. Then she said, "What we talk about is confidential, right?" to which I gave my standard reply: "Of course, unless we have reason to be concerned about your safety or worry that you might be dangerous to someone else."

She went on to share that her friend, Cassie, had started cutting, shown Lana several cuts on her arms, and asked Lana to keep the cuts a secret. Lana felt torn. She didn't want to break Cassie's trust, but she was losing sleep over concerns that Cassie might continue to hurt herself. On top of that, she felt obliged to keep a close eye on Cassie when what she really wanted was a break from their stressful friendship.

Few girls will reach adulthood without knowing about the self-destructive behavior of a friend or classmate. Especially as they age, girls often ask their friends to keep their dangerous behavior a secret, but doing so puts the secret keeper in a terrible position. Teenage girls share a powerful sense of loyalty to their tribe members and are reluctant to go behind one another's backs, as they consider it, even to seek the help of adults. At the same time, they worry intensely about one another and may try to help a friend with problems far beyond what teenagers can manage. Actually, girls sometimes try to help one another with problems that even adults can't manage, unless that adult happens to be trained in a mental health field. I rush to point this out to girls who seem to feel that they're failing their friend by bringing her problem my way.

When girls tell me that they have a friend who is cutting, drinking excessively, using drugs, suicidal, suffering from an eating disorder, or engaging in any other type of dangerous behavior, I start by reassuring them that they were wise to let me know, and that's what I did with Lana. I said, "You're right to be worried, and you're right that Cassie needs more help than you can give—she's lucky to have you looking out for her." Lana's shoulders relaxed, but her face remained serious. She knew that we still had work to do.

Next, we strategized about how Lana could make sure that Cassie's parents—the only people who could get Cassie the help she needed—knew what was happening. Lana and I agreed that she could return to Cassie and say something such as, "I'm glad you told me you were cutting. Clearly, part of you is worried about it and I want to stick up for that part of you. Your parents need to know so that they can get you the help you deserve. What's the best way to tell them?" We agreed that Lana could suggest two options, namely that Cassie could tell her parents and ask them to confirm to Lana that they'd been told, or Cassie could go with Lana to tell a trusted adult at school and ask that adult to inform Cassie's parents. Not surprisingly, Lana suspected that Cassie would reject both of those options. If that happened, I encouraged her to say, "An adult needs to know what's going on. If you don't want to tell anyone, then I need to. I know you'll be mad, but I care more about your safety than about having you be happy with me all of the time."

It's important to remember that teenagers form tribes with

the express purpose of creating a group that *doesn't* include adults, so going outside of their group to get help from an adult—even for life-threatening behavior—can feel like a huge betrayal. If your daughter comes to you about a friend's problems, make a point of letting her know she's made the right call. If you're really worried about your daughter's friend, you might be compelled to make what I consider to be the *wrong* call: the one where you immediately dial the parents of your daughter's friend, even if your own daughter doesn't want you to. When your daughter comes to you for help, supporting her should be your priority. Going around your daughter to act on something that she has told you in confidence will damage her willingness to trust you with sensitive information and may keep her from coming to you for help, guidance, or a reality check in the future. Barring immediate life-or-death concerns, reassure your daughter that she's not responsible for her friend's care and that the kindest thing she can do will be to connect her friend with an adult who can help.

I learned about the importance of respecting girls' loyalty to one another, even when addressing dangerous behavior, while conducting research on preventing eating disorders. Traditionally, eating disorder prevention programs have focused on helping girls to manage stress, feel good about their bodies, or become critical consumers of media imagery. In general, these programs are more effective at changing what girls know about stress, body image, and the media than they are at changing how they care for their own bodies. This is a frightening reality given that eating disorders often go undetected by adults until they are severe, so my colleagues and I designed a program to encourage girls to tell an adult if they saw the early signs of an eating disorder in one of their friends.

Before testing the program with girls in years 9 and 10, we met with a focus group of Year 11 girls at Laurel School to get feedback on the study design. After we described the plan for the study, the Year 11 girls told us that they would be open to telling an adult if a friend showed signs of an eating disorder, except for one thing: they didn't want to be seen as disloyal. They were fiercely committed to supporting one another and keeping one another's secrets, and they worried that telling an adult about a troubling change in a peer's eating would be a social transgression. With help from the Year 11 girls, we came up with a solution. We would give girls the option of leaving unsigned notes detailing their concerns for trusted adults at Laurel School (e.g., "Maggie has skipped lunch for the past week"). From there, the adults would find an opportunity to observe what the peers shared and—if appropriate—broach the concern with the girl and her family without mentioning the tip-off.

Ultimately, we developed a successful program that educated girls about the dangers of eating disorders and the importance of early intervention while emphasizing the anonymous mechanism by which girls could share concerns about their friends. Looking back, I'm sure that we owe the success of our approach to the candid feedback from our Year 11 focus group. From them we learned that girls are much more likely to seek help for a suffering friend if they can count on adults to respect their tribal loyalties.

Even when girls do get help for serious problems, things don't always get better right away. In our next session, Lana told me that Cassie had actually agreed that she needed more support than Lana could provide and, with Lana in tow, told the school counselor about her cutting. Cassie later told Lana that the counselor had referred her to a therapist in their community. Lana was relieved that her friend was getting professional help but found that her relationship with Cassie was just as stressful as before. Two or three nights a week she texted Lana to say that she was feeling very upset and on the verge of cutting. Lana had no idea how to respond. She was incredibly worried about Cassie, ill-equipped to counsel her, and resentful about losing homework time because she was feeling upset or busily trying to care for her friend.

We *want* girls to call on one another for support, and usually they do a great job of it. In other words, the help they provide their tribe members usually has a positive effect. For Cassie, though, Lana's efforts didn't help—the problem was bigger than the two of them. Should your daughter find herself in Lana's spot, support her as she draws some boundaries in her relationship with a needy friend.

Here's what I said to Lana when she told me about the recent texts: "Cassie's dark feelings are like a haunted house that she carries around inside her. When she's drawn to her haunted house, she, understandably, doesn't want to go in alone. That's when she sends you a text that gets you almost as upset as she is. It's not your job to go into Cassie's haunted house with her—that's her therapist's job. The next time Cassie sends you a text like that, encourage her to share her painful feelings with her therapist. If that's not working, we can think together about how you, or Cassie, can let her parents know that Cassie's troubles outmatch the professional support she's getting right now."

Girls will often set aside their own wishes to help a needy friend. But if the help doesn't solve the problem, stand ready to offer your daughter some kind, assertive language she can use to protect herself while pointing her friend toward the right resources. A few weeks later, Lana told me that our approach had worked. When Cassie next sent a scary text, Lana asked her if she was sharing her difficult feelings with her therapist. She then sought Cassie out at school the next day to talk about an upcoming history test, intentionally not mentioning the texts from the night before. To Lana's relief, an unspoken agreement developed between them. They were still friends, but Lana stopped being the recipient of Cassie's awful feelings.

For the most part, the work of joining a new tribe today looks a lot like it did back when we were teenagers. But Lana and Cassie's relationship reflects the one huge exception to this rule: your daughter will advance along this developmental strand while cultivating her social life on multiple channels. Today's girl must build and maintain her friendships while connecting in both real and virtual ways.

Social (Media) Skills

Most parents are stupefied by how attached girls become to their phones. The best explanation I've heard for this comes from danah boyd,* an activist and scholar who studies the role of technology in teens' social lives. In her words, "Teens aren't addicted to social media. They're addicted to each other." If you think about it, we were also addicted to each other as teenagers, but all we had was the Pliocene-era technology of our times: the landline phone. Every night, I turned myself into a one-girl fire hazard by using a ridiculously long phone cord to pull the family phone into my bedroom—strapping doorways closed and blocking the hallway in the process. And what did I do on the phone? Usually, not much. I'm sure I'm not the only one who sometimes held the phone to my ear, hardly talking, while doing homework "with" the person on the other end of the line. I even remember watching television while on the phone with a friend who watched the

---

* Note that dr. boyd elects to spell her name in lowercase letters.

same show at her house, sometimes commenting on what we saw, but mostly just quietly enjoying each other's company. For most of us, being on the phone with our friends was a second choice—what we really wanted to do was hang out together. And when we could, we did.

When we compare the experience of today's teenager with our own, two things are starkly different. First, they want to be connected, just as we did, but today's technology allows for the kind of easy, pervasive communication that we could have only dreamed of while dozing off on our corded phones. Second, many of today's teens spend fewer long afternoons hanging out together than we did. Families who wish to give their children every opportunity (and have the resources to do so) often keep their kids tightly booked. Girls who are doing ungodly amounts of homework, playing three sports, developing as a musician, or engaged in some other demanding combination of activities, have little downtime. We already know that too much unsupervised time can lead to trouble for teenagers, but some girls are actually so busy that it's hard to find unstructured time with their friends.

At its best, digital technology gives teens a way to build and maintain their friendships even when they can't be together in person. At its worst, digital technology undermines a teen's capacity to cultivate meaningful in-person connections and actually amplifies the negative aspects of their relationships. New research finds that, when it comes to teens' social lives, what happens online reflects what happens in real life. Girls who enjoy happy, supportive friendships in real life use their digital communications to build those friendships, and girls who are having trouble getting along in person also have trouble getting along online. Put simply, the online environment brings the possibility of tribal activity, good or bad, to every minute of a girl's day.

Even for girls who have supportive on- and off-line relationships, research shows that intense use of digital technology can impair young girls' social skills and interfere with their healthy, face-to-face relationships. Not surprisingly, healthy relationships depend on complex and subtle social skills that are best learned in the context of real, not virtual, interactions. For this reason, I encourage parents to ban technology (including their own) from the places where humans learn and practice social skills. This includes the dinner table, your designated family nights, and perhaps even short car rides. And this is where the many demands on girls' time can be a good thing as girls benefit from participating in activities that suspend phone use while requiring interpersonal interaction.

We all know that digital communication can bring out the worst in how humans relate to one another. Talk with your daughter about unkind online behavior and make it clear that rules for virtual social behavior are the same as the rules for social behavior in the real world: she doesn't have to like everybody, but she should never conduct herself in ways that are less than polite. How much you need to supervise your daughter's social media activity will depend a lot on your daughter. Some girls use social media to stay in touch with good friends and would instinctively avoid conflict if they saw it online. Other girls interact with as many peers as possible online and can easily find themselves caught up in unpleasant social drama.

If your daughter isn't yet texting or interacting online, wait until she *really wants* a phone or social media accounts and make your right to supervise her activity a condition of gaining access to the digital world. Go with the begin-strict-then-loosen-up approach (known by teachers as "Don't smile till December") and start with frequent monitoring. It's always easier to relax your rules than to create new ones when things already feel out of control. And remember that supervising your daughter's digital activity isn't all about busting bad behavior. You can use what you notice while monitoring to comment on how teens talk to one another and to discuss what should, and shouldn't, be shared digitally. If you know that your daughter is being sarcastic in her texts but aren't sure her friends can tell, gently point that out. Teenagers are learning what it means to be a friend both in person and online. So long as you don't overdo it, you may be able to offer some feedback and guidance.

If your daughter already has a phone and social media accounts, you might implement some rules if you haven't already. To do so, you'll need to say something like, "I know that I've given you total privacy with your phone and social media until now, but I'm thinking that was a mistake. If the whole world can know what you're doing digitally, I should have access too. So I'm going to start checking your phone and social media accounts from time to time." Should your daughter balk (a likely response), there are a couple of routes to consider. If you're paying for her phone, her computer, and her online access, you can stick to your guns and decide that _ funding her technology use means you can monitor it. Alternatively, you can talk with your daughter about who *can* monitor her digital activity. I know of one insightful thirteen-year-old who explained, "It's not that I'm doing anything bad on my phone. We mostly just talk about who has crushes on who. When my friends come over, it's really weird if my mom and dad know all that." She and her parents came up with the solution of having her levelheaded seventeen-year-old cousin keep an eye on her digital activity. The thirteen-year-old didn't care if her cousin knew about the crushes in her tribe.

Most parents get to a point where it stops making sense to keep close tabs on their daughter's phone. If you are there, or when you get there, you can say, "If I hear that you are being unkind or inappropriate online, I'll let you know and we're going to figure out what to do. And remember that deleting information from your accounts doesn't mean it's gone—it's still out there somewhere." So long as you are financing your daughter's technology use, you can make the case to regulate her online activity. That said, we do well to remember that our parents had almost no idea how we acted with our friends. We made mistakes and we learned from them. For better or worse, we are in the first generation of parents who have detailed access to how our teens interact with one another. This means that we have a useful record of interactions that go poorly, but it can also mean that we have too much access to what should be private communications among teenagers.

When parents monitor their daughter's online activities, they often do so in an effort to keep her from making a permanent record of unseemly behavior. This is a valid rationale and one that we'll delve into in chapter 5, "Planning for the Future." As you consider the question of how much to monitor your daughter's social interactions online, it may help to ask yourself, "Am I doing this because I truly worry that she might do terrible things online, or am I doing this simply because I can?"

Joining a New Tribe: When to Worry

There are three conditions regarding your daughter's social life that should cause you to worry: if your daughter has no tribe, if your daughter is a victim of bullying, or if your daughter bullies her peers.

Social Isolation

A girl doesn't need more than one good buddy, but she's in trouble if she doesn't even have that. Studies of teens who become socially isolated haven't teased out whether the isolation causes or is caused by feelings of depression and low self-worth, but being alone and feeling terrible are closely linked in adolescence. And research finds that having a close relationship with one's parents, or doing well at school, can't make up for the harm of being socially isolated. Loneliness should be taken seriously. The longer a girl goes without a tribe, the worse she will feel and the harder it will be for her to build new friendships.

Further, girls who are friendless become prime targets for bullying. As we know, conflict comes with human interaction, but I have watched girls withstand a surprising amount of friction with their peers when they have comrades who will defend them or reassure them that they are loved, even if not by everyone. Girls without friends face the social slings and arrows of adolescence without any armor to protect them. Run-ins that are painful for well-connected teens become unbearable for girls with no one on their side.

Though some meanness comes with the territory in any large group of teenagers, comparatively few adolescents are directly involved, either as the culprit or victim, in true bullying situations where one person is repeatedly mistreated and unable to defend herself. But most teens are aware that bullying occurs, and research consistently demonstrates that bystanders who witness bullying are the individuals best equipped to prevent it. Sadly, research also shows that bystanders tend to ignore or avoid their isolated peers.

If your daughter becomes socially isolated, take aggressive measures to help her connect with a tribe. For starters, you might ask trusted adults at your daughter's school for insights about her social situation. Teachers and administrators know more about the dynamics that unfold between students than anyone. See if there are changes that you or your daughter could make to improve her prospects and ask if there is anything the school can do to connect her with potential friends. I've seen thoughtful teachers assign seating and work groups to create social openings for girls who need them.

Find summer and after-school opportunities that might help your daughter connect with new peers. Girls without friends can become socially pigeonholed at school and have few opportunities to try out the interpersonal skills needed to spark new connections. Happily, when girls are given a blank slate to build new friendships (such as going to a summer camp), they often return to school feeling more confident about themselves and enjoy more social success than before. If your daughter struggles to connect to her peers no matter what you do, talk with your pediatrician or family doctor about a referral to a seasoned psychotherapist. Your daughter is suffering. She needs support and may benefit from having a neutral third party who can help her figure out what keeps her from finding a tribe.

Being Bullied

One morning in early December, I received a phone call from a mother who was looking for help for her Year 9 daughter. Over the phone, the mom explained she had just learned that Lucy was being bullied at their local parochial school. The bullying came to light when the school nurse called home to share that Lucy usually came to her office complaining of headaches on gym days and appeared to have a panic attack in response to the suggestion that she go to class despite not feeling well. Lucy's mother mentioned the call when her daughter came home that afternoon. To her mother's surprise, Lucy fell apart and described, with heaving sobs, what was happening at school. Not knowing what to do next, Lucy's mom called me.

Lucy didn't want to meet with me alone but was willing to come to my practice with her parents. At our first appointment, she sat next to her mom on the couch while her dad pulled my extra chair close to be near her on the other side. Lucy—a pretty and somewhat overweight Year 9 student—was polite but very tense. Clearly, she felt like a specimen waiting to be examined under my microscope. Hoping to put her at ease, I began.

"Lucy, it sounds like things have been really hard at school— your mom told me over the phone that you've been dealing with some rough treatment for a long time. What would be best? Do you want me to ask questions, do you want to share what it would be helpful for me to know, or do you want your folks to tell me what you've told them?"

Quietly, but visibly relieved to have options, she said, "They can tell you."

Together—sometimes finishing each other's sentences—her parents recounted what their daughter had shared. Before and after gym class, Lucy was often cornered in the locker room by three of her Year 9 classmates. They teased her about her weight and cruelly joked within earshot about how hard it must be for some girls to find exercise clothes big enough to fit. Once, they stole her bra while she showered and told the boys in their class that she was not wearing a bra later on that day. The boys gladly joined in on the teasing and carried on loudly for weeks afterward about the fact that Lucy was "letting it all hang out." The rest of her classmates knew what was going on but remained silent. Lucy's parents imagined that they were in no rush to paint targets on their own backs.

Girls can be incredibly cruel to one another, but that doesn't mean they have the market cornered on bullying. Lucy discovered what research demonstrates: boys bully girls (while girls rarely bully boys), and the mistaken belief that girls will only be bullied by other girls can keep adults from getting a clear picture of some bullying situations.

The effects of bullying can be lasting and profound. We have long known that the trauma of child abuse can leave psychological scars that endure into adulthood; new research also suggests that verbal harassment from peers can make a lasting imprint on the corpus callosum, the part of the brain that coordinates the functioning of the brain's left and right hemispheres. As uncomfortable as it was for Lucy to be in my office, I welcomed the opportunity to address the emotionally toxic treatment she'd suffered and to help her parents protect her from further harassment.

If you think that your daughter is being bullied, you must step in. Carefully. Start by reaching out to adults at your daughter's school to see if they have any helpful information for you. Though you may feel very upset, be as calm as you can when sharing your concerns with teachers and administrators. Bullying situations can be highly volatile for schools, all the more so as some states have laws holding them accountable if bullying occurs among students. The adults at your daughter's school are more likely to take you and your concerns seriously, and be less defensive, if your approach isn't confrontational. I encouraged Lucy's parents to make notes on what she told them and to begin by sharing their information with the person most likely to be able to evaluate the situation directly—for them, a kind and earnest gym teacher. We agreed that they would move up the chain of command if the gym teacher was unhelpful or if she lacked the authority to address their concerns.

Lucy's father wondered if he should also contact the parents of the students who were mistreating Lucy. I strongly encouraged him to hold off and pointed out that his wish to stand up for his daughter grew out of a protective instinct shared by most parents. Regardless of what was actually happening in the locker room, the parents of the teens who were harassing Lucy were likely to stick up for their kids, which would only make matters worse. In my experience, it's rarely a good idea to tackle bullying by calling other kids' parents because some girls tell their parents they are being mistreated at school without owning up to the fact that they dish out more than their share of misery. You would rather find out from your daughter's teacher that she gives as good as she gets than discover this by calling an alleged bully's parents.

As a side note, I also discourage parents from calling one another about girls who are in conflict. I have never seen situations made better by such calls, and they are often made worse. For example, a parent who wonders why her daughter has been dropped by a longtime friend might feel compelled to call the friend's mom to inquire. Parents on the receiving end of such calls are unlikely to offer good information about what's happening (assuming, of course, that they even know) and making the call stands to harm the social reputation of the girl who has been dropped. If you're worrying about your daughter's friendships, support her efforts to repair her relationships or build new ones, or seek advice from a neutral third party such as a teacher or coach who might have insight into a tricky social dynamic. Should another parent call you about a friendship issue, feel free to say, "Thanks so much for letting me know. I am really confident that the girls will find a way to come to their own resolution."

Having met with Lucy's dad, the gym teacher immediately notified the headteacher about what she'd learned. After meeting with Lucy and her parents to hear the details firsthand, the headteacher met separately with bystanders who confirmed Lucy's account, then began disciplinary proceedings with the students who had targeted Lucy. The headteacher handled the situation remarkably well. Experts on bullying counsel against having the bully and victim meet to sort things out. In a true bullying situation, doing so seriously risks exposing the victim to future mistreatment. The students who targeted Lucy were required to perform community service at the school, and they and their parents were warned that any evidence of further harassment would be grounds for expulsion. Lucy never had to confront her tormentors directly and was, to her relief, soon ignored by them at school.

After several meetings with her parents joining us, Lucy felt ready to meet with me on her own. When we got to know each other better, she told me that she had been so hurt by the passivity of her bystanding classmates that she had thought about killing herself. Lucy explained that she doubted that things would ever get better and added that having suicidal thoughts only seemed to confirm her sense that she was damaged and crazy. Together, we worked our way through her painful feelings and developed strategies to help her manage the panic attacks that sometimes came on when sitting near one of the students who had harassed her. Lucy's burden seemed to lighten as we talked. In the words of one of my colleagues, "Things seem so much worse when they are on the inside than when they are on the outside." By the spring of

Year 9, she'd connected with two bright, easygoing girls who happily included her in their weekend plans and sought her company during the school day.

Being a Bully

Research suggests that girls who bully other girls often do so to create a sense of belonging or to alleviate boredom in their group by creating excitement. In other words, girls sometimes find their place in a tribe by harassing or excluding girls who don't fit with the group norms. They may also target their peers to create social "glue"—something to talk about, something to do—when they lack the maturity to come together around positive interests.

If you discover that your daughter engages in bullying, don't blame her behavior on anyone else. No parent wants to believe that his or her child could be a bully, but denying reality will keep you from helping your daughter. Studies tracking teens who engage in bullying find that, over time, they are at heightened risk for depression, anxiety, drug abuse, and antisocial behavior. Let your daughter know that bullying is unacceptable and punishable, and keep a close eye to prevent it from happening again. Consider having your daughter work with a therapist to help her understand why she's been abusing her peers, repair any damage she has caused, and build positive social skills.

Even if your daughter doesn't have firsthand experience with bullying, point out the critical role that bystanders play in helping victims. Let her know that you don't expect her to confront a bully, but, unlike the girls in Lucy's locker room, she should take action if she knows a classmate is being harassed. Tell her that she should act regardless of her personal feelings about the victim and that you stand ready to think with her about how she can advocate for a classmate who is being bullied.

Sometimes, the elements of adolescent development come together to form their own perfect storm. This is especially true when we combine the two strands we've covered so far ("Parting with Childhood" and "Joining a New Tribe") with the strand we'll turn to next: "Harnessing Emotions." We already know that teens are shifting away from their families and toward tribes of peers, and that they are seeking (and sometimes competing for) tribe membership at the same moment as everyone else they know. With so much at stake for girls, it's no surprise that they get upset when their social lives aren't going well. But you may have already discovered that getting upset can be a stunningly intense experience once your daughter becomes a teenager. It's hard enough for girls to try to figure out how they fit into the broader world; the job is made that much more challenging by the fact that most teenage girls feel as if their emotions can spin out of control.

THREE

. . . .

Harnessing Emotions

WHEN I WAS IN MY FIRST SEMESTER OF GRADUATE SCHOOL, THE professor teaching my psychological testing course handed me a stack of Rorschach inkblot tests to score. Before sending me on my way, he offhandedly said, "Double-check the age of the person whose test you are scoring. If it's a teenager, but you think it's a grown-up, you'll conclude that you have a psychotic adult. But that's just a normal teenager."

Two years later, I came across this account of adolescence, written by Anna Freud:

> I take it that it is normal for an adolescent to behave for a considerable length of time in an inconsistent and unpredictable manner; to fight her impulses and accept them; to love her parents and to hate them; to revolt against them and be dependent on them; to be deeply ashamed to acknowledge her mother before others and, unexpectedly, to desire heart-to-heart talks with her; to thrive on imitation of others while searching unceasingly for her own identity; to be more idealistic, artistic, generous, and unselfish than she will ever be again, but also the opposite: self-centered, egoistic, calculating. *Such fluctuations and extreme opposites would be deemed highly abnormal at any other time of life.* At this

time they may signify no more than that an adult structure
of personality takes a long time to emerge, that the individual in question does not cease to experiment and is in no
hurry to close down on possibilities.

I thought, "Wow. There it is again: in teenagers, normal
seems crazy."

Twenty years later, I don't need to score inkblot tests or read
Anna Freud to know that healthy teenage development can
look pretty irrational. Parents tell me about it every day. They
describe how a minor annoyance—such as when a girl finds
out that the jeans she wants are still riding out the rinse cycle—
can turn into an emotional earthquake that knocks everyone
in the house off balance. They describe how their formerly
mild-mannered daughter now actually screams when excited,
and how their girl who was resilient at age eleven has melt-
downs over small disappointments at age fourteen. And it's
not just that teenagers' feelings are potent, they're also erratic.
I hear about how the "worst day in the history of the universe"
can suddenly become the "best day, ever!" if a crush-worthy
peer sends a flirty text. As one of my friends put it, "My daughter has five different, extreme emotions before eight in the
morning."

The sudden force of a teenager's feelings can catch parents
off guard because, between the ages of six and eleven, children
go through a phase of development that psychologists call *latency*. As the term implies, the mercurial moods of early childhood simmer down and girls are pretty easygoing until they
become teenagers and their emotions kick up again. Recent
developments in brain science offer new insight into why latency ends when it does. Though we used to assume that the
brain stopped developing somewhere around age twelve, we
now know that the brain remodels dramatically during the

teenage years. The renovation project follows the pattern in which the brain grew in the womb. It starts with the lower, primal portions (the limbic system) then moves to the upper, outer areas (the cortex), where the functions that separate humans from other animals live.

Updates to the limbic system heighten the brain's emotional reactions with research indicating that the feeling centers beneath the cortex are actually more sensitive in teens than in children or adults. For example, one straightforward study used functional magnetic resonance imaging to watch teenage brains respond, in real time, to emotional input. The research team showed images of fearful, happy, and calm faces to children, teens, and adults while monitoring the activity of the amygdala, a key player in the emotional reactions of the limbic system. Compared to the brain activity of children and adults, the teens' amygdalas reacted strongly to fearful or happy faces. In other words, emotional input rings like a gong for teenagers and a chime for everyone else.

With the lower-to-higher remodeling of the brain, the frontal cortex—the part of the brain that exerts a calming, rational influence—doesn't come fully online until adulthood. This means that limbic system reactions outstrip frontal cortex controls. Put simply, intense emotions burst through and introduce you, and your daughter, to a new period of emotional upheaval.

Adults often tell teens that their feelings are at full blast because of "hormones." This usually doesn't go over very well, plus it's probably inaccurate. Despite the obvious coincidence between the beginnings of puberty—with its acne, growth spurts, and dawning smelliness—and the intensification of your daughter's emotions, research evidence suggests that the impact of pubertal hormones on teenagers' moods is indirect, at best. In fact, studies find that hormones respond to, or may even be trumped by, other factors that influence your daughter's mood, such as stressful events or the quality of her relationship with you. In other words, the changes in your daughter's brain and the events that occur around her are more likely to shape her mood than the hormonal shifts occurring inside of her.

Here's the bottom line: what your daughter broadcasts matches what she actually experiences. Really, it's just that intense, so take her feelings seriously, regardless of how overblown they might seem. The upsurge in your daughter's feelings brings us to the developmental strand we'll consider in this chapter—the one where she learns how to harness all of those emotions. Girls may start adolescence in a whirl of passions, but we want them to arrive at adulthood with the confidence that they can manage, indeed make good use of, their feelings.

Parents who are surprised by their daughter's dramatic ups and downs can lose sight of the fact that she is pretty shocked, too. Early in my career, a senior colleague offered some of the best professional advice I've ever received. She said, "You must work with the assumption that every teenager secretly worries that she's crazy." Since my Rorschach-scoring days I'd been thinking about the fact that healthy teens can *seem* crazy to adults, but it hadn't yet occurred to me that teens, themselves, are worrying about their own sanity. But of course they are. A girl can dissolve over unavailable jeans while simultaneously thinking, "What's happening to me?" Teenagers remember the calm waters of latency and are often as unsettled as their parents are by the stormy seas of adolescence.

I always bear my colleague's advice in mind when, in my professional capacity, I meet a girl for the first time. However eager she may be to talk to me, however understandable her challenges are, I assume that some part of her is thinking, "It's true. I'm nuts. Because here I am sitting with a psychologist." I use every tool at my disposal—my words, my tone, my demeanor—to let her know that I see her as capable and whole and that we will be equal partners in the effort to make sense of whatever has brought her my way. To paraphrase the great neurologist Oliver Sacks, I try not to meet girls thinking, "What difficulty does this girl have?" but instead, "What girl has this difficulty?"

So if your teenage daughter is developing normally, you are living with someone who secretly worries that she is crazy and who might have the psychological assessment results of a psychotic adult. And we might as well add that you are living with a girl whose key support system—her tribe—consists of peers who are also as reactive and erratic as they will ever be. Your daughter works hard every day to harness powerful and unpredictable emotions so that she can get on with doing everything else she means to do.

To manage all of that intensity and to keep from feeling crazy, she'll recruit your help. Depending on the moment, she might ask for your support directly, she might unload her feelings on you, or she might find a way for you to have a feeling on her behalf. Sometimes you'll recognize the role you are being asked to play, other times you'll only appreciate your part in retrospect, if at all. Understanding your daughter's efforts to harness emotions will allow you to maintain your sanity while you're busy helping her feel confident in her own.

You: The Emotional Dumping Ground

Teenagers often manage their feelings by dumping the uncomfortable ones on their parents, so don't be surprised if you find that the arrival of adolescence comes with a surge in complaining. Overnight, the Year 6 girl who shared amusing accounts of the games she and her friends invented over lunch turns into the Year 7 student whose stories run together in a din of grumbling. No parents enjoy listening to their daughter's endless stream of complaints, but it's a lot easier to stand if we appreciate that her griping serves a valuable purpose.

Complaining to you allows your daughter to bring the best of herself to school. Adults generally hold sugarcoated memories of what it's like to spend a school day with one's peers. We think teens are lucky to get to hang out all day with their friends, but the reality of school is usually a far cry from what we think we remember. If you were to follow your daughter invisibly through her school day, I can all but guarantee the three reactions you would have. First, you would think, "Geez, her day is as demanding as it is tedious; that clock in her history class actually seems to go backward." Second, "A lot of these kids are really *annoying*. I'm never going to make it to lunch period." And finally, "Wow. She handles her day with incredible grace—I don't know how she does it. Especially when she's being told what to do all day and can't even go to the bathroom without permission."

Of course, children must adapt to peers, teachers, and the demands of school starting in preschool, but they tend not to vigorously *complain* about their days until they are teenagers. Why is this? With every feeling turned up to the maximum, the classmate who was merely bothersome in Year 5 becomes downright unbearable in Year 8. And teenagers have much less patience with adults (because they are far better at seeing through them) than children do. Further, younger children often go ahead and *act* on their annoyance by letting their impulses take over; they hit, push, call names, or find other ways to misbehave at school. Teenagers (and plenty of adults) still have the same impulses but use their willpower to contain their negative feelings and keep themselves out of trouble during the school day.

Here's where you come in.

Instead of being rude or aggressive toward peers or teachers at school, your daughter contains her irritation and waits until she is safely in your company to express it. If she can hold it together all day at school, you might wonder why your daughter can't hold it together a little bit longer so that she can also be pleasant with you. As it turns out, willpower is a limited resource—a finding demonstrated by one of my favorite semisadistic but harmless and creative research studies. The psychologists conducting the research asked undergraduates to participate in what the students thought was a study of taste perception. The subjects were sent alone into a room where they found two plates on a table. One plate held freshly baked chocolate chip cookies that had been cooked right in the lab so as to fill the entire space with their scrumptious smell. The other plate held raw radishes. Half of the subjects were instructed to enjoy a couple of cookies while the remaining subjects were told to eat some radishes and not to touch the cookies. (If you're wondering if the researchers spied on the undergraduates to make sure they only ate the assigned food, the answer is yes.)

After the subjects ate their assigned food, the researchers gave them a poppycock reason for why they needed to stay in the lab for an extra fifteen minutes. While the subjects waited, the researchers invited them to kill time by helping the investigators study problem-solving abilities. In their final move, the researchers gave the subjects an unsolvable puzzle and timed how long each participant worked on the puzzle before giving up. By now, you've probably guessed where this is going. On average, the cookie eaters used their willpower to work on the puzzle for more than twice as long as the radish eaters who, presumably, had used up all of their willpower resisting the cookies. For many teens, school is a plate of radishes. By the time they get to the end of the day, there's just no energy left to contain their annoyance, and the complaining begins.

Girls who get a chance to talk about the abundant frustrations of their day usually feel better once they've unloaded their distress on you. Any adult who has spent dinnertime grumbling about a coworker, neighbor, or boss understands that sharing one's true feelings at home makes it a lot easier to be charming out in public. Teenagers are no different. Having used you as their emotional dumping ground, they are prepared to return to school and play the part of the good citizen. Indeed, they may be able to act as a good citizen at school *precisely because* they are spending some of their time imagining the colorful complaints they will share once their school day has ended.

When your daughter complains, listen quietly and remind yourself that you are providing her with a way to unload the stress of her day. Many parents find that they want to *do* something as they listen to their daughter's distress—to offer advice, point out their daughter's misconceptions, make a plan to address her troubles, and so on. Do not feel pressed to solve your daughter's problems; you've probably tried and already found that she routinely rejects your suggestions, even the especially brilliant ones. If you really want to help your daughter manage her distress, help her see the difference between complaining and venting. Complaining generally communicates a sense that "someone should fix this," while venting communicates that "I'll feel better when someone who cares about me hears me out." Most of what teens complain about can't be fixed. No magic wand can make her peers, teachers, coaches, locker location, or homework any less irritating. Better for her to do a little less complaining about such realities and a little more venting. In doing so, she moves away from the childlike idea that the world should bend to her wishes to the adult idea that life comes with many unavoidable bumps.

How do you get her to do this? When she starts rolling out the complaints, consider asking, "Do you want my help with what you're describing, or do you just need to vent?" If she wants your help, she'll tell you. Even better, she might take your advice having actually asked for it. If she wants to vent, she'll tell you and you can sit back and know that just by listening you are offering meaningful support. More important, *she'll* start to learn that sometimes, just by listening, you are providing all the help she needs. Your daughter may be suspicious of your motives the first time you offer her the opportunity for unbridled venting. If she has grown used to getting (and, of course, reflexively rejecting) your advice when she complains, she may wonder what you're up to. But stick with it and be clear that you believe in the healing powers of "just venting." Soon, she'll come around. Don't expect that venting will—or should—fully replace complaining. But do take advantage of opportunities to help your daughter distinguish between problems that can and should be solved and problems that are best addressed by sharing them with someone who cares.

If the content of your daughter's venting strikes you as totally unfair and you feel compelled to weigh in, consider saying, "I have a different take on the situation. Do you want to hear it?" Should she say yes, carry on. Should she say no, bite your tongue and find comfort in the knowledge that your daughter is now aware that she shouldn't mistake your silence for a tacit endorsement of her views.

Congratulate yourself when you can get your daughter to advance to venting, because there will be times when you won't even be able to get how she expresses her displeasure *up* to the level of complaining (much less venting). These are the days when she simply takes out her annoyance on anyone in her path—a particularly unpleasant, and common, form of using you (your other children, or the family dog) as an emotional dumping ground. If your daughter feels that she must punish your family for her bad day, you might let one or two cutting comments pass. But, if it becomes clear that she plans to be wretched all evening, go ahead and say, "You may not be in a good mood, but you are not allowed to mistreat us. If you want to talk about what's bugging you, I'm all ears. If you're going to be nasty all night, don't do it here."

I'm Upset, Now You're Upset

When I get to my Harry Potter office on the days I spend at Laurel School, the first thing I do is check the messages on my desk phone. One morning, I found three messages in a row from the same dad.

The first, anxious message:

> Hi Dr. Damour, this is Mark B., calling at seven fifteen on Tuesday night. When I came home from work I found Samantha's chemistry test on the kitchen table—she got a D on it. I'm not sure how well you know Sammy, but she's never gotten a grade lower than a B. I tried to talk with her about the test but she said that it's no big deal and that I'm overreacting. I can't tell what's worrying me more: her bad grade or the fact that she doesn't seem to care about it. This is totally unlike her because she's usually really serious about school. I'm confused and wondering if you can call me tomorrow.

The second, utterly exasperated message:

Hi Lisa, Mark again, it's about ten thirty Tuesday night. I just tried to talk to Sammy about the test but she's holed up in her room and won't discuss it. She's such a good student—I just don't get it. I'm thinking that maybe she shouldn't go to the summer camp she was planning on and it would be better for her to go to a science program I just found online. I've got a small window for getting the camp deposit back, so please call as soon as you can.

The third, relieved-but-still-confused message:

Mark here, it's six forty-five on Wednesday morning. I just saw Sammy and she told me that she emailed her chemistry teacher last night and he got right back to her. They've arranged to go over what she didn't understand and he's going to let Sammy correct her test to recover some lost points. Sorry about all the messages. No need to call me back.

I called him back. It was clear that Samantha had put her dad through an emotional wringer and that he deserved some empathy, as well as an explanation for his daughter's confusing behavior. I knew Mr. B. well enough to know that he was a calm and reasonable guy who was likely baffled by what had transpired with his daughter. And I knew Samantha well enough to know that she had probably been upset from the minute she got her chemistry test back, yet she gave her dad the impression that she didn't care about the grade and accused him of overreacting. What gives? Externalization, that's what. Externalization is a technical term describing how teenagers sometimes manage their feelings by getting their par-ents to have their feelings instead. In other words, they toss you an emotional hot potato.

Your adolescent daughter doesn't wake up one day and say to herself, "I think I'll start handing off my uncomfortable feelings to my parents." The decision to use externalization for emotional relief occurs outside her conscious awareness. Unconscious processes can be powerful. If we could hold up a microphone to your daughter's unconscious mind, it would say, "You know, I've had a long day of being upset about this grade—the whole thing has become exhausting. I don't have a solution to the problem, but I need a break from being upset. I'll leave the test where Dad will surely find it so that *he* can be upset about it. Now, he might try to get me to remain upset about this grade, so I'll tell him he's overreacting and walk away—that should keep the upset feeling in his lap and out of mine for a while."

Here's another example. One night early in my first year of college on the East Coast, I was feeling particularly unsure, lonely, and far from my Colorado home. I called my mother to share my misery and my certainty that things would never get better. She tried to offer comfort and advice, but I abruptly ended the phone call on a despairing note, letting her know that I would find a way to muddle through, sadly and alone. When I hung up, I felt much better. My roommate showed up and we went out for the evening and had a great time.

The next morning, my mother called to check in. "Are you okay?" she asked in a voice warped by fatigue and concern. "Of course I am, what's wrong with you?" I asked back, but not in the kind, sensitive way you might be generously imagining. Later, I learned from my dad that she had stayed awake most of the night worrying about me.

Externalization happens when your daughter wants to get

rid of an uncomfortable feeling. And not just anyone will take on her uncomfortable feeling; it has to be someone who really loves her. Externalization is a profound form of empathy. It goes beyond feeling *with* your daughter to the point of actually feeling something *on her behalf.* When teens complain, they own their discomfort, will often accept your empathy, and may even allow you to help them address the source of their misery. When they externalize, they want you to accept ownership of the offending feeling and will prevent you from giving it back.

It's the difference between "Mom, I want to tell you how uncomfortable this very hot potato I'm holding is and see if you've got any good ideas for how I might manage it" and "Mom, take this hot potato, I don't want to hold it anymore. And hang on to it for a while."

Externalization is a strange and subtle process that helps make adolescence manageable—for your daughter. Teenagers spend the better part of their time with peers who are also trying to harness their emotions and may not be able to offer useful support. Put another way, how do you get your best friend to take your hot potato if she can barely manage the potatoes she's already got? When teenagers feel overwhelmed by their feelings and need to do *something*, they find a loving parent and start handing out potatoes. Lucky for your girl, but not so lucky for you. Parents on the receiving end of an externalization often don't know what hit them. All they know is that they, like Samantha's father, suddenly feel really upset about their daughter's problem but can't engage her in addressing it.

For the most part, there's not much that you can do about externalizations. You will rarely, if ever, be able to identify an externalization at the moment it occurs. And talking with your daughter about her behavior won't prevent her from doing it. Teens don't consciously decide to externalize, so they can't consciously decide not to. The process unfolds as rapidly for her as it does for you. Even if you could talk your daughter into taking responsibility for all of her difficult feelings all of the time, would you want to? Your willingness to hold your daughter's emotional hot potatoes from time to time is a thankless and charitable act, but it will help her get through some of the roughest patches of her adolescence. Given the opportunity to unload their discomfort, most teens will gather their resources and work through what went wrong or discover, with the benefit of time, that the problem comes down to size on its own. While Samantha's father worried in the kitchen about her indifference toward a D, she emailed her teacher about finding a time to review her test. Having made my mother upset on my behalf, I was able to go out and have fun with my roommate. (If I were a teen today, I would have simply sent my mom a distressing text message, then refused to acknowledge her response or answer my phone.)

What becomes of an externalized feeling? Well, now it's yours to manage, and many parents feel compelled to leap into action. Samantha's dad was ready to upend her summer plans. My mom seriously considered throwing some sandwiches in the car and driving across the plains to rescue me from my plight. If you find yourself compelled into radical action after a brief but painful encounter with your daughter, I've got two words for you: do nothing.

At an appointment in early November when Camille was in Year 9, Maya told me that she'd really blown it the prior weekend. Halloween had fallen on Friday night, so Maya was surprised that Camille stayed home to give out candy instead of going out with friends. The next morning, Maya casually asked what Camille's friends had done the night before. Camille indifferently responded that "pretty much everyone was at Sara's Halloween party." Maya was floored. Camille and Sara had found their way to a truce by the end of Year 8 and, without rekindling their old friendship, got along well enough to spend the summer hanging out in the same large group at the community pool. In fact, Camille and Sara had recently had a good time working together on a group project, and Maya had hopefully assumed that they'd put their Year 8 squabble behind them.

Without offering an explanation for why she hadn't been invited, Camille showed Maya the party pictures Sara had posted online. Clearly, Camille was one of the few Year 9 girls not at the party. The sight of the pictures poked the bruise Maya carried from Sara having told classmates about Camille's bedwetting. Hurt and angry, Maya impulsively called Sara's mother, a longtime acquaintance, to ask why Camille had been left out of the party. Sara's mom, offended by Maya's tone, explained that Camille had posted online that "Halloween parties are for babies" shortly after news got out that Sara was planning to host one. Not surprisingly, Sara decided that it was best not to invite Camille.

By calling Sara's home, Maya made things worse between the girls and created an awkward situation with Sara's mother. The impulse to call came from a loving, protective place, but the call was a mistake. In retrospect, Maya saw that Camille was probably angry with herself for the fresh conflict she had created and was unsure about how to straighten things out. Camille's hot potato handoff was subtle, but effective. Had Camille gone to her mother and tearfully said, "Things were going better with Sara and now I've made a mess and I don't know what to do," Maya would have tried to help Camille repair the damage. By seeming neutral while showing Maya pictures of the party, Camille got Maya to become upset on her behalf.

So what's a parent to do? When you are on the receiving end of an externalization, avoid taking urgent action. You love your daughter, and you are suddenly the reluctant owner of some of her intense teenage-sized pain. In this moment, you risk bringing a sledgehammer down on a thumbtack of a problem. Though a teenager will experience her fight with a friend as a full-blown crisis, it's our job as adults to remember that it's not. In fact, we can do a lot to help adolescents bring feelings down to size by not reacting like teenagers ourselves. Our overreactions only seem to confirm that *it really is that bad* and usually make the situation worse.

Camille would have resisted any immediate effort on Maya's part to talk about why she was left out of the party. Camille was in pain about her relationship with Sara but really wanted her mother to be in pain about it instead. Ideally, Maya might have called me or looked to her husband or a discreet friend for support. Talking with a trustworthy adult about what's happening with your teenager is usually the perfect salve to the discomfort of being on the receiving end of an externalization. By sharing the situation with someone who *isn't* holding an emotional hot potato, most parents start to see things more clearly and to regain an adult perspective on the problem.

Had Maya talked it through, she might have guessed that there was more to the story and that it would be best to stay out of it or offer moral support to Camille as she tried to patch things up, again, with Sara. Sometimes another adult isn't available or the content of the externalization feels too sensitive to be shared. Under these conditions—and absent pressing safety concerns—wait at least a day before taking any action. Waiting gives the hot potato time to cool and gives you and your daughter time to craft a rational plan. And you'd be surprised by how rarely a plan even needs to be made once some time has passed.

Befriending Distress

Girls get upset about getting upset. Sometimes, a girl knows what's wrong but is confused by the intensity of her feelings. At other times, she's rattled by emotions that seem to come out of left field. For instance, one of my friends recently told me that her fourteen-year-old daughter came to her in a panic saying, "I'm crying, but I don't know why!" When I find myself with a girl who is shaken by a feeling she doesn't understand, I start by reassuring her that mental health is like physical health: mentally healthy people get upset, just like physically healthy people get sick. We only worry when a person can't recover.

Of course it's exhausting for you and your daughter if she contracts and recovers from several emotional maladies each week, but as we know from Anna Freud, "fluctuations and extreme opposites" are to be expected in teenagers. In the "When to Worry" section at the end of this chapter, we'll address what you should do if your daughter *doesn't* recover from her psychological flus. But most of the time, girls do bounce back, and they are helped when adults reassure them that ups and downs are part of life. Better yet, we can let girls know that their emotions are actually the product of a highly developed (but, for teenagers, not so finely tuned) system that provides critical feedback about how their lives are going and the quality of the choices they're making. If being with a particular friend always leaves your daughter feeling as if she's been stepped on, it's probably time for her to reconsider that friendship. If your daughter experiences a jolt of anxiety when she realizes that there are no adults at a party and things are getting shifty in the basement, we'd want her to tune in to that feeling and call it a night.

Psychological discomfort is an amazing thing. It not only helps teenagers make good decisions, it sparks maturation. A girl who feels guilty because she didn't follow through on a promise will likely keep her promises in the future. Feeling the sting of a mistake keeps us from making the same mistake again. When you can, help your daughter to look upon a hard feeling as a really useful piece of information. If she pays attention to it and learns from it, she can expect to have fewer hard feelings going forward.

We want our daughters to learn from their emotional discomfort and use it to direct and drive their growth. But try telling that to your daughter (or yourself, for that matter) when she's apoplectic about an upcoming job interview or sobbing because she lost her varsity spot. Emotional pain can be a good thing, but we have to account for the fact that teenagers often have the right feeling on the wrong scale. They sometimes become swamped by their emotions, and no one can learn and grow when she feels as if she's drowning.

If your daughter becomes emotionally overwhelmed, you might feel overwhelmed, too. We love our daughters, hate to see them suffer, and can be tempted to react in proportion to their overreactions. As with emotional hot potatoes, you can help by making sure that your response matches the actual size of the problem. Losing a varsity spot is disappointing, but it's not grounds for you or your daughter to feel that she'll "never be good at anything, ever." If your daughter will allow it, see if you can help put her feelings into words.

By some magic that I can't fully explain (despite the fact that my entire career as a clinician rests on this magic), having

a name for a feeling and talking about that feeling with someone who cares go a long way toward bringing it down to size.
Try, "I know how much you wanted to be on varsity and that
you are really disappointed. The outcome hurts." Using specific words to describe the cause of her tears ("disappointed"
and "hurts") helps to contain her uncomfortable feelings. For
this tactic to work, your tune must match your lyrics. Regardless of the accuracy of your words, they're only useful if delivered in a tone that expresses warmth *and* your total confidence
that your daughter will find a way to bounce back. If you're
obviously alarmed while offering verbal comfort, only the
alarm comes through. Your calm, empathetic, and detailed description of what she's going through helps to ease painful
emotions by communicating that your daughter's not in it
alone. Once her feeling comes down to size, she may be ready
to learn from it or let it go. It's hers to do with as she wishes.

You might worry that putting words to your daughter's
emotions will only make them more real and, as a result,
worse. But that's not what usually happens. If you want to
make things worse, try talking your daughter *out of* what she's
feeling. Perhaps you've already attempted this (most loving
parents have) and discovered that she only tightened her grip
on her distress. It might have gone something like this:

Your daughter: "MOM—we can't go out of town *that* weekend! That's two weeks before finals! I will NEVER get my work
done."

You: "Oh honey, you'll be fine. You can review in the car and
you'll have plenty of time to study when we get back."

Your daughter: "Are you NUTS! It's like you *want* me to
fail!"

When feelings are minimized, girls often turn up the volume to make sure they, and their feelings, are heard. This is
unpleasant for you and it definitely doesn't help your daugh-

ter feel better. Trust me, you're both better off when you validate her emotions. Once a girl believes that her parents understand where she's coming from, she's usually willing to consider their advice or find her own solution. And don't try to guilt your daughter out of a feeling. If you tell her she shouldn't complain about a weekend trip away from home she might calm down to appease you, but you haven't really helped. She probably still feels upset, but now she can add feeling dismissed and guilty to her pile of misery.

At times, your daughter won't be in the mood to talk about her distress, or she might reject your attempts to harness her feelings by putting them into words. Under these conditions, consider my favorite fallback line: "Is there anything I can do that won't make things worse?" Set to a compassionate tune, there's beauty in this phrasing. In just a few words, it communicates everything your daughter needs to know: you understand that her distress is real, you're not going to try to talk her out of her feelings, nor are you frightened of them, and you can live with your inability to make things better. The last bit does the most work. If your daughter's at the end of her rope, she needs to hear your confidence that she'll find her way to a soft landing. When my friend told me that her daughter flipped out over unexpected tears, I suggested that she could remind her that crying often brings emotional relief. Tears, even unexplainable ones, don't seem so alarming if parents aren't worried by them and, instead, point out the relief that usually results from a good cry.

Catalytic Reactions

When it comes to dealing with emotional distress, research tells us that girls discuss while boys distract. In other words, girls tend to manage their hard feelings by talking about them. The upside? By seeking out their friends or parents for help, girls put themselves in touch with valuable social support and take a smart, mature approach to dealing with stress. The downside? Talking about problems at length can turn into what psychologists call rumination—focused attention on distress—and cause feelings to take on a life of their own. Rumination can lead to depression and anxiety, especially in teenage girls.

In contrast, boys often deal with being upset by distracting themselves. They put their energy into not thinking about it or they focus on something else, such as their schoolwork, video games, or sports, if they are suffering. This isn't necessarily a good thing. As boys move through adolescence, they sometimes silence their emotions because, as scholars who study boys note, they learn to equate feelings with femininity and femininity with degradation. Sadly, boys punish one another—usually with slurs about sexual orientation—for doing anything that could be construed as effeminate. Whereas girls commune to dissect and analyze their feelings, boys save face with their peers by seeming invulnerable or insensitive. The upside? Boys are less likely than girls to ruminate and turn their distress into depression or anxiety. The downside? As the psychologists Dan Kindlon and Michael Thompson point out, boys learn to substitute anger for all other feelings and are more likely than girls to get into trouble for aggressive behavior.

When used in moderation, distracting oneself can be a terrific strategy for harnessing painful emotions. To be sure, focusing on problems, putting them into words, and learning from distress can be useful *to a point*, but many girls continue to discuss problems well past the helpful mark. If you see that happening, encourage your daughter to take a page out of the boys' book and find a distraction. Normal teenagers become deeply preoccupied with their own world, all the more so when things aren't going well. Teenage girls can forget that taking a break from a problem might be part of the solution.

Shortly after she got off the phone with Sara's mom, Maya sent her an email apologizing for her call and for Camille's "Halloween parties are for babies" posting. Maya then confronted Camille about her mean message and asked what was behind it. Camille tearfully told Maya that she regretted the posting almost immediately but had hoped (unrealistically) that Sara would take it as a joke, even though Camille knew it wasn't funny. With Maya's help, Camille apologized, by text, to Sara late Saturday evening. On Sunday morning, it was clear that Camille had hardly slept because she'd spent most of the night checking her phone for a response. Stone-faced, Camille continued to check her phone for a reply until early Sunday afternoon, when Maya sent her outside to rake leaves. Though hardly chipper about the chore, Camille's mood lightened with the physical activity, fresh air, and break from her phone. Late Sunday, Sara sent a brief reply accepting Camille's apology, and on Monday they sat together at the same lunch table. Camille reported to Maya that lunch was "kinda awkward, but okay."

If your daughter doesn't welcome your suggestions about how to distract herself, try pointing her toward her best coping strategies. Every girl has her preferred ways of managing emotional distress, even if she doesn't always appreciate that that's what she's doing. Some girls feel better if they go for a run, others take long showers. They organize their rooms, shoot hoops in the driveway, do crafts, paint their nails, listen to music that fits or counters their mood, make lists, go on hikes, take naps, cook comfort foods, or try on clothes.

Many girls turn to the things they loved when they were

younger because the touchstones of childhood connect them with simpler, less emotional times. As we know, girls like to retreat to established base camps when the world feels overwhelming. Well into late adolescence girls will sometimes snuggle stuffed animals, watch children's movies, or reread their favorite childhood books when stressed. If she's not in the mood to talk, see if your daughter wants to watch *The Incredibles* (because really, what *can't* be cured by watching every scene with Edna, the supersuit designer?). If that doesn't work, see if she wants to join you for a trip to the gym or help you make holiday decorations. Here's the point: girls can seem to be hiding from a problem or messing around when, in fact, they are using effective tactics for helping themselves feel better. Tune in to how *your* daughter gets a handle on her feelings—the approach will be entirely her own—and suggest or support her strategies when she needs them.

At times, you may be able to anticipate situations where providing distraction or wordless emotional support might be in order. If you know that the job interview might not go well, consider having the family dog join you in the car when you pick your daughter up from it. Or pack her favorite comfort food for a snack. For your sake and your daughter's, remember that there are lots of ways to harness feelings, and only some of them involve talking. Wordless gestures go a long way, do their best work when presented without flourish, and do not foreclose the possibility of talking about feelings later.

Rumination isn't the only emotional challenge that favors girls. Studies find that girls, more than boys, experience *vicarious* social stress. In other words, when a girl talks to her friend about her emotional distress, the friend is likely to become distressed as well. And what do girls do when they become upset? They talk with one another. As a result, one girl's psychological pain can catalyze a powerful response in the complex chemistry of her tribe and trigger far-reaching chain reactions. This is not to say that boys don't care about what happens with their friends; it is to say that boys seem to be less likely than girls to take on a peer's problem as their own. They're more likely to express the equivalent of, "Sorry to hear that you're struggling, buddy. Let me know how it shakes out."

Lana, from chapter 2, was discreet about Cassie's cutting and didn't talk about it with the other girls in their tribe, who would have also fretted about their friend. Instead, Lana worried about Cassie privately, lost a lot of sleep in the process, and needed help to get out from under the burden of caring for her friend. When your daughter has a close friend who is suffering, there's a good chance your daughter will suffer too, even if the problem isn't as worrisome as Cassie's. If a girl can't focus on her homework because her best friend's parents are splitting up, try, "You're a great friend—and you're upset because Tia is upset. But not getting your homework done doesn't help Tia feel better. What if you push pause on your worries just for tonight and get to bed at a reasonable hour? In the morning, you can come up with some fun ways to pull her attention away from her parents' troubles. Given that there's nothing either of you can do to change what's happening, that would be a really kind thing to do."

Coping by Posting

As a psychologist who began practicing long before digital media invaded our lives, I've been blown away by the power of technology to stunt girls' ability to recognize and manage their own feelings. Unfortunately, the end of latency (and the upsurge in emotions) occurs around the same time that many young teens become regular users of computers and cell phones. This coincidence can cripple developing emotion-regulation skills if teenagers get into the habit of reaching for their phones or computers at the first whiff of a feeling. Girls who go online instead of sitting with their emotions—even if that emotion is just boredom—don't learn from what they are feeling or develop the skills they need to help themselves feel better.

It's not unusual for me to see girls in my practice who turn to technology when they're upset, but the most compelling example of this was Brooke, a boisterous Year 9 student sent to me by a local neurologist. Brooke had stress headaches, and the neurologist was hopeful that psychotherapy would ease them by getting to the bottom of what was causing her stress. In our sessions, Brooke spent a lot of time telling me about the social drama that she and the other members of her tribe stirred up throughout the school day and then continued into the evening over social media. She fought frequently with the boys and girls in her circle and would describe to me—with what seemed to be remarkably *little* stress—the creative insults she delivered online to "even the score" for any meanness that came her way. From what I could tell, the artistry of Brooke's insults gave her a great deal of social power with girls in her group, but the guys weren't afraid to take her down a few pegs.

In the autumn of her Year 10, Brooke's boyfriend announced the end of their relationship online and cruelly detailed his complaints about her on a site used by their friends. Proudly, Brooke told me about how she had paid him back by posting screen shots of the affectionate texts he'd sent during their relationship, embellished now, of course, with her special flavor of ridiculing commentary.

Given that I often find myself taking care of teens on the *receiving* end of social cruelty, it was hard to hear Brooke's delight in her retaliatory skills and to resist lecturing her about how hurtful her behavior was for everyone else. But my job was to get to the bottom of Brooke's stress, so I worked to remember that her hurtful behavior was evidence that she, too, suffered.

Brooke's distress was well hidden; it lived outside of everyone's awareness, even her own. The instant that Brooke felt any emotional pain—shame, humiliation, rejection, fear—she turned the tables. In the short term, her strategy worked. She no longer felt small when she made someone else feel smaller. She no longer felt frightened of rejection when she proved that she could push others away with an even bigger shove. Of course there are many, far better ways to soothe distress and solve problems, but there have always been people who manage pain by inflicting it on someone else. Unfortunately, digital technology gives new power and potential to this unpleasant human impulse.

There's something to be said for detaching from others. When we are alone and disconnected from technology, we can reflect on our feelings, vent silently to ourselves or our diaries, and imagine what we might say or do while considering the impact of any real action. Everyone who grew up without digital technology recalls having written a letter we're glad we never sent or having a rant we're glad no one heard. Using private time to express and get to know a feeling lets the feeling come down to size, teaches us a great deal about ourselves, and acquaints us with our internal resources for managing distress. Social disconnection also allows time to develop a considered plan about how (or if!) we want to act on hard feelings. In other words, we have time to keep our thoughts and our feelings separate from our actions.

Obviously, digital technology takes away social isolation. Brooke never had to sit, alone, with an uncomfortable feeling.

She never had to reflect on what was happening inside of her or find a way to help herself feel better. The instant Brooke sensed a feeling she didn't like, she grabbed her phone and visited the feeling on someone else. She never even knew that she was in pain. All she knew was that she *needed* her phone.

There's more to how Brooke's system "worked." The far and instantaneous reach of digital technology made it easy for her to stir up a lot of drama, and do so quickly. Brooke didn't have to focus on her painful feelings when she could focus on the social explosions she was setting off. At root, I believe that Brooke was badly hurt when her boyfriend dumped her. Rather than tuning in to her distress about the end of the relationship, she turned her attention to following the social media storm her retaliatory messages inspired. Brooke's well-oiled reflex to go on the offensive created a destructive, self-reinforcing cycle. When she was upset, she attacked. When she attacked, she felt better because she was in the driver's seat, not the one being run over. From there, she could focus on the unfolding social drama, not her own painful feelings. Brooke's attacks provided short-term pain relief while setting the stage for more emotional distress (and, sadly, headaches) to come. She was mistreating her peers and they would soon return the favor. And when they did, she'd attack.

Brooke provides one example of how girls turn to digital technology to manage painful feelings instead of finding ways to ease their own distress or seeking the support of kind, non-virtual relationships. I've seen other girls turn to their phones every time they feel lonely. Rather than wondering about the reasons for their loneliness or making plans to get together with a potential friend, they search online for an instant connection or at least an immediate distraction from their isolation. Or girls start posting when they feel forgotten or marginalized. Instead of losing themselves in a book they overshare online to pull attention their way. Or girls scan social media when they worry they've done something gossip worthy. Instead of taking stock of their anxiety and what they can learn from it, they eagerly search for evidence that they are being discussed. Girls also turn to digital technology when excited, using it to announce good news or hard-won accomplishments. Even here, the digital world can interfere with a girl's ability to enjoy a good thing. Rather than savoring her happiness or sharing it with nonvirtual friends and family, she may find herself anxiously checking her posts to see if they are being "liked" or commented upon favorably.

As already suggested, hold off on giving your daughter ready access to social media for as long as you can. The longer she goes without knowing the drug-like buzz of connecting to peers digitally, the more internal resources she'll build up for managing hard feelings and solving problems. Next, also as already suggested, set some boundaries around where and when your daughter can access social media. Consider limiting or banning digital activity (for you and your daughter) while out and about together, at meals, and in the hour or so before bedtime—prime times when you might be able to have a meaningful conversation with her about what she's thinking and how she's feeling.

You can also help regulate your daughter's digital technology use by supporting, or, if necessary, requiring, her participation in extracurricular activities. While engaged with sports, plays, volunteering or paid positions, or any of the other amazing things teenage girls do, girls not only build their social skills, they invariably face emotional challenges that they have to manage. With limited access to their phones, they learn to summon their own resources or capitalize on in-person support. Without question, there are dangers to over-scheduling. Girls who run from one activity to the next can suffer from unnecessary stress and, as we know, become disconnected from their families. But girls with too much time on their hands are more likely to misuse digital technology. As with most things in life, you'll want to help your teenager strike a healthy balance between these two extremes.

Look for opportunities to separate your daughter from technology for extended stretches of time. Demanding jobs, summer camps, and family trips can require—or inspire—long breaks from digital technology. Teenagers can be more willing to go along with no-tech trips if they are allowed to catch up with the digital world at preplanned times. While away from home, some families develop a rule that everyone is allowed to check his or her phone and computer for a half hour each morning and evening but otherwise agree to go off the grid.

Containing the amount of time your daughter spends on digital media—either through daily limits or longer periods of separation—will not, in and of itself, build her capacity to harness her emotions and become a self-sufficient problem solver. But limiting her digital access helps create the conditions that allow her to get to know her feelings. If she can't turn to a digital device every time she's upset, she will find other—probably better—ways to manage.

I wish I could tell you that I was able to help Brooke tune in to her distress and check her impulses to go online. In truth, she was reluctant to trade in her well-worn and surprisingly effective (if costly) tactics for what I was offering: the suggestion that getting to know her emotional pain might help her to make better choices *and* decrease the physical pain of her headaches. To make matters worse, Brooke's mother had long supported Brooke's habit of turning to digital technology when anything went wrong.

How to Become an Accidental Helicopter Parent

It's not just peer interactions over digital technology that undermine a girl's capacity to deal with hard feelings. Parents sometimes play their part, too. Helicopter parents are widely, and often fairly, critiqued. But the rant against helicopter parents usually addresses the outcome—the parent who seems to manage even the smallest details of a teenager's life—and misses the steps that lead to that result. My experience with parents and teenagers suggests that many helicopter parents earn their title as a result of a complex interaction between parent *and child* that unfolds over many years.

In my private practice, I usually meet with new teenage clients a couple of times before I meet with their parents because, ultimately, it's my job to serve the teenager; it makes sense for her to be the first to assess whether I'm likely to be a good fit. Over the years, I have developed a practice of asking girls to tell me what they think their parents will share when we meet. Girls almost always know exactly what their parents will say and, though I don't ask for this, the order in which they will say it. When I asked Brooke what her mother would tell me when we met, she surmised that her mom would link Brooke's headaches to Brooke's near-constant social drama, and then describe how neglected she, herself, felt as a child and how hard she has worked to be available to her own children, despite having a demanding job.

In our meeting, Sandra, a petite, edgy woman, made good on Brooke's guesses but also added that she worried about Brooke's intense dependence upon her. Sandra explained that in Year 7, when Brooke first got a phone, she started texting Sandra from school anytime she hit a snag. In Sandra's words, "Brooke would text in a total meltdown over a missing math book or because she hated what they had for lunch and was 'starving.'" Sandra didn't like being interrupted at work but couldn't resist offering solutions or advice. Before long, Sandra found herself spending part of each evening trying to help Brooke predict the next day's challenges. Even in Year 10, Sandra was still helping Brooke pack her book bag each night, study for upcoming tests, and tackle every problem she could anticipate.

With her detailed knowledge and guidance of Brooke's school life, Sandra looks like the all-time helicopter parent. And while there are certainly some teens who resist their helicopter parent's intrusions, Brooke belonged to the large group who invite and come to depend on them. In other words, helicopter parents are often created via a two-way process: the daughter seeks the parent's help for managing nearly every problem that comes her way and the parent agrees to provide the help. The more help the parent provides, the less capable the daughter becomes at managing on her own. As time goes on and challenges grow, the girl seeks more help from her parent and the parent continues to step in, recognizing that the stakes are higher than ever before. While it may be easy to let a girl go without lunch in Year 7, few parents would feel comfortable telling their imploding daughter to just figure it out when it comes to registering for college entrance exams.

Looked at from the outside, the solution to Brooke and Sandra's dilemma seems easy. Sandra should cut Brooke off, stop answering every text, and expect Brooke to manage her feelings or figure out her problems on her own. In the big picture, Sandra was well aware that Brooke was too dependent on her and lacked basic coping skills. But in the day-to-day, Sandra couldn't resist helping her daughter when asked because she, like all loving parents, hated to see her child struggle. And every good parent tries to improve on the parenting they got;

a key element here was that Sandra wished to be a better, more available parent to Brooke than her own parents had been to her. I've also seen adults drawn into helicopter parenting because they are worried about losing their connection to their teen and welcome the invitation to stay close. I've seen others who fret that they spend too much time at work and so welcome the opportunity to be present digitally. Put simply, the instant connection provided by digital technology can put parents and teenagers on a loving road to an unfortunate outcome.

No parents look at their infant daughter and think, "How can we raise our girl in a way that will be sure to turn her into an emotionally impaired, overly dependent young woman?" We all aim to raise self-sufficient, problem-solving girls, so we need to appreciate that digital technology poses a real threat to this goal. You can avoid becoming an accidental helicopter parent by paying close attention to how your daughter uses technology to engage with you. If she's checking in to let you know she's running late, terrific. If she's texting you because she's upset about a grade that just got handed back, be careful about how—and how quickly—you respond. Waiting to reply will give her time to come up with a solution that doesn't involve you. You can't fix the grade, and if you don't respond right away (or at all), she'll get help from a friend or teacher, or find a way to manage her upset feelings on her own. If you worry that going dark will be experienced as cruelly withholding, send a warm text message that cheers on her ability to come to a resolution. Let her know that you're there to support her, not there to solve problems for her. Something like, "Bummer—but definitely a challenge you can handle. Xoxo, Mom."

Harnessing Emotions: When to Worry

Though it's exhausting for you, your daughter, and, some-times, everyone in a five-mile radius, try to keep in mind that all is well if your daughter's feelings swing from high to low. As we know, normally developing teenagers are calm and rational one minute, wildly elated the next, and brooding not long after. So long as your daughter's feelings are all over the map, she's probably doing fine. You should worry if your daughter's mood is consistently somber or crabby, goes to frightening extremes, is dominated by anxiety, or if she uses self-destructive measures to cope with her feelings.

Recognizing Adolescent Mood and Anxiety Disorders

Teenagers have ups and downs, but if they're down day after day something could be wrong. Clinical depression, a psycho-logical illness that goes far beyond feeling blue, affects roughly 5 percent of all teenagers and is more likely to occur in girls than boys. If your daughter shows several of the classic signs of clinical depression—sadness, not enjoying life, changes in her appetite, sleep, or activity levels, fatigue or loss of energy, feelings of guilt or worthlessness, or difficulty concentrating—for many days in a row, consider having her evaluated for a mood disorder. Should your daughter express suicidal feel-ings, call her primary care provider immediately; if she indi-cates that she might hurt herself, take her to an emergency room.

Unfortunately, it is not widely known that the symptoms of depression in teenagers are rarely the same as the symptoms in adults. Instead of being sad and gloomy, depressed teens are more likely to be highly irritable with most people, most of the time. Living with a teenager who suffers from this form of depression is like living with a touchy porcupine. When teens are testy all the time, it's easy for adults to write their behavior off as stereotypically teenaged and simply annoying. That's a mistake, and one that causes us to miss many highly treatable cases of adolescent depression. If you tense up every time you try to interact with your daughter because you expect her to be prickly, you should consider the possibility that something's really wrong.

Bipolar disorders—mood disorders that involve both manic highs and depressive lows—often begin during adolescence. Teenagers who suffer from manic episodes may have periods in which they sleep little, talk fast, and dash from one activity to the next, often with little regard for their own safety. Though mania is often associated in the popular culture with joyful giddiness and high levels of productivity, adults and teenagers in a manic phase are likely to become agitated or irritated and to accomplish little even while being endlessly active. Recent years have seen a sharp, controversial increase in the diagnoses of these disorders in teenagers. On one side of the debate you'll find clinicians who worry that we're now carelessly stretching an old diagnostic category to include what are really just common, if extreme, adolescent mood swings. On the other side, you'll find clinicians who feel that bipolar disorders have long been underdiagnosed in teens because their manic symptoms sometimes look like mere troublesome outbursts, not the hyperactivity we typically see in manic adults.

And then there's anxiety, a feeling that can be a useful signal that something's amiss, but only when it occurs in certain contexts and with sufficient intensity. As we know, anxiety can be a girl's best friend if it helps her to be on her toes when she's in a dangerous situation. Unfortunately, anxiety can also grow out of control and ring a deafening emotional alarm when there's no real threat to be managed, or even when the threat is a small one, such as a test on a topic the girl knows well. Girls often talk about being stressed or anxious, so it can be easy to dismiss their concerns, but a full 10 percent of teenagers may suffer from full-blown anxiety disorders, which, like clinical depression, are also more likely to occur in girls than boys.

If you're feeling overwhelmed by the murky picture I'm painting of adolescent mood and anxiety disorders, I've got good news for you. First, you don't need to try to make any subtle diagnostic distinctions before seeking help. Psychiatric diagnoses morph constantly and have become vastly complex. If you're worried that something's wrong, get an evaluation from a trusted clinician. A second bit of good news is that there's an easy way to know if something's wrong. Your daughter's moods are grounds for concern if they interfere with her progressive development.

Several years ago I worked with a seventeen-year-old girl suffering from such profound social anxiety that she refused to attend school. She was certain that she was being scrutinized by classmates who stood ready to ridicule her if she got mayonnaise on her cheek while eating her sandwich or if she stammered while speaking in class. She rarely left her home, was so self-conscious that she wouldn't order her own meal if she went out to dinner with her parents, and was completing her Year 12 through an online program. We threw our weight behind getting her anxiety under control. Though she was progressing academically, her out-of-control emotions had stopped her from parting with childhood (her parents still had to care for her as if she were very young) or joining a new tribe.

It's your daughter's job to grow along the strands described in this book, and if her moods are getting in the way, she needs help. If she can't part with childhood because she's anxiously clinging to you, be concerned. If she can't join a new tribe because she's so depressed that she won't reach out to classmates, it's time to worry. The same rule applies to the strands yet to come. It's normal for girls to be temperamental, but they shouldn't be so out of sorts that they offend every adult (chapter 4), can't plan for the future (chapter 5), won't pursue romantic relationships (chapter 6), or don't care for themselves (chapter 7).

Self-Destructive Coping

Some teens rely on self-destructive tactics to harness painful feelings. Drinking, using drugs, engaging in eating-disordered behavior, and cutting are disastrous long-term solutions for psychological distress, but in the short term, they do an incredibly effective job of numbing emotional pain. Teens, like some adults, can come to depend on the nearly instantaneous psychological relief that comes with getting high or harming themselves in another way, especially if they see no other path toward feeling better. Even leaning heavily on peers, as Cassie did with Lana, might bring short-term solace but long-term trouble as peers eventually back away to save themselves.

If you suspect that your daughter relies on self-destructive practices to manage unwanted feelings, there are two reasons you'll want to seek professional help immediately. Most obviously, the behaviors themselves are dangerous and need to stop. Less obviously, the self-destructive behaviors interfere with the crucial psychological maturation that comes with experiencing and learning from emotional pain. As clinicians who specialize in treating substance abuse say, "A person stops maturing at the age that they start abusing substances," and I have always found this to be true in my own practice. People who fall into the habit of using self-destructive tactics to numb pain will *age* as time passes, but they don't *grow up*.

Your daughter isn't just leaving childhood behind, fitting herself into a network of peers, and trying to get a handle on her supercharged emotions—she's also figuring out what to make of the adults she has to deal with every day. When girls become teenagers, they stop buying everything we're selling. They still trust some adults, but they watch us carefully and are quick to see our flaws. They know our rules but often feel compelled to chart their own course. Next, let's consider how these forces, and others, play out as teenagers come to terms with adults and the power they exercise.

FOUR

. . . .

Contending with Adult Authority

YOU KNOW THE SCENE IN *THE WIZARD OF OZ* WHEN TOTO PULLS back the curtain and reveals that the great and powerful Oz is just a guy frantically pulling levers behind a curtain? If we put your daughter in the role of Dorothy and you, my friend, in the place of the Wizard, the scene perfectly explains why girls start to challenge adults, break rules, and engage in other forms of rebellion once they become teenagers. Before adolescence, girls don't see behind the curtain; they respect their elders and usually do as they're told. Children do push the limits, but they tend to go along with adults, especially if we get mad. When the curtain is pulled back, girls see that we aren't infallible, omnipotent Wizards. In fact, we sometimes abuse our office and issue arbitrary rules. Once they're armed with this insight, it's hardly surprising that girls stop acquiescing to age-given rank and start questioning our authority.

It's humbling to lose the absolute power that comes with being the Wizard, but your daughter's new perspective is actually a good thing. Figuring out how best to contend with authority is one of the developmental strands of adolescence. We're not looking to raise sheep who give in to threats or do everything they're told. By the time they're adults, we want our daughters to know how to evaluate authority figures while making thoughtful, even tactical choices about when to resist orders and when to toe the line. This chapter will help you guide your daughter's sudden inclination to contend with adult authority, even as she challenges you, your rules, and the wisdom of most grown-ups.

Seeing Behind the Curtain

What pulls the curtain back? Why do girls follow our rules one week then scoff at them the next? Our answer comes from Jean Piaget, a towering figure in the field of psychology who, in the mid-1950s, was the first to describe the dramatic mental shift that occurs at the end of childhood. Somewhere around age eleven, girls stop seeing the world in strictly concrete terms because they develop the capacity for abstract reasoning. Before then, children can only reflect upon specific events that they have, or could have, actually observed. In other words, if you ask a ten-year-old, "What would make someone throw a cell phone out of a moving car?" she could likely assure you that the phone would be a goner, but she probably couldn't imagine compelling reasons for *why* a person might toss the phone. By age eleven, however, girls start to think in abstract terms. They weigh theoretical concepts like retribution, reflect on their own thoughts, and make inferences about what might drive someone else's actions. An eleven-year-old could imagine any number of plausible explanations for phone throwing, even if she had never been tempted to try it herself. Perhaps the phone was tossed to bring a dramatic (and stupid) end to a frustrating conversation. Or maybe it was chucked by an exasperated parent making an expensive point to a teenager. The eleven-year-old might tell you that she couldn't really know, but still be able to come up with a list of possible motives.

What does abstract reasoning have to do with questioning authority? Everything. When teenagers start thinking in abstract terms, they make stunning inferential leaps. In the words of one insightful fifteen-year-old, "I realized that if I can be dishonest with adults, that means they can be dishonest with me."

With the curtain pulled back, teens watch adults closely and soon notice that many of our edicts are, in fact, hypocritical, nonsensical, or simply self-serving. Of course some of our rules make tons of sense (and we'll address how you can continue to enforce them once your Wizarding days end), but plenty of our rules don't. I recently caught myself making a totally meaningless rule when my older daughter grabbed a pen to write a reminder on the back of her hand. Before I could stop myself I said, "What are you doing? Get some paper!" But really, there are very few reasons *not* to write reminders on the backs of our hands and plenty of good reasons to do it. I've come to admit that, like all other parents, I regularly call my own authority into question by citing "laws" that are merely preferences.

How will you know when your daughter has seen behind the curtain? Oh, you'll know. Your first hint might be when she serves up a trenchant, even funny, critique of adults and the beliefs they hold dear. My favorite example is the girl who announced at dinner, "You know, Odysseus was kind of a dick." She captured a truism (Homer's hero does, in fact, specialize in deceit) while using her choice of words to communicate that she was prepared to discuss classical literature with adults but would be doing so on her terms. And if she hasn't already, your daughter will call on the two signals girls most commonly use to let us know that they are questioning our authority: rolling her eyes and taking a sassy tone.

Sometimes girls recruit eye rolling, tone taking, and other nonverbal cues to express their dissent while still following the rules. When you ask her to change into an outfit that's appropriate for dinner out as a family, she might roll her eyes or issue a sharp "Fine!" before stomping off to her room to change. This scene should feel familiar because you've been around this block before, back when your daughter was a toddler. Teenagers and toddlers have a lot in common—I've heard some parents refer to their teens as "toddlers on hormones"—with a key commonality being their need to establish that they are an independent state while still submitting to the laws of the reigning government. When your daughter was a toddler, this took the form of loudly refusing to take a bath while simultaneously stripping down and heading toward the tub. As a teenager, she rolls her eyes or takes a tone while doing what you asked her to do. Though your daughter's resistance will almost certainly irritate you, consider letting it slide. More than that, you could silently admire the impressive defying-while-complying solution that allows her to be a good kid even as she expresses her opposition.

Periodically, your daughter's eye rolling or tone might strike you as provocative and rude—designed to jerk your chain more than solve a dilemma. At these times, you might ask her to communicate her dissent in a more mature way. You could say, "I can't stop you from rolling your eyes at me, but I think it's rude. If you can tell me what's wrong, we could talk about it," or "I'm not okay with your tone—try again," or "I'm open to negotiating, but not when you're acting like that." Your daughter is letting you know that she disagrees with you, and that is certainly her right. And it's your right to expect that she will be civil while objecting. As we know, it takes girls time to learn to be assertive. Don't miss the opportunity to invite your daughter to practice her assertiveness skills on you.

The End of "Because I Said So"

Having figured out that adults routinely create arbitrary rules, girls determinedly undertake the massive task of testing the established regulations. Your daughter will test plenty of rules on her own time. She'll blast music while driving, watch movies you've banned, go out in the cold with wet hair, and see for herself that the world does not, in fact, come to an end. And she'll test plenty of rules on your time. It's truly exhausting when your daughter questions nearly everything you say, but you should honor her newfound insight by having real conversations about your rules.

So how will you respond? At times, you'll stick to your position while nevertheless acknowledging that yours is one of many valid perspectives:

Attending church as a family is important to your mom and me, so we expect that you'll come with us. When you move out, you can make your own choices about going to church.

At other times, you'll offer a fuller explanation than you have in the past:

Here's my problem with the way you keep your room: I hate to see the nice clothes we've paid for thrown all around. I don't feel comfortable buying you anything new while good stuff lies on the floor.

At still others, you'll negotiate:

> *I don't want you to put a streak in your hair because your grandma will be visiting next month and I'm not up for hearing about it from her. If you'll hold off until after that visit, I'm open to it.*

Occasionally, you'll see her point:

> *You're right, I'm wrong. Go ahead and write on your hand. And pass the pen when you're done.*

When your daughter questions your authority, take her seriously and offer an explanation, a compromise, or your agreement. As one teen told me, "There's nothing better than beating an adult in an argument." If your daughter has a point, recognize it. If she's right and you're wrong, grant her the joy of changing your mind. The best way to maintain your daughter's respect will be to welcome her budding insight. When it comes to engaging with your daughter as she questions your authority, there are many ways to get it right. And there are two things you should *not* do: don't insist that you are still the Wizard, and don't give up.

A particularly painful example of what happens when a parent insists that he's still the Great and Powerful Wizard showed up in my private practice. For several months, I worked with Chloe, a poised, artsy teen whose parents divorced when she was twelve. When Chloe was seventeen, her father—a man with an impressive track record of insensitive behavior—married a woman who prided herself on her cooking. Chloe, a vegetarian who enjoyed a terrific variety of healthy foods, spent Tuesday evenings and alternate weekends with her dad and stepmother and on her first visit to their new home, Chloe's stepmother served chicken cacciatore. Chloe quietly focused on eating her vegetables until her father (but, interestingly, not her stepmother) pressed her to share in the main course. Despite Chloe's protest that she hadn't eaten meat in over a year, her father insisted that she was being rude to her stepmother by refusing to eat what was served and threatened to take her phone if she didn't give in. Chloe stood her ground. Her father took her phone.

I'm sure that I don't have to tell you that taking a teenager's phone, especially at age seventeen, amounts to a very severe punishment. Chloe hung in for two weeks until she could no longer get along without her phone. She choked down a few bites of meat on the nights she ate at her dad's house, got her phone back, and toughed it out for a month until she turned eighteen. The divorce agreement did not require Chloe to stick to the visitation plan once she became an adult in the eyes of the law, so after her birthday, Chloe packed her bags, moved out of her father's house, and stayed full-time with her mother. Chloe's mom empathized with Chloe's position, all the while worried about the harm her ex-husband had done to his relationship with their daughter.

Sad as this story is, I was thankful that Chloe had a way out. When teens are trapped with parents who would rather flaunt their power than negotiate on even minor points, it doesn't always end so well. These parents don't just damage their relationships with their daughters, they can also provoke girls into proving that they will not be controlled. Under such conditions I've seen girls sneak around to do things that are frighteningly out of control. It's far better for your Dorothy—and your relationship with her—for you to come out from behind the curtain, even when doing so gives rise to a series of tough negotiations.

And don't give up.

I think here of Veronica, a fifteen-year-old referred to my private practice by a school counselor who received a desperate Monday-morning call from her parents. They told the counselor, then me, that on the preceding Saturday night Veronica had gone to a party with some older teens who offered to pick her up and bring her back home. Though reluctant to let her go, Veronica's parents set an early curfew of ten thirty, figuring that she couldn't find much trouble before then. When she wasn't home at eleven, they started calling her phone but got no answer. At midnight Veronica finally rolled in. Remorseless about being late, she flippantly explained that she had "accidently" turned off her phone.

As I got to know Veronica—a smart, disaffected girl—and her parents, the rest of the story came out. When she was thirteen, Veronica started to break small rules. She began by playing music loudly in her room. When her father asked her to turn it down, she'd grumble, comply, then soon turn the music up again. Before long, her father gave up and asked the rest of the family to put up with the noise. Next, Veronica started wearing black lipstick that her mom hated. Her mother asked her to save the lipstick for Halloween, or at least for the weekends, but Veronica wore it to school every day. Several contentious mornings later, her mother gave up about the lipstick, figuring that even if she made Veronica take it off before school, she could put it back on while riding the bus, so there was really no point in fighting about it. In one of our meetings, Veronica's mom, a soft-spoken woman with a worried face, told me that she nearly blew up when Veronica got in the car wearing the lipstick to go to church on Easter Sunday. She was hurt and offended (and knew this wasn't lost on her daughter) but bit her tongue because she feared their relationship was already under too much strain and, on top of that, she didn't want to ruin the morning for the rest of the family.

Teens are eager to contend with adult authority and they often do it by testing the adults closest to them. In my experience, teenagers usually start with small stuff. They do things that annoy us but that don't really have the potential for negative and lasting consequences. Adolescent misdemeanors reflect teens' creativity, interests, and knowledge of what will push their parents' buttons. Girls leave dishes in the sink when they've been told not to, listen to offensive music, read off-putting novels, wear weird clothes, lobby for a nose piercing, decide to become Democrats if their parents are Republicans (or the other way round), and so on.

When girls don't find the friction they're looking for with adults on the small stuff, they sometimes ramp things up by moving on to the predictable list of things we *really* don't want our daughters to do—things that could matter down the line. Unable to get her parents to stay toe-to-toe with her about her loud music and her lipstick, Veronica ups the ante and does something that's harder to ignore.

Why do teenagers move on to risky business when they don't meet resistance on the small stuff? Because teens want to know where the lines are and that they'll be called out of bounds if they cross them. It's daunting to be a teenager and have access to tempting but dangerous attractions; it's terrifying to think that no one is watching. As one of my clinical colleagues commented, when teens like Veronica act out, they are posing the question, "So what does a girl have to do around here to get the grown-ups to act like grown-ups?" If Veronica had to sneak her lipstick out of the house and apply it when she got on the bus, she might have felt comforted by the presence of rules, even as she broke them, and left it at that. Indeed, research has long established that teens whose parents are highly permissive—whether they are indulgent, neglectful, or just reluctant to step in—are more likely to abuse substances and misbehave at school than teens whose parents articulate and enforce limits.

I saw this principle in action early in my training when I spent a graduate school summer staffing a psychiatric unit for teenagers. These adolescents lived in the inpatient setting because they were too troubled to be cared for outside of a hospital. Many of the teens were defiant and belligerent—as staff we spent a lot of time preventing physical fights—so there was an elaborate system of points, rewards, and penalties designed to control, and hopefully improve, their conduct. Early in my days on the unit I made a rookie mistake: while supervising a group of teens I didn't know well, I let a few infractions slide in the hopes of securing the group's good behavior by establishing that I was friendly and easygoing. Bad idea. When I didn't tell the first teen to take her feet off the table, a second teen turned on the radio without asking permission. Then a third would bicker about the station selection. Before long, a wise supervisor pointed out what was happening. They weren't just misbehaving—they were *scared*. They were looking for reassurance that I would keep things under control and I wasn't providing it. So they kept looking. A rookie no more, I put myself on high alert for the first misdeed committed in any new group of teens. I quickly and publicly (but still nicely) docked the proper number of points from the offending teen's tally and watched the whole group breathe a sigh of relief.

So make it easier on yourself and safer for your daughter by engaging with some of her annoying behaviors. What you oppose and how will be unique to you and your family. You don't have to resist each bothersome move your daughter makes (having a teenager, after all, can help us grow in our acceptance and flexibility), but you shouldn't ignore every small thing. If she won't turn her music down after being asked, ask again. If it's still loud, stand in her doorway and make that face she hates until she turns it down. And even when you can't really control the outcome, go ahead and have the fight. Remember Andy, my globe-trotting friend who gamely withstood the teasing dished out by his daughter Grace? When we were in high school, Andy wore his favorite T-shirt to school most days despite being forbidden by his mother to wear it outside of the house. She was right. The shirt was so worn that Andy could hide it by jamming the whole thing in the back pocket of his jeans, which he did most mornings as he left for school. He changed into the threadbare shirt before he got to the end of his block and headed off secure in the knowledge that the adults hadn't given up or rolled over.

I encouraged Veronica's parents to go ahead and challenge some of the small stuff she did, even if that meant increasing the friction around the house. At times, Veronica rudely told her mother to stop talking, and her mother had fallen into the habit of obliging. With my support, Veronica's mom started to push back and say, as calmly as she could, "Hey, that's rude. I don't speak to you that way, and you shouldn't speak to me that way. If you're angry, let's talk about it." Veronica never took the bid—she usually walked away in a huff—but she didn't escalate the situation either.

Veronica's parents had adopted an uncomfortable pattern of avoiding their daughter and her snarky attitude. They didn't enjoy her and she didn't enjoy them so I recommended that they look for new ways to connect. When Veronica asked to join a drama program in a neighboring community, they signed her up and used the long drive to rehearsal to discuss her growing interest in theater. Gradually, Veronica's attitude toward her parents improved for two reasons I could see: she felt comforted by the knowledge that they would respond when she misbehaved, and their support of her theatrical interests had put money in their shared relational bank. In other words, when she wrangled with her parents, as she occasionally still did, it now came at the expense of the generally pleasant time they were having with one another.

Perhaps most important, the lines of communication had reopened between Veronica and her parents. As a clinician I'll take friction over a stalemate any day. Here's why: your daughter will be given many opportunities to do hazardous things while she's a teenager, and you want to be talking with her about the risks teens take. You can't have these all-important conversations when you're in a standoff.

Framing Danger

Parents of teenagers must live with the painful truth that teenagers can and do engage in dangerous behavior—behavior that goes way beyond wearing questionable lipstick or a banned T-shirt. You're not alone if you've lost sleep worrying that your daughter might get hurt if she and her friends decide to try out some of the careless things that teenagers sometimes do. More than a few parents secretly wish that they could lock their daughter away until she's an adult or follow her around all weekend as her personal (and profoundly unwelcome) bodyguard.

Our fears about teen safety aren't crazy. Statistically, people take more risks as teenagers than they do at any other time of life. Reckless driving, drug use, and unprotected sex all peak during adolescence. Yet contrary to popular belief, research *doesn't* support the myths that teenagers push limits because they are highly irrational, think they're invulnerable, or can't calculate risks. Rather, when something bad happens to a teenager, it's usually because her capacity for wise decision making has been swept away by powerful contextual factors. Remember the video game study in chapter 2 that showed young drivers throw caution to the wind when their friends are nearby? That's what we're talking about here. A teenager's wish to connect with her friends and be seen as cool in their eyes can readily trump her better judgment.

But even under the sway of social influence, teenagers don't disregard the issue of rules completely. In my experience they still think about it, but in the wrong way. Instead of reflecting on *why* we have rules, teens focus on trying not to get caught while breaking them. I've got Sasha, a fun-loving Year 12 student, to thank for this insight.

One Thursday afternoon Sasha, whose parents initially sought my help because she was routinely cutting class, brought herself to our regular appointment at my practice. Excited to share her plans for the weekend, she dropped her book bag on the floor of my office, plunked down on my couch, and happily began.

"So, listen to this! There's a guy at school who I sorta know who asked me to a sleepover on his parents' houseboat this weekend. From how he asked, I can't tell if anyone else will be there. He said that he knows where his folks keep the keys to the boat, so we won't have any problem getting in. My mom would never be okay with this, so I'm gonna tell her that I'm sleeping over at Julia's." Julia was Sasha's best friend and sometimes accomplice. As I listened to Sasha's plans, my heart rate skyrocketed and my mind left its psychologist mode and switched fully to "I'm a mother too!" mode. All I could think was, "Forget your confidentiality, kiddo, I am *so* calling your mom."

I should note here that many excellent therapists refuse to work with teenagers because they don't want to deal with the challenges that come up when teens talk about risky behavior in therapy. As clinicians, it's our job to protect our clients' confidentiality. But it's also our job to keep teenagers safe, so we must break confidentiality if we think a teenager might do something truly dangerous. A lot of what teens talk about in therapy falls into a tricky gray area that requires us to make a judgment call about whether we should alert parents to potentially harmful behavior, even if that means damaging our relationship with a teenage client.

In telling me this story, Sasha was clearly counting on my confidentiality. She must have sensed my discomfort about what I was hearing because next she said, "This should totally work because I have thought it all through. Yep . . . thought it all through." From there, Sasha described the elaborate scheme she and Julia had crafted to keep her mom from figuring out where she really was. Listening, I realized that by "thinking it all through," Sasha meant that she'd given a lot of thought to figuring out how to make sure she wouldn't get caught. I collected myself and got back into psychologist mode.

Assuming that every teenager has a wise, mature side (even if she does a great job of hiding it), I spoke to that part of Sasha and said, "Look, you and I both know that getting caught by your mother is the *least* dangerous thing that could happen to you this weekend." Thankfully, Sasha's mature side suddenly surfaced and spared me an awkward (and borderline unethical) phone call to her mother. Once I suggested that there might be some genuine risks to consider, Sasha named them for us: she didn't really know this boy, she might be alone with him off some dock on Lake Erie, if something went wrong she'd be on her own, and so on. To my enormous relief, she talked herself into canceling her plans.

When our daughters assess risk, we want them to assess the

right risks. We want them to focus not on escaping adult detection but on the real dangers they might face. How do you make this happen? To begin, think carefully about your response when your daughter tells you about her peers' risky behavior. As frightening as these tales can be, consider each and every one of them a gift. News of what so-and-so did gives you an open invitation to have critical conversations with your teenager—the kind of conversations that would come off as unwelcome lectures if broached directly.

If she mentions a friend who texts while driving, resist your impulse to say something such as, "That's horrible—if I were her parent I'd ground her indefinitely!" and use the opportunity to comment on the actual perils of what you're hearing. Consider, "Yikes! Can you help her stop doing that? I'd hate for her to hurt or kill herself or someone else." If she tells you about a classmate who uses her cell phone to lie about her location when calling home to check in, you might say, "I hope she's also focused on making sure she's somewhere safe and not just thinking about how to throw her parents off her trail."

Similarly, make good use of the hypothetical situations your daughter puts before you. If she asks, "What would you do if you caught me smoking?" talk with her about nicotine's highly addictive chemistry and the lethality of lung cancer. Don't tell her that you'd routinely search her room for cigarettes and give her a close sniff every time she walked through the door. Parents who threaten their daughter usually come from a well-meaning place—they don't want anything bad to happen to her and hope that they can scare her straight. But parental threats focus a girl's attention on avoiding the short-term menace posed by the rules, not the long-term damage that could result from the risks she's considering. It's logistically impossible to supervise teenagers all the time and with cell phones, cars, and friends like Julia, teenagers can get away with all kinds of dangerous mischief. If you set up the game as "don't get caught by me," your daughter can win that game, even at her own frightening expense.

Come out from behind your curtain and offer the real reasons for your rules. Frame conversations about dangerous behavior in terms of the bottom-line risks your daughter might face, not what will happen if she gets busted. And as you take this tack, know that the research is on your side. A long-standing area of study in academic psychology demonstrates that teens with *authoritative* parents—parents who are warm yet firm and emphasize the reasons for rules—consistently take fewer risks than the teens of *authoritarian* parents who simply lay down the law and try to gain compliance through punishment. In chapter 7 we'll discuss in specific terms the risky things girls sometimes do, how to talk with your daughter about those risks, and how to respond if your daughter takes them. For now, our aim is to encourage our daughters to consider the actual hazards of risk taking, not the logistics of defying authority.

Rupture and Repair

I'm at lunch with a close colleague—a psychologist who treats adults and who, like me, is the mother of two girls. Her daughters are eight and eleven, and when we get to talking about the older daughter's impending adolescence my friend apprehensively says, "I think we'll be okay ... we've got a really good relationship right now, so I'm hoping that we won't have a rough time with each other when she's a teenager." To which I reply, "Well, you *will* get into rough times with each other, what matters is how you get *out* of them. We both want to help our girls build their emotional intelligence, and having healthy fights with you will help your daughter grow that intelligence." We got refills on our coffees and kept talking about what we mean when we say *emotional intelligence* and how the right kind of conflict can build it.

Emotional intelligence is a widely used term, but there's no consensus among psychologists about its definition. I favor the approach of Peter Fonagy, the head of the Clinical, Educational and Health Psychology Department at University College London and director of the Anna Freud Centre. Dr. Fonagy and his research team describe emotional intelligence as the capacity to reflect on our own thoughts, feelings, and actions *and* to be aware of complex mental states—the wishes, beliefs, and feelings—of the people around us. We are using our emotional intelligence when we wonder, "What's gotten into me? Why am I so short-tempered today?" and our daughters are using their emotional intelligence when they think, "What's up with Mom? Did I do something that ticked her off?" In other words, it's both "seeing ourselves from the outside and seeing others from the inside." Often, emotional intelligence is just common sense; we use it all the time without even noticing. Almost everyone comes wired for emotional intelligence, and some people have more of it than others. But it's also a skill, and like any other skill, emotional intelligence can be developed.

What does emotional intelligence have to do with telling my psychologist friend to go ahead and fight with her soon-to-be teenager? Research demonstrates that emotional intelligence requires the collaboration of the two areas of the brain we've considered before: the lower, primal portion of the brain (the limbic system), which processes emotional information and generates emotional reactions, and the upper, outer area of the brain (the cortex), where rational thinking lives.

When we feel threatened or when our feelings are running high, the limbic system can take over and send us into an attacking or defensively self-protecting mode. This is especially true for teenagers whose brains, as we know, are in the middle of a renovation project that upgrades the limbic system before bringing the higher-order, rational system fully online.

Teenagers are prone to having strong emotional reactions that override their better judgment. They become all emotion and no intelligence. And what's likely to trigger this unfortunate state of affairs? Coming into conflict with you. But there's good news: working your way through a conflict with your daughter brings her brain back into balance and builds her emotional intelligence.

Let's consider an invented interaction between a father and his teenage daughter.

Father: "Hey, it's time for you to set the table for dinner."

Daughter: "Shhh! I'm in the middle of my favorite show and I've been waiting all day to watch it."

Father (firmly): "Doesn't matter. Set the table. Now."

Daughter (snotty): "Geez! Doesn't a girl have the right to watch television around here? Last I looked, kids were no longer considered chattel. If the laws have changed, someone should have let me know."

Father (now mad): "Stop acting like a lazy freeloader! Set the table now or forget about using the car this weekend."

Daughter (stomping off to her room): "Screw you!"

After cooling off for twenty minutes, the father knocks on his daughter's door, gains permission to open it, and stands in her doorway to calmly say: "I don't like what just happened between us, and I want to apologize for my part in it. I'm not okay with how you acted, but I know your days are long and that you love your show. That said, you need to find a better way to respond when I ask you to do something you're not ready to do. On top of that, you shouldn't have taken that tone with me and when you do, you know I'll get mad. Regardless of what you said, I shouldn't have called you a lazy freeloader—that was mean and untrue. I had a long day myself, but that's just an explanation, not an excuse. We're going to eat soon—please come on down and set the table."

If the daughter rolls her eyes, says nothing in response, resentfully sets the table, and sits silently while she eats, I'd still call this exchange a terrific step on the path toward building her emotional intelligence!

Research done by Dr. Fonagy and his team shows that we build emotional intelligence in teens when we help them consider their own, and other people's, mental states. By wondering if his daughter's long day might have contributed to her testy reaction, the father encouraged the kind of self-reflection we want girls to develop ("seeing ourselves from the outside"). In apologizing for his bad behavior, the father reminded his daughter about how he reacted to her snotty tone and connected his harsh words to his own long day. Laying out what unfolded in his mind as the conflict escalated gave his daughter a window into his mental state ("seeing others from the inside") and an impressive primer in emotional intelligence.

But wait, there's more! In our invented interaction, the father didn't just build his daughter's emotional intelligence, he helped to rewire her brain. Emotional intelligence requires the integrated functioning of the prefrontal, rational parts of the brain with the limbic, emotional parts. This is what happens when we *think* about *feelings*, whether they are our own or someone else's. In a gross oversimplification of how the brain works (but a terrifically catchy phrase), "what fires together wires together." The repeated practice of reflecting on the patterns of *her own* mental states and *your* mental states will help your daughter bring her frontal cortex more fully online and pave her path toward an emotionally intelligent adulthood.

Don't expect your daughter to thank you for your efforts to talk with her about your mental states and to appreciate hers. That would be weird. But do expect that, over time, these conversations will help your daughter to be curious about where you (and others) are coming from and to think about what drives her own thoughts, feelings, and actions. And honoring your daughter's complexity while reminding her of yours will keep the lines of communication open when you need them most.

You may be all for building your daughter's emotional intelligence but still wonder, "Must we fight? Can't we build emotional intelligence while we're getting along?"

Not really.

When we're getting along, we only need elementary levels of emotional intelligence. If you and your daughter want to listen to the same song, you don't really have to think about your inner state (as in, "Why *do* I want to hear that song? And is it immature of me to say it's my turn to choose the music?") or your daughter's ("Perhaps she's had a bad day and would feel better if she listens to music she likes"). Only when we are at odds with each other do we start to build our advanced emotional intelligence skills. When we reflect on *competing* mental states—when what I want isn't what you want, but I'm holding both of our perspectives in mind—we start to become emotional geniuses.

You may be on board with the idea of supporting your daughter's growing emotional intelligence and rewiring brain, yet you're still thinking, "But must she fight with *me*? Can't she get the same mental workout fighting with someone else?"

Actually, no.

It has to be you, or some other emotionally intelligent person who really knows and loves her. Because it's not the fighting that builds your daughter's emotional intelligence; it's the path toward resolution where the magic happens. The repair that occurred when the father spoke to his daughter after their blowout depended heavily on the unique bond between a parent and child. To start, he used a calm tone to communicate that the fight was behind him and that they were back in a safe, familiar place with each other. We know that emotional intelligence first grows in the context of loving relationships in which people feel secure. It's almost impossible to ponder our own mental states, much less anyone else's, when we feel threatened. Next, the resolution the father offered involved his past knowledge of his daughter (wondering if her insolence was because of her long day) and her past knowledge of him ("you shouldn't have taken that tone with me and when you do, you know I'll get mad"). Emotional intelligence skills grow when we use our insights about each other to find a way back across a breach. In order to have emotional-intelligence-building relationship repair, you have to have a rupture with someone who cares and knows enough to make it right.

This might seem like a lot of work just to get a girl to sit begrudgingly at the dinner table, but believe me, it's worth it. Every healthy relationship your daughter will ever have depends on her emotional intelligence. When you tune in to your teenager's mental states and help her tune in to yours, you send a strong message. You let her know that she *deserves* to be in relationships with people who are interested in her perspective, can reflect on their own, and are willing to do the hard, humble work of using conflict to deepen and improve a connection. She may never step back to think about the emotionally intelligent relationships you are working to create at home, but her positive experiences with you will encourage her to steer clear of anyone who doesn't treat her with the same dignity.

What if the father hadn't worked toward repair? What if he had let his daughter seethe in her room while he stewed through dinner? He certainly had a right to be mad—her words and actions were out of line—and he could have reasonably expected, even demanded, an apology. But the father left the conversation on a shaming note ("Stop acting like a lazy freeloader!"), and shame is one of the last places we, as parents, want to land with our kids. Indeed, the capacity to shame a child is one of the most dangerous weapons in our parenting arsenal. Shame goes after a girl's character, not her actions. It goes after *who she is,* not *what she did.* Shame has toxic, lasting effects and no real benefits. Once shamed, teens are left two terrible options: a girl can agree with the shaming parent and conclude that she is, indeed, the bad one, or she can keep her self-esteem intact by concluding that the parent is the bad one. Either way, someone loses.

Teenagers can be reactive, they can be rude, and we already know that their intense emotionality can provoke adults to act in ways they later regret. If you say something you don't mean, if you use shame or throw your power around when in conflict with your daughter, apologize. It's the right thing to do, and it's the first step in the critical process of repairing relational ruptures. Don't worry that owning your mistakes will reveal flaws your daughter hasn't noticed before. She already knows you're not perfect. In fact, she can probably list your faults better than anyone.

Crazy Spots

Every parent comes with limitations and, with the curtain pulled back, teenagers can see our limitations clearly and become adept at naming them. This doesn't mean you deserve every criticism your daughter levels at you—you're not parenting very well if your teen agrees with all the decisions you make—but don't rush to dismiss your daughter's critiques of your character. Painful as it can be, there will be times when she names your shortcomings and irrational behavior—what I like to call "crazy spots"—with astounding accuracy.

Some parents know their warts and will not be surprised when their daughters see them, too. If you spent years in therapy mapping the landscape of your neuroses, you'll be impressed when your daughter lays it all out for you in three blunt sentences. Other parents can't tolerate the idea that they have shortcomings. They deny their faults and get defensive when their daughters try to point them out. Most of us fall somewhere in between.

How will you know when to take her critiques seriously? Your daughter is probably on the right track when she's accusing you of something you've been accused of before. Perhaps you're irrational about money, perhaps you aren't as reliable as you should be, or perhaps you have strong reactions to small mistakes. She may also be on the right track if you feel hurt by her accusations. For most of us, the critiques that sting are the ones with some truth to them.

Our daughters have a good reason to point out our limitations: they want us to be better. They will only ever have one set of parents and they are newly aware that we are far from perfect. Ever hopeful, our daughters think we'll improve if they point out our flaws. That said, constructive feedback ("When you are late to pick me up, I feel anxious and frustrated") would make their critiques easier to take. Don't hold your breath waiting for it.

If you suspect that your daughter has accurately identified real limitations in your parenting, you could consider checking her observations with someone else who knows and loves you, perhaps your partner, a sibling, or a gentle friend. Don't be ashamed to admit that your parenting's not perfect. There is no such thing as a perfect parent and there doesn't need to be. Being honest with yourself about your faults will improve your relationship with your daughter and help her thrive in parts of her life that have nothing to do with you. There are a lot of upsides to owning your crazy spots.

Let's say you've confronted your limitations. You've looked yourself in the mirror and said, "You know, she's right, I'm less reliable than I should be. I say I'll pick her up at six o'clock, and I rarely make it before six twenty." What happens now? You've got a couple of options. First, see if you can change. People grow and evolve throughout their lifetimes—having an insightful teenager in your house can make you a better person. Tell your daughter, "You are right, I'm bad about being on time and it's not fair to you. I apologize. I'm trying to change." If you can't change, own your shortcomings.

I have plenty of crazy spots myself and will confess in print to my irrational attachment to having my home be both tidy and clean. It doesn't need to be operating-room clean, but I really (really, really) like to have things shipshape. Left to my own devices, I will spend an entire weekend scrubbing and organizing our already clean kitchen. My affliction predates parenthood: before we married, my now-husband once remarked, "Your idea of fun doesn't seem to be the same as everybody else's." So he knew what he was getting into.

When I stumble upon an unexpected mess—like mud tracked into the house and left to dry—I will sometimes go bananas. I know that my reaction can be totally out of proportion to the size of the problem, so I've worked to own my crazy spot. I've explained to my daughters that my overreactions should not be taken personally; they grow from the many years I happily controlled my surroundings as an only child. We have come to the understanding that I'll do what I can to contain my irrational response, and they'll work with the awareness that things might get ugly if they leave messes around the house. Interestingly, my girls have discovered through trial and error that I don't mind any mess left on a tiled landing right inside our back door. In a display of sisterly solidarity they have come to refer to the area as "Mom's not-crazy spot" (as in, "Whoa, that's really muddy—leave it in Mom's not-crazy spot").

It takes guts to admit one's limitations, especially to a teenager. You might worry that owning your crazy spots will compromise your authority, but the effect is usually the opposite. Teens generally have more respect for adults who admit what they as adolescents can plainly see.

Talking about your crazy spots not only saves your daughter the work of trying to change your fully formed personality, it also builds her emotional intelligence. In its more basic form, your daughter's emotional intelligence will help her to consider competing mental states. But when you teach her about your crazy spots, you are taking her emotional intelligence up several notches: you are inviting her to think about your motivations in a broad perspective that includes past experiences and relationships. By encouraging her to expand her insight beyond what's happening in the moment, you'll advance your daughter from amateur-level emotional intelligence ("Why does Mom act psychotic when I track mud through the house?") to the pros ("Mom acts psychotic because she didn't have to share her space when she was growing up, so she doesn't always handle it well now").

Owning your limitations and helping your daughter not take them personally opens up a whole new world for her. Though teenagers can recognize their parents' shortcomings, the egocentricity of adolescence causes them to see our crazy spots as something we are doing "to" them, and they believe that if they point out our faults, they can bring us closer to being the ideal parents they want us to be. Few moments in life spark more maturation than when a young person recognizes that her parents have strengths and limitations that were in place long before she came along and that will be there long after she moves out. In letting go of the dream of turning you into the perfect parent, your daughter recovers a lot of energy that has been devoted to being angry with you, feeling hurt by you, or trying to change you. And there are many more important directions for an adolescent's energy to go: toward her studies, toward building healthy friendships, toward planning her future, and, of course, toward enjoying the strengths of her less-than-perfect parents.

In good marriages, partners can help their children appreciate what they should and shouldn't take personally in the other parent's behavior. My husband has told our daughters that I've been clean crazy for as long as he's known me and that he stopped taking it personally years ago. Done carefully, and with everyone's best interest in mind, crazy spot naming can also be a feature of good divorces. Those of us who work with divorced parents universally counsel them not to bad-mouth their exes to their children, but it's still possible to help teens with an ex's crazy spots in a way that supports the teen and her relationship with both parents.

Chloe (the vegetarian) and her mom came to an appointment together so that we could address the fallout from her dad's insistence that she eat meat at his home. As Chloe complained about her father's high-handed tactics, her mother matter-of-factly commented that he had never been one for negotiation. Indeed, she explained that that was one of the reasons their marriage had failed. She went on to offer suggestions for how Chloe might reach out to her dad when she felt ready and added that, shortcomings aside, he really adored Chloe and that many of her own wonderful qualities were ones she had in common with her father. If I'd had a "Divorced Parent of the Century" prize on hand, I would have given it out right there.

So go ahead and own your crazy spots and help your daughter with your partner's (or ex's) spots if you can do it in a kind way. And take comfort: girls don't reserve their character critiques for their parents—they see through other adults, too.

Adults with Faults

When I was in Year 11, I had an awful trigonometry teacher. His explanations of problems added to my confusion, his tests didn't cover what he said they would cover, and he took forever to grade and return our homework. I was stuck with Mr. Martin (or that's what we'll call him) and complained constantly about him at home. When my mother had her fill of my griping, she offered one of the least welcome and most helpful things anyone has ever said to me: "There will be no place on your school marksheet to explain that you didn't like Mr. Martin. You'd better figure out how to manage."

These situations are not rare. Every school has teachers who are incompetent, disorganized, callous, provocative, or deadly boring. Welcome this reality. If you could staff your daughter's school with nothing but the most engaging, talented, and conscientious teachers, she'd have an amazing educational experience but would graduate without the skills needed to thrive in the outside world. Once your daughter leaves school, she will need to know how to manage unpleasant bosses, difficult college instructors, and other challenging people in positions of authority. So when she encounters a problematic teacher, seize the opportunity to help your daughter develop strategies that will serve her for the rest of her life.

Don't hesitate to validate your daughter's experience when she complains to you about another adult. Unless you have reason to believe otherwise, her description is likely accurate; teenagers are particularly clear-eyed and can provide descriptions of adults' characters that would put a Brontë sister to shame. If your daughter has been lucky enough to spend her childhood surrounded by reasonable grown-ups, she may be confused when a less-than-impressive one first crosses her path. Spare her the trouble of doubting her perceptions while calmly acknowledging that she will need to learn to deal with all sorts of people.

Indeed, when girls in my practice complain to me about the adults in their lives, I rarely question their assessment. If a girl seems stymied by her parents' shortcomings, I try to boost her emotional intelligence by asking her to theorize about their alleged crazy spots (as in, "So what do you make of the fact that your dad seems to prefer time in his workshop to time at the dinner table?"). Or I empathize with the girl's position without allowing it to become an excuse for her difficulties. Once, when I was sitting with a bright teenager who could not stand her parents and was protesting their deficiencies by failing in school, I found myself saying, "I'll take you at your word that your parents aren't fit for the job—but then you've got to help me understand why you are setting yourself up to live with them indefinitely."

Our old friend Camille made a smooth transition into Year 10. She welcomed the smorgasbord of extracurricular opportunities that became available and the influx of new kids from other schools. Camille had always been a strong student, so Maya was surprised when her first end-of-year report showed a high C in French. When Maya asked her what was going on, she got an earful about Camille's own Mr. Martin, her Year 10 French teacher, Mrs. Clayton. By Camille's report, Mrs. Clayton spoke only in French, sometimes ridiculed students, and gave out worksheets that were graded entirely on whether they were handed in on time. Camille complained over dinner that she should not be expected to put forth her best effort given Mrs. Clayton's ridiculous policies and obvious disdain for her students.

Maya told me that she was tempted to pull Camille from the class and switch her into Latin, but, before she did, we decided to try to help Camille get things back on track. As we talked, Maya reflected on a narrow-minded boss she had had in one of her first jobs. At our next meeting, Maya reported that her conversation with her daughter had gone well. She had shared with Camille how miserable it was to work for a mean and petty boss yet how useful it had been to walk away from that job with a strong recommendation. From there, Maya went on to help Camille rise to the challenge of dealing with her difficult teacher. She openly agreed with her daughter regarding Mrs. Clayton's grading policies but pointed out that Camille could play by the stupid rules to get the grade she wanted. When her daughter objected that she wasn't even catching all of the assignments Mrs. Clayton gave in rapid-fire French, Maya suggested that she compare notes with several classmates about what they believed the assignments were, trusting that among them they were likely to get everything. Later that week, when Camille couldn't make sense of a grammatical rule while studying for an upcoming test, Maya helped her search online until they found a video tutorial that addressed the question.

By engaging seriously with the dilemma posed by Mrs. Clayton, Maya sent several important messages: that Camille would have to deal with problematic authority figures throughout life, so wishing it were different was only a waste of energy; that she had total confidence that Camille could develop solutions to the problems Mrs. Clayton presented; and—perhaps most important—that she fully expected that Camille would figure out how to manage her lousy situation. Maya later told me that she said to Camille, "Look, I know that Mrs. Clayton bugs you. Getting good at dealing with her will pay off for you in the end. The most successful people I know do their best work under any conditions, for anyone. You can use this year with Mrs. Clayton to help you develop that capacity."

Sending Camille in to deal with Mrs. Clayton amounted to a powerful vote of confidence. In effect, Maya was saying, "You are not so fragile that you need everything to go your way. I trust that you can solve this." Had she simply moved Camille to Latin, Maya would have signaled that the problem in her French class was unusual and should be dodged. Even worse, switching classes would have sent Camille the message that she wasn't resilient enough to deal with Mrs. Clayton.

There are, of course, times when parents should intervene. Teenagers should not be expected to manage authority figures who are grossly unfair to students, make it impossible for any student to succeed in class, harass students, or mistreat them on the basis of their sex, race, class, religion, culture, or sexual or gender identity. If you are unsure about whether you should step in, start by doing everything you can to support your daughter as she tries to manage the situation. If she can't address the difficulty posed by a teacher or coach, or if the situation worsens, contact the school and advocate for your girl.

Camille was unambivalent about Mrs. Clayton, and understandably so. There wasn't much to like. But there will be times when your daughter's move into adolescence—with its dawning insight into adult character—will bring about mixed feelings regarding an adult she felt really good about before.

Away from my private practice and back under the stairs in my office at Laurel, I waited for Carly, a quiet Year 11 student who had requested an appointment. As is often the case, she arrived with two additional girls in tow. Even girls who request my help can feel unsure about meeting with me (because, as we know, they secretly worry that they are crazy) and often show up with companions.

Accustomed to this procedure, I lightly asked, "Are you guys the delivery service, or are you planning to stay?"

Carly looked anxiously at her friends, then at me, before saying, "Is it okay if they stay?"

I said, "Sure. If it's okay with you, it's fine by me."

They squeezed in. Carly sat in the chair across from mine, and I pushed my bag and books aside so that her friends could huddle on my bench. The Laurel uniform is a kilt that girls usually wear with low socks and sneakers. The more girls I have sitting in cramped positions in my office at once, the more the space becomes dominated by their bare knees.

Carly began, "I want to talk to you about my figure skating coach, Maureen. I've been working with her since I was ten and she's one of the best coaches in town. She's always been really good to me, but she's said some stuff that I'm not sure about."

"What kind of stuff?" I asked.

"Well, a couple of years ago I had a growth spurt and since then she's been making comments about my size." Let me add here that Carly was a capable and fit athlete who enjoyed skating but was not planning to compete beyond school. She went on, "I haven't done as well in competition lately, but that's because I've moved up a level and the girls I'm going against now are really good. I emailed you after practice last week because Maureen told me to 'choose water over food' before the next competition, and I'm not sure what to do with that comment." Carly's friends nodded sympathetically and looked to me for a response.

This wasn't the first time I'd heard about a skating coach or ballet teacher saying something that tempts me to show up at the rink or studio and give them what-for about the dangers of eating disorders. But I could hear that Carly was fond of Maureen, so I tried to cloak my outrage while sticking up for reality. I said, "It sounds as if there's a lot to like about Maureen, but that comment is really inappropriate."

Carly's friends nodded, and Carly said, "Yeah, I thought so, too."

"Do *you* think you need to lose weight?" I asked.

"No. Well at least I didn't before she made that comment last week. But I talked with my mom about what Maureen said and my mom's a doctor. She showed me a chart and my weight is exactly where it's supposed to be for my height."

"What did your mom make of Maureen's comment?"

"She didn't like it either, but she knows I really like working with Maureen and don't want a new coach."

"So, where does that leave you?"

"I don't know." Carly paused, looked at her friends, looked down at her hands, jiggled her legs, then said, "I still think she's a good coach, and the right coach for me. It just changes how I feel about her."

I asked, "Would you want to say something to Maureen about her comment?"

"No, that probably wouldn't work. But I think that I can ignore what she says about my weight. I think that it's her issue—it's not really about me."

"That's your call to make, and certainly a reasonable one. Let's do this: if she says something that gets to you, or if you start to worry about your weight, will you let me or your folks know?"

"Yeah," Carly said, "of course."

I went on, "I'm sorry that you've gotten to know a side of Maureen that's not so great and am impressed that you can see past it to make the most of her good coaching. Adults are human, which means we're imperfect—so you'll need to figure out how to make the most of us anyway. It seems like you're doing a good job sorting this out."

Carly and her friends nodded in agreement, promised to return if needed, then made their way to lunch.

All relationships come with ambivalence. Knowing some-one well means that we enjoy the best of what he or she has to offer and must reconcile ourselves to being frustrated and disappointed at times, too. Acknowledging your own crazy spots (and, perhaps, your partner's) welcomes your daughter to these facts of life. Don't hesitate to extend this same lesson to adults beyond your home as well. When we help girls let go of the idea that there are perfect people or perfect relation-ships, they move into a vastly more mature way of dealing with people as they are and the world as it is. And on your end, too, remembering how to hold on to good feelings when we are angry or disappointed will come in handy because sometimes your daughter will do things she's not supposed to do.

Holding the Line

Most teens step over the line with their parents at some point during adolescence, often through open displays of disrespect. If your daughter was one of the world's sweetest little girls, you will be taken aback—even hurt—the first time she's belligerent with you. Of course, getting ugly differs from family to family because every household has its own emotional thermometer. Some run hot—shouting and swearing are used both in happiness and anger—and others run so cool that interrupting amounts to a verbal assault. There's no right or wrong emotional thermometer so long as everyone is held to the same standard. In other words, you can't curse at your daughter and then call it a violation when she returns the favor. Expect that wherever your family draws the line for acceptable communication, your daughter will almost certainly cross it.

When your daughter is no sugar and all spice, you might find yourself reacting in ways that you don't feel good about. Instead, consider taking an approach that I learned when I landed on the television show *Cops* during some late-night channel surfing. The scene I caught featured a policeman in his cruiser as he talked to the camera about his "three F's" for dealing with surly criminals. Cynically, I thought to myself, "Oh! This should be rich," but then he said, "Just be fair, firm, and friendly." To translate this brilliant approach from the mean streets to your kitchen, take a breath and remember that—regardless of what your daughter just said—there is that thoughtful, grown-up part of every teenage girl to which you *can* respond. In a genuine and kind way consider saying, "Clearly you're very mad—I'm open to having a real conversation about what's bothering you as soon as you feel ready." You may need to repeat your same line in the same even-tempered tone if the bile keeps coming. If so, you will find that it's *very* rare for a teenager to continue to hurl insults at an adult who persistently offers to address her concerns in a civil manner.

Teenagers also do things they shouldn't—even things they've been specifically told not to do. On a Sunday afternoon I got an urgent message on my practice voicemail from Ben, the father of Dara, a girl I had seen in psychotherapy for separation anxiety when she was in Year 4. When I returned his call, he picked up right away and spoke rapidly.

"Hi, Dr. Damour, thanks for getting back to me quickly. I think you remember Dara—she's now seventeen. Well, her grandmother just died so her mom and I were out of town for three days emptying her house. We left Dara at home and told her not to have anyone over. I got back a few hours ago—my wife is still dealing with her mom's affairs—and could tell that Dara had a party. Our outdoor plants are trashed and the basement carpet reeks of beer. Dara admitted that she invited a few friends over and that the party got out of hand when a bunch of kids she didn't know showed up. She says she got everyone to leave by telling them that she'd call the police. I don't know what to do and I want to keep this off of my wife's plate for now because she's already overwhelmed."

When teens act out, they do shortsighted, even dangerous things, and parents can wonder what constitutes a "reasonable" reaction. There are no hard-and-fast rules, but here are a few guidelines to consider. We already know that you shouldn't try to correct your daughter's behavior by shaming her, and research on disciplinary practices finds that yelling at teenagers actually exacerbates problem behavior instead of fixing it. From what I can tell, angry lectures serve the sole purpose of providing relief for frustrated parents.

Over the phone I encouraged Ben to sit down with Dara and talk about the many bad outcomes that they, as a family, were lucky enough to avoid. He could start by seeing if she could lay out the dangers for him, and if not, he should: someone could have been hurt, the house could have been badly damaged, the neighbors might have called the police, and, had anyone been injured at or even after the party, Ben and his wife could have been held liable. In other words, it's important for adults to point out that we don't exercise our authority for the sake of displaying our power—we ask teenagers to play by the rules in the name of safety.

Discipline should always come with the opportunity to make things right again. Ben checked in with me a couple of days later to share that he had required Dara to buy and plant new greenery and to rent a steam cleaner from the local hardware store to clean the carpet. To his credit, Ben wasn't deterred when she grumbled about her punishment, and he made her use her babysitting money to cover the costs. Giving a teenager a way to make reparations is the opposite of shaming her. If shame says, "You are bad," repair says, "You messed up, but you can make it right." We want teenagers to learn from their mistakes, and we want them to have a way back to a clear conscience so that they don't, unconsciously, seek out further punishment to bring the scales into balance.

Within a month Ben and his wife, Trudy, were meeting with me in my office. Trudy, who was visibly depleted by the death of her mother and the recent challenges with Dara, now limply explained, "Dara has a friend who has some piercings and dyed her hair purple a couple of weeks ago. We're not big fans of this girl, but we've known her a long time and she and Dara are pretty tight. After sleeping over at the girl's house last weekend"—Trudy now wrinkled her nose—"our daughter came home with one piercing in her ear cartilage and three in her eyebrow."

Ben joined in. "We got mad at her and feel like we should punish her but aren't sure how—I mean she's seventeen and we just don't have much say about who she hangs out with or how she looks."

"I think you're right that punishment doesn't really make sense," I said. "What she's doing annoys you, but it's not actually dangerous. You *could* say, 'We're concerned about your new piercings and here's why: adults will—even unfairly—make judgments about them. Some will mistrust you and others will assume that you're not as smart as you really are. We don't want any doors to be closed to you and I don't want you to be denied any opportunities. We can't make you take out the piercings, but we're here to think with you about when it may not work out for you to rub adults the wrong way.'"

Trudy nodded. "Yeah, part of the problem is that she's going to start looking for summer jobs next week."

"Perfect," I said. "You could add, 'You *do* need to get a job this summer and, right or wrong, employers may not hire you, or even pay you as much, if your look makes them uncomfortable.'" In other words, they didn't need to stand between Dara and the natural consequences of her choices, but they could point out the consequences and express their hope that she wouldn't make decisions she'd regret.

Ben and Trudy were on the same page about Dara's behavior, but it's worth noting that parents don't need to be fully aligned for their girls to thrive. It's tricky when parents occupy opposite ends of any parenting spectrum—and we'll address those difficulties in the "When to Worry" section—but for the sake of healthy development, teens need each of their parents to be internally consistent more than they need them to be in lockstep with each other. In other words, teenagers (and children, for that matter) need for their parents to be predictable.

Girls who know what each of their parents will generally allow, consider, and flat-out refuse can usually find ways to operate within those known parameters. It's when the rules constantly shift that girls suffer. For instance, a stressed, distracted parent might let his daughter go to a faraway party one weekend but then be appalled by a similar request the next. In these cases girls don't know what to expect so they give up or, more likely, become sneaky. Neither outcome serves any girl's best interests.

Parents can usually live with each other's slightly different but predictable styles, and when they can't, they should try to come to an agreement on their own time. And they might do so while appreciating the luxury of having an invested partner as they raise their daughter. Making and enforcing rules as a single parent demands incredible fortitude. It's unpleasant to come into conflict with a teenager under any circumstances, and it's that much worse when you don't have another adult nearby to offer backup or comfort. I have enormous respect for parents who raise teenagers alone, and advising them is some of the most gratifying clinical work I do.

If you are a single parent, you deserve as much support as you can find. Seek out trusted friends who care about you and your daughter and can take calls at crazy hours. If you have the resources, consider setting up regular appointments for yourself with a clinician who specializes in working with teens and their parents. Consulting with a supportive psychotherapist doesn't mean that you aren't doing a great job already—it means that you will have regular access to the kind of sounding board that all parents need and deserve when their teen pushes the limits.

Contending with Adult Authority: When to Worry

When it comes to the work of contending with adult authority, three scenarios are grounds for concern: when your teenager never rubs an adult the wrong way, when your teen rubs
most adults the wrong way, and when key authority figures
work against each other.

Too Good to Be True

Adults might enjoy the teenage girl who never contends with
their authority, but something is usually wrong with that picture. A teenage girl should be finding friction with some adult
somewhere, and if she isn't, we should wonder why. Thinking
back to chapter 1, we might ask if the grown-ups who sur-
round the girl are too fragile to withstand the normal, healthy
opposition that adolescent girls should raise against the adult
world. Totally compliant behavior seems pretty safe—especially
compared to the worrisome things teenagers do—but it might
signal a problem below the surface. Research has long demonstrated that boys are more likely than girls to express distress
by acting out in ways that annoy adults, while girls are more
likely to develop depression, anxiety, and eating disorders.
Adults should be mindful that girls who are depressed or anxious (or both) may have little energy to oppose us because they
are suffering quietly and caving in on themselves. If you feel as
if you recognize your daughter in this description, share your
observations with her doctor or a mental health professional.

There's an exception worth noting: girls whose parents
have chosen to make enormous sacrifices on behalf of their
daughter such as moving from another country to give her
opportunities or living very simply so that she can enjoy an
abundance of options. This can put girls in a tricky spot.

While they may have a normal, rebellious itch, these girls do not always feel that they have a right to revolt against such altruistic parents. I've seen girls in this position ward off their impulses toward "bad" behavior by going all the way to the other extreme and adhering to the highest imaginable standards. They get terrific grades, are leaders within their schools, and dutifully help out at home. Such tactics serve them well in the long run, but I'd still prefer to see even a minor insurrection. Luckily, girls who are fantastically mature often find safe ways to undermine key adults. They declare themselves vegetarians in a meat-loving family or insist on giving their allowance to charity when their parents hope they'll use it to have fun. It's healthy for teenage girls to find a way to buck authority—even as they meet or exceed adult standards—and we should worry about girls who never oppose adults.

Constantly Contending

Teenagers should get along with—indeed make good use of—grown-ups, and we should be concerned about girls who persistently rub adults the wrong way. You'll note that I refer broadly here to "adults," because I have known teenage girls with deeply troubled parents who maintain strong, supportive relationships with adults outside the home. These resourceful girls rely on positive connections with teachers, coaches, and other mentors to get through adolescence effectively, even as they avoid their own parents or weather overwhelmingly negative interactions at home. But if that's not the case, if a girl is insolent with nearly every adult she knows, we should worry.

The stereotype of the unrelentingly horrible teenager is inaccurate and destructive. In the words of Brett Laursen and W. Andrew Collins, psychologists who specialize in studying the parent-teenager relationship, "Disagreement is common, but serious conflict is not." Studies consistently find that most teenagers get along with their parents and other adults most of the time, and new research suggests that parents who hold negative stereotypes about the teenage years can actually create a self-fulfilling prophecy with their own children.

A fascinating longitudinal research study—the kind that follows the same families for many years—measured the beliefs that parents of Year 8 students held about teenagers in general, then waited several years to ask how those same students were doing when they reached Year 10. Some parents in the study held generally positive views of adolescents while others stereotyped teenagers as being difficult, obsessed with their looks and their friends, and immune to adult influence. By Year 10, the teens with parents who took a dark view of adolescence were more likely to report that they ran with a risky crowd and fought with their folks than those with parents who reported feeling good about teenagers several years prior. Put simply, teenagers live up to expectations, and they live down to them, too.

Negative stereotyping is a double whammy when it comes to teens: it can provoke them to act out and it can cause us to mistake a girl's real psychological distress for willful behavior. Teenagers who are chronically nasty or routinely act out are distressed; they are probably suffering from the kind of porcupine depression described at the end of chapter 3. If you recognize your daughter here, consult with her primary care physician or a mental health professional about how to turn things around. Teenagers should have positive connections to grown-ups—especially their parents—and a disheartening line of research shows that girls who alienate themselves from adults are at heightened risk for depression, early sexual behavior, and drug and alcohol use. Don't fall for the stereotype that your daughter's teen years will be an inevitable, endless barrage of storm and stress. Get support for yourself and help for your daughter if it feels as though your relationship is always on the rocks.

Adults Contending with Each Other

Girls should not find themselves caught between parents who undercut each other. When parents disagree about how to raise their daughters it's common for one parent to adopt a highly permissive stance while the other tries to cancel his or her partner out by becoming excessively rigid. This dynamic can unfold between parents who are married or divorced, and it tends to worsen with time. In a perfect example, a teen once shared with me this description of what had transpired over the weekend between her divorced parents: "My mom was pissed about my midsemester grades, so she told me that I couldn't go out with my friends for a week. But I was at my dad's house this weekend so she called him to tell him about my punishment. When I got to his house he said he thought she was totally overreacting to my grades, so he loaned me his car and gave me forty dollars and told me to call my friends and go out to lunch with them. At lunch I ran into one of my mom's coworkers who then, go figure, mentioned to my mom that she'd seen me out with my friends. So then my mom got really mad and grounded me for a month."

A teenager should not be given the opportunity to play her parents off of each other and should not become a pawn in a disagreement between them. Any normally developing teenager would take advantage of such a situation while guiltily knowing that she is getting away with something she shouldn't. Add to that the discomfort that teens feel when the rules aren't clear, and you've got a real mess. If you find yourself caught in a dynamic where you are working against your daughter's other parent, get help from a neutral third party. Together, or on your own, find a clinician or mediator who can help you reach a compromise or learn to support each other's parenting decisions. Your daughter needs rules that make sense, and she should not be recruited onto one parent's team or the other's. If there are teams in family life, parents should be on the same one.

Healthy teenagers contend with adult authority, but not all of the time. Teenagers shouldn't be hung up on the inadequacies of surrounding adults, working against every adult they encounter, or stymied by unpredictable or feuding parents. When teens put all of their energy into contending with adults, they don't have any resources left over to prepare for what lies ahead.

FIVE

. . . .

Planning for the Future

MOST CHILDREN AND TWEENS DON'T THINK TOO FAR AHEAD—
and they don't need to. At ages eleven and twelve, we expect
girls to look no farther into the future than their next class
project or the guest lists for their birthday parties. But by the
time they approach the end of adolescence, however, girls
should have real goals and should be making plans in pursuit
of them. Some teens race along this developmental strand. They
have an unusually clear view of what they want for themselves—perhaps taking steps at sixteen and seventeen to carefully
hone their personal statements—but they are more the exception than the rule. Usually, girls are unsure of their future
plans or often change their minds about what they want to do
next. Shifting interests aren't a problem so long as our daughters arrive at young adulthood with hopes for the future and
the basic skills they'll need to go after them.

No one feels more invested in your daughter's future than
you do. You love her and want to smooth her path toward a
fulfilling life. But you may have already found that when you
try to help her think ahead, she can be indifferent, if not
downright resistant, to your sensible guidance. On top of that,
some girls seem to lose interest in a goal the minute their parents get behind it. Why wouldn't a girl take well-meaning ad-

vice from the people who care about her most? Why would she give up her dream to become an artist just when her parents present her with a gift of painting classes? Because, for most teenagers, the drive toward autonomy trumps everything else.

The craving for autonomy—for independence and self-determination—kicks in hard during adolescence. This is a good thing and a sign of normal, healthy development. But in the day-to-day of raising a teenager, the adolescent drive toward autonomy can take the form of a teenager refusing to do something, even something that she should do and might even have been *about* to do, simply because a parent has suggested it. I remember the exact moment in my private practice when a teenager taught me just how powerful the drive toward autonomy can be. Every Friday for several months I met with an insightful, levelheaded Year 12 student who arrived, one day, in a particularly sour mood. When I asked what was wrong, she explained: "My schoolwork is all over our dining room table and I had time before this appointment to organize it and put it away. I've been looking forward to dealing with it all week because it's been driving me crazy, but I've been too busy. I came home from school and was walking toward the dining room when my mother told me that I had to get my stuff off the table. So I got in a fight with her about how I didn't want to put my work away, and the fight took up all of the time that I was planning to spend picking up. Now I'm here, and my work's still a mess, and I'm really mad about it."

She smiled as she got to the end of the story. It was pretty funny and she knew it. Yet, in a testament to the power of the teen drive toward independence, my client truly believed that the frustrating outcome was inevitable from the moment her mother told her to move her schoolwork. Even having her own plans to do exactly what her mother ordered could not override the urge to rebuff her parent's request.

Your daughter's need to plan for her future presents you with a unique challenge: you want to guide and support her as she moves along this developmental strand, but you don't want your input to cause her to do the very opposite of what you suggest. This chapter will help you channel your daughter's press for independence toward meaningful future plans. We'll start with how you can leverage your daughter's own goals to help manage her online behavior.

Impulses, Meet the Internet

Parents rightfully worry about how teenagers conduct themselves online. With today's technology, a teenager can make, record, and broadly transmit evidence of impulsive misjudgment that can harm her at some point in the future. Anyone who spends time with teenagers knows that they routinely use technology to share things that they would not, ultimately, want a future boss or college admissions officer to see. For example, sexting—the practice of sending or receiving racy texts and pictures—is surprisingly common among teens: roughly 12 to 15 percent of teenagers report having sent sexts, while 15 to 35 percent (depending on the study) say they've received them. Research consistently finds that girls are more likely than boys to be asked (often pressured) to send sexts, though it is not clear that girls actually sext more than boys do. It's easy to vilify any teen who uses her phone to transmit bedroom content, but doing so points our attention in the wrong direction. Teenagers are and always have been impulsive. And really great teenagers sometimes do really dumb things. Unfortunately, digital technology makes it possible for teenagers to act on their impulses in ways that are immediate, public, and permanent.

Let's put it another way. If a popular Year 9 boy had asked me to share a titillating photo when I was in Year 8, I probably would have given the request some consideration. Had I decided to go through with it, I would have had to find the family camera, make sure that it had film, take the photo, shoot off the rest of the roll, figure out what to do with the photos already on the roll, make sure I had money to replace the roll and pay to develop the photos, get myself to a one-hour photo developer (for speed and efficiency, of course!), wait for the pictures, and then figure out how to get my picture to the boy. Somewhere along the way I like to think that I would have reconsidered the wisdom of my plan and concluded that I was acting like an idiot. Today's teens exist without the benefit of the many behavioral speed bumps we had when we were teenagers. Not only can they act on their impulses with ease, they can create a sharable record in the process.

From this perspective we see that the issue isn't the impulses that come with adolescence, it's the potential that digital technology gives to them. Adolescent girls have always wondered about their power to draw attention, but they haven't always been able to send sexy photos or connect with strangers from their bedrooms. Teenagers have long experimented with illegal behaviors such as underage drinking, but they haven't always been able to post a photograph of their behavior where almost anyone can see it. Looking back on their own teenage years, most adults feel grateful that there's no easy-to-access document of all the dumb things they did.

It takes time to grow up, and making mistakes comes with the process. We couldn't whitewash adolescence and even if we could, we wouldn't want to because the vibrancy of adolescence serves some developmental purposes. But still, we should aim to have girls arrive at adulthood without a damaging record of their youthful behavior hanging around their necks. The best way to address your daughter's online behavior will be to frame your concerns in terms of protecting *her own* long-term plans. We must help our daughters appreciate the real implications of a permanently recorded and readily shared adolescence.

Conveniently, the news is replete with stories of how regrettable emails, photos, or posts ultimately cost people their reputations or their jobs, so you'll have plenty of conversation starters on hand when your daughter gains regular access to digital technology. While you're at it, look up the sexting laws in your state. The legislation on this topic is changing rapidly. You and your daughter should be aware of the legal consequences of creating, sending, requesting, or even receiving a sexually explicit image of a minor.

When the time comes, talk with your daughter about the fact that she's about to create a record of her adolescence, sympathize with the unfortunate outcomes made possible by digital technology, and share with her how lucky the generations before her were to have tech-free teenage years. Be clear that you do not expect her to be an angel throughout her adolescence, but you are hoping—for her sake—that she doesn't make a digital record of any of her less-than-angelic impulses. By framing the conversation this way, you put the emphasis where it belongs, namely on your role as her ally in the effort to ensure that none of her regrettable impulses follow her indefinitely.

In addition to talking with your daughter about the importance of keeping her impulses away from the Internet, you'll want to put some digital speed bumps in place. When your daughter first gets regular access to a phone or computer, you can, as I've already suggested, make her use of digital technology contingent upon your right to monitor her activity and have her passwords. If your daughter balks at this, remind her that you are doing so to reduce the chance that she'll act impulsively online. Let her know that if she'd like privacy, you're glad to leave her alone while she makes phone calls or to give her plenty of space to interact with friends in person.

Some parents think that they can better monitor their daughter's online activity if they do so in secret. Of course it's possible for girls to delete out-of-bounds content if they know you'll be checking their technology, but there are two good reasons why you should be honest about the fact that you are keeping an eye on your daughter's digital activity. First, knowing that you'll be checking not only gives your daughter an important speed bump, it provides her with a convenient excuse for bowing out of some digital naughtiness ("Guys, stop posting that junk on my page—my mom checks my account!"). Second, if you come across troublesome content while secretly monitoring your daughter's use, you're stuck. You can't confront your daughter without owning up to your sly behavior, and you may fear that if you admit to your snooping, you'll miss out on future valuable information. I've seen too many parents struggle with this exact dilemma while their daughter digs herself deeper into a bad situation.

Trustworthy older adolescents who are willing to talk with your daughter about her online persona may be one of the best speed bumps of all. Teenagers are quick to dismiss most adult perspectives on digital technology—they feel that we don't understand their technological world (I'm not sure they're wrong) and that the threats we point to ("You know, someone looking to hire you might check to see what you've been doing online") are too far in the future to be meaningful to most teens. But young teenagers take very seriously the perspectives shared by older teenagers they respect. Sixth formers occupy a future that Year 8 students daydream about, and they can use their influence to shape your daughter's online activity. If you have access to trustworthy older cousins, neighbors, or beloved babysitters, ask them to talk with your daughter about the digital mistakes they regret making and their seasoned policies for technology use.

As your daughter ages, you'll need to renegotiate how, and how often, you supervise her technology use. The path forward depends heavily on how responsibly she's used technology so far. There are few truisms in psychology—humans are too complex to be reduced to one-liners—but here's one: the best predictor of future behavior is always, *always,* past behavior. If you want to know what someone is going to do, look at what she has done. If your daughter has handled technology well and hardly needed your monitoring, you're probably safe to let her proceed into late adolescence with minimal supervision and perhaps a simple warning that you'll revisit your loosened policy if news of any digital naughtiness comes your way. If your daughter's impulses routinely get the best of her online, continue to keep a close eye on her technology use or recruit the help of a trustworthy relative or young adult until she establishes a track record of responsible online behavior.

The Road to the Future: Who Drives?

The most immediate road to your daughter's future runs through her life at school, and by nearly every available measure girls, as a group, do well academically. They get better grades than boys, are less likely than boys to repeat a grade or drop out of school, consistently outperform boys in reading and writing, do as well as boys in mathematics, are more likely than boys to go to university immediately after leaving school, outnumber male university students, and are more likely than boys to complete university.

Girls' academic advantage seems to arise from a combination of nature and nurture. Fine motor skills develop faster in girls than in boys and these promote written and verbal abilities by enabling girls to use pens and pencils and articulate words. Young girls seek one another out as playmates and together they talk, make up stories, and favor other language-heavy activities that reinforce their verbal skills. Further, the areas of the brain associated with self-control develop more rapidly in girls than in boys and make it easier for girls to sit quietly and build early literacy skills. Indeed, many girls begin their academic careers as attentive, persistent, and eager students and continue on that trajectory. Despite all this good news, along the way most girls run into some sort of difficulty at school. And when a teenager hits an academic snag, parents can be unsure of their role in helping her address the challenge.

Trina, a visibly angry Year 11 student, and her mother, Michelle, sat beside each other on my couch in my office the first time we met. Trina refused to speak. She had been dragged to the appointment and, frankly, I hadn't expected that she'd be joining us. In setting up the appointment over the phone, Michelle indicated that she was coming in for some guidance regarding Trina's schoolwork, so I was surprised when I went to my waiting room to find Trina sitting opposite Michelle, a casually dressed woman holding a large, worn purse on her lap. Standing in the doorway of my waiting room, I nodded to Michelle before turning to Trina.

"Hi," I said, in a tone that expressed my surprise to see her.

"I'm Dr. Damour. You must be Trina." She raised one eyebrow, pursed her lips, gave me a wry "no shit, Sherlock" look, and said, "Yeah." Hoping to make it clear that I did not have a dog in Trina's fight with her mother, I asked, "Will you be joining my meeting with your mom?" Though I was offering Trina a choice about attending our appointment, her mom clearly wasn't. Trina looked at her mother, looked at me, did the mental math, groaned, "Okay, fine," then stood up and trailed behind her mother and me as we went to my office.

This is another reason why many talented clinicians won't work with adolescents: they don't want to get pulled into a fight between a parent and a teenager. One advantage of working with adults is that they come to psychotherapy under their own steam and they, or their benefits, pay for it. Those of us who work with teenagers routinely juggle competing agendas and the fact that the wishes of the client we are retained to serve (the teen) may not line up with the wishes of those who are footing our bill (the parents). Like any practiced clinician who works with adolescents, I have a developed choreography for the tricky dance of aligning myself with, and only with, the teen's best interest. The dance step I used that day was the one where *I* never insist that a teen come into my office. But I'll allow a parent to require it while being clear that I'm hoping to be useful to both parties.

Once situated in my office, Michelle spoke first. She began despairingly. "As I mentioned on the phone, Trina was a good student up until last year, when she started Year 10 and joined up with a party crowd that doesn't care about school. She did okay in Year 10 but not great. This year, her initial grades were two B's, two C's, and a D in math—and she's a really smart girl. I tried to help by making her do her homework in the kitchen where I could keep an eye on her while I

cooked dinner and answered email. That didn't work, so I
started checking her homework to see that it was done, and
done right, before she took it to school. I even stood there and
made sure that it went into the right folders in her binder so
she would remember to give it to her teachers. I called you
right after I got a message from Trina's Year 11 advisor. Apparently Trina stopped turning in her work and might fail two of
her classes."

When I think of teenagers and their schoolwork, I'm reminded of the delightful movie *The Princess Bride* and Vizzini's
great line, "You fell victim to one of the classic blunders—the
most famous of which is 'Never get involved in a land war
in Asia.'" Michelle fell victim to a treacherous parenting blun-
der: never get into a power struggle with a teenager in an area
where she holds all the power. When it comes to their schoolwork, teenagers have almost total control and you have none.
If your daughter chooses to take responsibility for her schoolwork, chances are that it will go well. If she chooses not to, she
cannot be overridden by parental force. Unless your daughter
has a diagnosis that prevents her from doing well in school,
such as a learning or attention-deficit disorder, by adolescence
she is in the driver's seat when it comes to how she handles
her academics. As the driver, she may request or accept your
help or the support of others who have her best interests in
mind. But, as Michelle learned, if a teenager does not want
things to go well at school, she can easily get her way.

Why would a teenager sabotage herself? Trina was clearly
annoyed by Michelle's efforts to help her with her homework,
but why can't Trina see that her *own* plans for the future might
benefit from her academic success? Unfortunately, some teenagers lack the maturity to see it this way, especially if they feel
that doing well in school compromises their drive toward au-

tonomy. Michelle's efforts to improve Trina's grades inspired Trina's need to prove that her mother didn't have that kind of power. Trina was willing to torpedo her overall marks to make her point. Not a mature move, but definitely one I've seen teenagers make.

Trina sat sullenly through our meeting and alternated between giving me a dead-eyed stare and looking out the window behind me. After Michelle explained why they had come, I asked Trina if she had anything she wanted to add. I wasn't surprised when all I got back was a flat "No." It was abundantly clear that they were playing out in front of me the exact dynamic that brought them to my office in the first place. Michelle could make Trina do her homework, but she couldn't make her turn it in. Michelle could drag Trina to psychotherapy, but she couldn't make her talk.

Autonomy. For the win.

I struck a pragmatic tone (because teens cannot stand any sort of "therapisty" speak) and shared what I was thinking. "Clearly, you're in a standoff. Michelle, you can't figure out how to get Trina to improve at school, and Trina, you don't want to be controlled by your mom. I think we can find our way through this, but I'm not sure it makes sense for Trina to join our meetings. Trina, if you ever feel that I can be of help to you, my door is open. I'd be happy to meet with you on your own or with your folks. Michelle, I'm wondering if you and your husband would be willing to meet with me to see if we can find our way out of this impasse. You want what's best for Trina, but what you're doing right now isn't working." Trina was clearly relieved to be uninvited to our future meetings and Michelle accepted my offer to return with Trina's dad so that we could figure out how to use Trina's drive toward autonomy to encourage her to take school more seriously.

Making the Grade

It wasn't long into my first meeting with Michelle and her husband before I could see that they didn't enjoy pressing Trina and they didn't care if she went to a top university—they were simply worried that, at fifteen, she had started to close off options that she might want to have available at eighteen. Not knowing what else to do, Michelle had tried to micromanage Trina's homework.

I only have time to teach graduate students now, but before I had two children I also taught college courses in psychology. My classes were huge (swelling to more than four hundred in an auditorium at the University of Michigan), so I was always acquainting myself with some new form of undergraduate misbehavior: the student who didn't come to class for three weeks and was wondering how to get the notes, the student who plagiarized a paper but then felt really sorry, and so on. My colleagues and I would confer in the Psychology Department's faculty lounge about how to handle these situations, and when the conversation went on too long, someone would always end it with the six smartest words: "People make choices, choices have consequences." Trina's parents understood this, and they needed to help Trina understand it, too.

For Trina, the distance between the choices she was making now (to turn in her homework or not) and the consequences she'd face later on (college options) was too big for her to take seriously. On top of that, Michelle had unwittingly set up a power struggle in which Trina felt that holding on to her autonomy meant letting go of her schoolwork. Trina's parents and I needed to shorten the distance between Trina's daily choices and the consequences she faced, and we needed to move Michelle out of the role of homework supervisor. We had to work with, not against, Trina's drive for autonomy.

Predictably, Trina received disappointing mid-term grades. After her parents and I met to craft a new game plan, they said to her: "We hate to see you shutting down options that you may want to have at the end of school. You'll probably have interests then that you're not aware of now. And there's something else. We know that you want to go to parties and concerts with your friends, but those come with risks that require maturity and good judgment on your part. You're not showing us maturity and good judgment at school, so we're not doing our job as parents if we let you go into risky situations without any proof you have the judgment needed to handle those situations well. Show us your maturity at school and we'll let you exercise that maturity when you spend time with your friends."

We worked carefully on the language Trina's parents would use to spell out their new approach, but much more important than their words was the spirit in which they were spoken. In order for our plan to have a shot at success, I coached Michelle and her husband to use a tone that conveyed that they were feeling hopeful, not hostile, and that they were comfortable with the fact that Trina held all the power when it came to her schoolwork. They needed to communicate that they *wanted* Trina to be able to go out with her friends but that it was up to her to choose that option.

Trina thought the new plan was ridiculous and told them so. Her parents proceeded anyway and suspended any risky socializing until they received her end-of-term grades in December. In the spirit of not putting her under house arrest without warning, they allowed her to have friends over and go to friends' houses if the parents were home. They also asked Trina to propose the grades that she thought she could get if she were to apply herself until the end of the term. She projected that she could pull B's in most of her classes but doubted that she could get above a C in math. Her parents accepted her proposal and said that she should let them know if she needed any tutoring support. They told her that she could go to parties and concerts if she got the promised grades and that she could keep those privileges at the start of the second term with the understanding that they would again be revoked if her grades fell below projections in the next marking period.

We might have considered other consequences for Trina's low grades, such as docking her allowance or increasing her chores. But many teenagers would choose poverty or laundry duty over doing their homework, and only a few would sacrifice their independence. And linking Trina's grades to her social life makes sense because Trina needs to demonstrate maturity for her parents to feel comfortable with her expanding social activity. Trina's grades provide an objective, if imperfect, measure of her ability to act responsibly. When Trina pushed back, I urged her parents to impassively point out that their new plan simply mirrored the realities of life beyond their home. When people are irresponsible (doing shoddy work, not paying speeding tickets) they tend to lose privileges (professional autonomy, their right to drive). Our plan wasn't a diabolical scheme to persecute Trina. It was a small-scale version of how the rest of the world works.

We proceeded in a two-steps-forward, one-step-back fashion. Trina did better at school from October to December to regain her privileges, then faltered in February and posted subpar grades in March. Trina was furious when her parents cut back her socializing pending her June grades. They made it clear that they were neither pleased nor angry about her backsliding and reminded Trina that, when it came to how she spent her summer, she was the one in the driver's seat. Trina tried to pull Michelle into a fight by pointing out that

her friends' parents allowed them to attend parties and concerts regardless of their grades, but Michelle warmly joked
back that her friends' parents must not love their daughters as
vigorously as they themselves loved Trina and reminded her
that they had her best interests in mind.

Trina's parents did an impressive job of maintaining their
neutrality in the face of her struggle. They calmly pointed out
that their rules were designed to keep her safe and her options
open. In the privacy of my office, they fretted over whether our
plan was working, but in front of Trina, they maintained a
united, practically indifferent front. To keep them on board
(while I *also* worried that our plan wouldn't work), I shared my
experience that girls who are struggling usually improve in the
same way that spring comes to Cleveland. The temperature
doesn't rise a degree or two each day as we move out of our
dreadful winter into our glorious spring. Instead, the ratio of
crummy days to decent days gradually shifts. No matter what,
March and April bring at least one ferocious ice storm, but
that doesn't put us back in January. I encouraged Michelle
and her husband to stay the course, to see the lapse in Trina's
grades as an unfortunate ice storm, and to work with the assumption that her spring would still come.

Trina put her folks through a fickle academic spring, but by
the end of the school year, she eked out the grades she'd promised and was rewarded with a summer of fun. I later learned
that when Trina thanked her mom for dropping her off at a
concert, Michelle took the opportunity to say, "Don't thank
me, you're the one who made this happen. I'm happy that you
get to do the things you want to do." Trina had gotten in gear
to change the direction her life was going.

If your teenager runs off the academic road (because I might
as well, ahem, "exhaust" this metaphor), start by eliminating
the possibility that her difficulties, unlike Trina's, are out of

her control. At times, girls have learning or attention disorders that go undiagnosed until adolescence because the diagnosis is mild enough to have been missed or because the girl's strategies for managing her limitations have been equal to the schoolwork faced in the early grades. You might suspect that your daughter has a learning disorder if her efforts don't yield expectable levels of academic success, if her grades are surprisingly uneven from one class to another, or if her teachers report gaps in her learning.

Some girls with an undiagnosed learning or attention disorder look as though they have a bad attitude because they feel discouraged and struggle to maintain their motivation. But their frustration is understandable. Most of us would want to give up if our hard work didn't bring good grades and if school seemed to come so much more easily to everyone else. Should your daughter's school raise the possibility that she might have a learning or attention disorder, work with the school counselor or psychologist to pursue an evaluation to rule out a disorder or to provide clarity if one exists.

You do not need to wait for your daughter's difficulties to be flagged at school to consider a diagnostic assessment. Schools may fail to alert parents that a child may be struggling with a learning or attention disorder for any number of reasons: teachers sometimes worry that parents will be hurt or offended by their observations, the school may be reluctant to take on the costs associated with assessing and supporting a student with this type of diagnosis or may lack the resources needed to collect and share specific, timely, and helpful feedback about how individual students are doing. In some cases, a girl will perform adequately or even quite well during the school day while only her parents know how overwhelmed and confused she feels in class or how many painful hours she spends on her homework each night.

If you suspect your daughter has a problem with learning or attention (or if someone in your family already has such a diagnosis and your daughter's patterns are starting to look very familiar) raise your concerns with her teachers or, if it makes you more comfortable, with your pediatrician or family doctor. Should a professional assessment yield a diagnosis, you will have critical information about the academic support your daughter needs. If nothing's amiss, you will have a clear picture of her intellectual profile and an objective measure of what expectations you can reasonably hold.

What if you don't think your daughter has a learning or attention disorder, but you're still concerned about her grades? Start by considering the possibility that your expectations are unrealistic. Some parents who were academic heavyweights themselves assume that their children will be whiz kids as well. But genes are complicated, and "normal" covers a wide range of students. Does your daughter take responsibility for her work, exert reasonable levels of effort, and maintain a positive attitude toward school? If so, she may be getting exactly the right grades. If you doubt your ability to take a neutral view of your daughter's capabilities—and who among us can be neutral when it comes to our own children?—ask your daughter's teachers for their take on her academic performance. Be clear that you want an honest appraisal and that you are making sure that your expectations are fair and realistic. Educators know more about teenagers and their schoolwork than anyone. Most teachers have their students' best interests in mind and will provide an accurate read on your daughter's efforts and abilities if you ask for it.

If you have ruled out a learning or attention disorder, weighed the fairness of your expectations, and *still* have concerns about your daughter's underperformance, it may be time to let her know, from the passenger seat, that you're wor-

ried about where she's headed. Point out the long-term consequences of low grades, and if that doesn't work, you, like
Trina's parents, may need to find ways to capitalize on your
daughter's drive for autonomy to help her feel motivated
about school.

Tense About Tests

Girls who are planning ahead sometimes feel that their futures ride on every exam and test they take, so it's no surprise
that they can experience intense test anxiety even if they usually do well in class, on their homework, and on the actual
tests. Girls, more than boys, feel threatened by evaluative situations. Accordingly, research demonstrates that they suffer
more test anxiety than boys do and that their test anxiety
hurts their scores. Anxiety influences how girls feel (nervous),
what they think ("I'm going to bomb this test!"), and their
physical state (racing heart, sweaty palms, dry mouth). Under
these conditions, a girl's mind goes blank because her working
memory shuts down and stops retrieving and applying the information she knew right before the test. From there, girls
tend to have one of two reactions. They give up and start filling in answers randomly, or they expend *too much* energy on
the test and fretfully double-check and change responses. Either way, their scores go down.

Though it's not a recognized diagnosis, girls often talk
about having test anxiety the same way that they talk about
their eye color—as if it were a factory setting that can't be
changed. But psychologists understand a lot about anxiety,
and we know that there are many ways to help students address it. If your daughter has test anxiety, a first step will be
to *normalize* her feelings, because our culture's discomfort

with psychological distress has given anxiety (and other troublesome feelings) an unnecessarily bad name. While too much anxiety can become crippling, we know that some degree of anxiety can serve as a signal that it's time to be on your toes. Research shows that moderate levels of anxiety actually energize test takers (and athletes, actors, and other performers) and contribute to their success. Performance only suffers when anxiety becomes too intense. Help your daughter appreciate that she should feel *some* tension on the way into a test because girls who aim for Zen-master levels of tranquillity freak out at the first whiff of nerves. It's a short step from there to feeling that the anxiety has won and all hope is lost.

More often than you might suspect, girls experience test anxiety simply because they haven't studied. If your daughter feels anxious and you know that she has yet to buckle down, say, in a nice way, "Of course you're nervous for the test—you're not ready. It's as if you're showing up for opening night without knowing your lines or having gone to rehearsal. When you study, your anxiety will go down."

Even girls who study can arrive at tests underprepared because, overwhelmingly, students get ready for tests by reviewing their notes, highlighting passages, or rereading material. While reviewing the material constitutes a good first step in studying, it should *only* be considered a first step because research finds that highlighting and rereading are among the most ineffective study strategies of all. To return to the theater analogy, reviewing the material is the equivalent of learning one's lines—you can't have a play without the actors knowing their lines—but memorizing lines doesn't make an actor ready for the play. Next, the actor needs to practice delivering her lines under playlike conditions—hence rehearsals. For test takers, this means applying their knowledge in conditions like the ones they'll face during actual tests, such as being quizzed at home or, best of all, writing and answering their own test questions. Some of the best students I know search online for sample tests on the topics they're studying and routinely find tests like the ones they'll be taking. When girls actively engage with test material under testlike conditions, studies find that they learn the material more thoroughly and get better scores than students who use passive review techniques.

Another recipe for test anxiety is believing that a test measures much more than it actually does. Some girls face tests thinking their scores will reflect their overall intelligence, likelihood of professional success, or worthiness to take up space on the planet. One bright girl in my practice approached every test as an opportunity to compete with her older brother, a superstar at their school. She worried that her test scores might prove that she didn't measure up. Not surprisingly, she became anxious during exams and got lower scores than she should have.

Girls aren't always aware of what they are loading onto a test, and the outstanding research on the phenomenon of *stereotype threat* has demonstrated that students who are negatively stereotyped (e.g., "African Americans aren't as smart as whites," "Girls are bad at math") tend to underperform in testing situations where they fear they might confirm the stereotype. In other words, a girl might bomb a math test precisely because she is worried that a low score will reinforce the wrongheaded belief that girls are bad at math. Interestingly, research suggests that the girls *most* eager to disprove the stereotype—girls who are proud of their female identity—may also be the most likely to suffer from the effects of stereotype threat. Tests take on awesome proportions for teens who feel charged with defending their sex with their math scores. As you'd expect, anxiety sets in and hurts performance.

To study the phenomenon of stereotype threat, researchers

subtly remind students of the stereotype and then see what happens. In one study, a team of psychologists put together two groups of undergraduate research subjects; both comprised men and women with strong math records (they had all received at least a B in calculus and scored above the eighty-fifth percentile on the SAT math subsection), and both were given the same challenging math test. The groups differed in only one way. Before the test began, the first group was told that they were taking a test that had yielded gender differences in the past and the second group was told that no gender differences had been found on the test they were taking. When mentioning gender differences, the researchers didn't even say that men had outperformed women, and yet here's what they found: in the first group, the men got much better scores than the women, and in the second group, the men and women performed equally well. The mere mention of a gendered pattern on the math test was enough to trigger stereotype threat and suppress the performance of strong female mathematicians.

Amazingly, research on stereotype threat shows that the phenomenon occurs entirely outside of the test taker's awareness. The girl doesn't realize that her anxiety arises from carrying the weight of her sex (and, for some girls, her negatively stereotyped racial or ethnic group) on her shoulders. All she knows is that she feels nervous and then, naturally, starts to link her anxiety to the test. She thinks, "Yikes . . . I'm sweating. These questions must be really hard" or "I must not be as ready as I thought I was!"

Help your daughter combat stereotype threat and manage text anxiety by limiting what she believes to be at stake on any one test. Remind her that a test only measures her mastery of the material on the day of the assessment. It does not reflect her value as a girl, daughter, or person. It doesn't even measure her promise in the subject being tested. If she worries that a test will determine her future, encourage her simply to focus on each test item, forget about everything else, and ask herself, "What do I know that will help me answer this question?"

We already know that adults do a great job of encouraging girls to be nice, but we don't always help them make good use of their angry or aggressive feelings. Our failure to help girls channel what psychologists call "healthy aggression" not only keeps them from standing up for themselves, it also gets in the way of their ability to attack tests because healthy aggression fuels the capacity to compete with gusto and show off hard-won skills.

Unfortunately, popular depictions of aggressive girls invariably feature the ones who specialize in *unhealthy* aggression, girls who put the mean in "mean girls." Examples of tough but kind girls aren't always easy to find in popular culture (with the important exceptions of Disney's Mulan and *The Hunger Games'* Katniss Everdeen), a fact that might contribute to girls' belief that they should stay away from aggression in any form. Some girls actually fear tests because they are uncomfortable employing the scrappiness that helps people to do well in competitive situations. In the same vein, many coaches of girls' teams complain that the girls are too worried about hurting their opponents' feelings to steal the ball, strike them out, or beat them on the field or in the water.

If you suspect that your daughter may be taking the "nice girl" thing too far, help her find her inner warrior at test time. Tell her to "get in there and show that test who's boss" and "kick those questions around a bit." When she does well on a test, commend her for being a go-getter and encourage her to keep fighting the good fight. If you watch sports together, comment on how the same athlete can be kind and humble off the field yet go for the gold at game time. With the right support, girls can learn to be fierce when it's time to compete or take tests and compassionate souls the rest of the time.

Practicing relaxation techniques serves as a final, excellent option for helping girls manage test anxiety. With the support of a therapist or, more conveniently, a quick online search, your daughter can learn about techniques including diaphragmatic breathing, progressive relaxation, and visualization. She should practice her preferred relaxation technique at home under low-anxiety conditions and call on it before her anxiety becomes too intense. Once she has a reliable tactic for managing her nerves, your daughter will be able to take a thirty-second test break to turn down the dial on her anxiety if needed.

Test anxiety happens when a girl's nerves take on an unhelpful life of their own. In contrast, procrastination—our next topic—happens when the healthy tension that helps girls stay on top of their work seems to be missing. If your daughter is a procrastinator, you might find yourself in the unpleasant and untenable position of feeling more worried about her work than she is.

Planning for Next Week

There are plenty of teens who care about school but fail to link what they do today with the grades they'll get next week. Teenage girls should be dreaming big about their futures, but they should also use incremental planning to tackle their immediate goals. Adults, who have the perspective and experience to link daily choices with short- and long-term outcomes, can come into conflict with girls who haven't figured out how to stay up-to-date on their schoolwork.

If you surveyed a large group of parents about their daughters' worst academic habit, the most common complaint would be that they procrastinate. Teenagers procrastinate, sometimes for the same reasons as adults and sometimes for other reasons. Like many adults, some teens struggle to delay gratification and would prefer to do fun things—and even not-so-fun things—before getting down to work they really don't want to do. Some teenagers (and adults) are under the impression that they turn in their best performance at the last minute when their fear of missing a deadline finally outmatches their wish to avoid the work to be done. And some teenagers procrastinate because they truly do not appreciate the amount of time their work will really take. Regardless of why your daughter procrastinates, your job will be to make sure that she sees the problem as hers, not yours.

Maya and I met less frequently after Camille's Year 10. By the end of that year Camille's relationship with Maya had warmed up, the drama of Camille's earlier social life had cooled down, and Camille had devoted herself to her friends, her growing interest in her science classes, and her place in the school's marching band. I didn't see Maya again until the end of Camille's Year 11, when she made an appointment to check in about a tough night they'd had the week before.

Maya explained that Camille tended to wait until the eleventh hour to get things done and, though she usually managed to pull off good grades, did so at the price of a lot of last-minute stress. Knowing that Camille had a major term paper coming up, Maya encouraged her to get going on the paper well before the deadline but was met with prickly resistance. True to form, Camille found herself looking at an all-nighter right before the paper was due. Panicked, she became testy over dinner, then tearful about the long night ahead, then insistent that Maya stay up with her as late as possible to keep her company while she hammered out the paper. Maya reluctantly agreed to stay up for much of the night—drinking coffee and attending to her own work while Camille typed away. Unhappy with (and exhausted by) the way things were going, Maya wanted to address her daughter's procrastination before Camille headed off to college but wasn't sure how to step in.

When teenagers are in conflict with themselves, they often seek out conflict with their parents. Procrastinators tend to be of two minds. Part of them would like to enjoy the benefits of getting their work done in a timely fashion, and part of them would prefer to watch reruns. Rather than wrestling with an uncomfortable internal struggle, teenagers will—unconsciously—look for an external fight with their parents. In other words, Camille dallied and let her mother take up the work of nagging her to start writing the paper. It's not particularly pleasant for most teenagers to be at odds with their parents, but they generally prefer it to being at odds with themselves. This dynamic doesn't limit itself to schoolwork—it's a recurrent theme in parenting a teenager. You'll know that you've been drawn into your daughter's internal conflict when you find yourself nagging her to do something that she knows full well she should do, such as get in shape before her basketball season starts or return an employer's call.

People only make changes when they are uncomfortable, and it's most uncomfortable for Camille to be at odds with herself. To help Camille stop procrastinating, I encouraged Maya to decline Camille's invitations to bug her about her schoolwork. Not surprisingly, soon after that Camille left a paper to the last minute and then wanted Maya's support through the night. Maya later told me that she said, "I'm sorry that you put yourself in this position. I have a long day tomorrow so I'm headed off to bed. Perhaps next time you'll get started earlier." Maya's response might seem harsh, but I could tell from her recounting that it was said in a loving way. In fact, it almost killed Maya to turn Camille down, but she knew that staying up with her would send the wrong message: that Maya had a hand in a predicament that Camille, alone, had created. Several weeks later, Maya called me to share that Camille had decided to join an after-school study group to help her get started on her schoolwork. Left to deal with her discomfort, Camille had come up with a smart solution that, happily, didn't involve Maya.

Some girls are quite at ease with putting off schoolwork and don't mind operating under the gun. If this is the case in your home, you may need to wait until your daughter is upset about her habits to comment on them. If your daughter feels disappointed with her grades or if they don't meet some agreed-upon standard, if she's tired from staying up too late to do her work the night before it's due, or if she misses out on a fun opportunity because she waited until the last minute to do an assignment, you might be in a position to say, "I don't have to tell you that getting started earlier would have solved this problem. Next time, you may want to do things differently."

Of course, girls procrastinate about things besides schoolwork. They put off taking out the trash, drag their feet when they should be finding summer jobs, or fail to turn in necessary forms to get paid for work they've already done. If your daughter's procrastination poses a problem only for her, stand back and let the natural consequences do their work. If it's a problem for you, create a logical repercussion. Let her know that you won't be giving her a ride to her friend's house if you end up having to take out the trash; give her a deadline for securing a job of her choosing while letting her know that you'll find her a job of *your* choosing if that deadline passes. Procrastination is no fun for anyone, but it's a common affliction among teenagers and one that many outgrow, especially if they are allowed to feel the impact of their choices.

Procrastinating isn't the only way girls struggle to manage their daily obligations. They may have trouble keeping track of due dates, lose their homework assignments, or study ineffectively. Unfortunately, schools that give parents an easy way to keep daily tabs on their daughters' assignments have opened up a new way for girls to recruit their parents' help with what should actually be each girl's own responsibility. Digital grade books have been a godsend for the parents whose daughters have real problems with executive functioning (shorthand for the capacity to plan, organize, and strategize) and cannot learn from their own academic mishaps. But for everyone else, monitoring a girl's daily work can interfere with her ability to plan for the future.

Girls who learn from small failures are more likely to avoid big ones. We don't like to let our teenagers falter, but stepping in to help with the small stuff and never stepping out keeps girls from growing. Parents who get into the habit of closely monitoring assignments can unwittingly involve themselves in a conflict that should have stayed between the part of their daughter that's being irresponsible and the part that wants to improve. If your daughter is frustrated with her grades, consider saying, "We know that you're disappointed about your marks. And you know that you're not taking charge of your schoolwork. We're happy to offer any support you'd like or help you connect to resources at school, but we trust that you'll figure out what you need to do differently to get the grades you want." If your daughter isn't disappointed, but you are, consider tying her freedom to her schoolwork as Trina's parents did. Though it might take a few grading periods, or even longer, to straighten things out, she'll start learning how to plan for the future, even if that future is only several days away.

Dealing with Disappointment

The arrival of adolescence coincides with new ways to be ranked and sorted. Adults measure teenagers against one another in very public ways. Some teens get into the sports team, some win academic awards, some get fast-tracked, and only one or two are picked for lead roles in the school play. Adolescents often craft ambitious—even grandiose—plans for the future and can become painfully disappointed when things start not to pan out or when they themselves don't measure up to their peers.

Girls, more than boys, may be derailed by disappointment because research shows that they explain failure differently than boys do, especially in traditionally male subjects such as mathematics. When a boy fails a test, doesn't get the lead in the play, or faces some other hitch in his plans, he's likely to attribute his difficulties to external or temporary factors. He'll say, "It was a dumb test," "The drama teacher doesn't like me," or "I didn't prepare enough." Right or wrong, a boy's explanations can help him to feel that he's still in the running. Girls, on the other hand, are more likely to explain failures in terms of internal, permanent factors: she's broken and can't be fixed. When faced with disappointment, a girl might say, "I'm no good at this," despite piles of contradictory evidence. Schools are full of girls who ace the first five tests in physics class but declare themselves bad at science when they get a B on the sixth. Worst of all, girls' explanations for failure take them out of the game. Once a girl decides that she's weak in a subject, it doesn't matter if she's smart or talented; she's likely to stop trying to build her skills and thus surrenders her chance at success.

Helping teens deal with disappointment is a timeworn problem that has been blown wide open by the game-changing research of psychologist Carol Dweck. Dr. Dweck identifies two kinds of people: those with a growth mindset, who believe that their talents can be expanded with effort, and those with a fixed mindset, who believe that their abilities are static and cannot be changed. Her research clearly demonstrates that people with a growth mindset outperform those whose mindset is fixed. Girls with a growth mindset *embrace* challenges because they know that hard work will expand their skills, *welcome* feedback from teachers and coaches because it provides information about where they need to aim their efforts, and feel *inspired* by talented peers. Girls with a fixed mindset, on the other hand, *fear* challenges because they worry that they've come to the limit of their abilities, feel *threatened* by feedback because it provides good or bad news about what they believe to be fixed traits, and feel *humiliated* by their talented peers.

When your daughter comes home in tears because she received a bad grade, lost her spot in the sports team, or was passed over for the lead in the play, you may be compelled to offer all sorts of well-meaning but fixed-mindset reassurance. You might say, "It's okay, honey, I was never good at math either!" (accidentally reinforcing the idea that math talent is a fixed trait) or "Maybe the coach doesn't really understand how talented you are" or "They chose *her* to play lead? Well, honey, I think that you're a *way* better actress than she is!" Ultimately, fixed-mindset reassurance backfires. When we support our daughters by telling them that they are special, or that they're great at *other* things, we suggest that success depends on luck, not effort. In the short term, her self-esteem may be salvaged. In the long term, she's left feeling that she's the helpless victim of circumstance, not someone who can use her diligence to make things happen.

How do we offer growth-mindset reassurance? We celebrate effort over outcome. We say, "You have come a long way in your skills as a pianist and you'll keep growing with practice. It's crummy to lose a competition, but you already know what you need to do to become better." Or, "I remember how stunned I was the day when I got put in the second team when I thought I was a really good soccer player. I wasn't ready for how good the other players were and how much more they knew about the game. It got better when I realized that there will always be stronger players and that my job was to try to learn from them." Words like these coupled with a reassuring tone will go a long way toward helping your daughter feel better. Don't share her humiliation when she encounters more talented peers—focus on helping your daughter to be *her* best, not *the* best. Say (and mean it when you say it), "I'm so glad that you're not leading the pack—it's easier to grow when you're surrounded by peers who can stretch and inspire you."

Girls who are very smart, or who have been hailed as gifted, can be at heightened risk for developing a fixed mindset. When we explain success in terms of smarts, girls can worry that having to actually work at something proves that they weren't so gifted in the first place. I'm not against telling girls that they're bright, but balance that praise with an admiration for her work habits and effort. If your daughter succeeds without breaking a sweat, consider saying, "You're doing well without having to work hard at all, but I also look forward to the day when you have to push yourself to understand the material. That's when the real learning begins."

Should your daughter falter when she meets hard work relatively late in the game, there's still time for her to adopt a growth mindset. Plenty of girls sail through primary and beyond and don't face their first real challenges until adolescence. Then, not knowing what's hit them they may give up, make excuses, or complain that they are suddenly "dumb." If this is your girl, empathize that it's hard to buckle down when the work has come so easily until now, but point out that many of her classmates developed their persistence years ago and she can too.

Though you may have celebrated your daughter's smarts in the past, it's time to remind her that talent only gets a girl so far. We all know gifted, lazy people who accomplish nothing and likewise tenacious, less gifted people who go far. Indeed, terrific new research on *grit* shows that the steadfast pursuit of long-term goals contributes to success over and above what can be explained by intelligence alone. Put another way, you can tell yourself and your daughter that it doesn't matter if she's a mental Ferrari if she won't step on the gas. A speeding Ford Taurus will beat an idling Ferrari any day.

Dr. Dweck's work hasn't just influenced my thinking, it has actually warped my parenting. I started reading Dweck's research when my older daughter was four and I became an instant convert. It's rare that academic psychology presents such a fresh, elegant, and practical idea, and growth-mindset thinking actually accomplishes the hat trick of raising confidence, improving grades, and helping girls embrace challenges. I realized how profoundly my parenting had been influenced when my daughter came home from kindergarten to say, "Mom, I want to tell you about a really cool thing a girl in my class built, but I don't want you to tell me that I could build something like it if I worked really hard." Clearly, the message (which I was undoubtedly beating to death) had gotten through.

Planning for the Future: When to Worry

There are many effective ways for girls to look to the future. Some girls lay careful groundwork for distant plans. Others aren't sure what they want to do after school but leave the door open for unforeseen interests to come along. Still others give little thought to what's ahead then suddenly become consumed by a worthy goal. In fact, one of my favorite things about working with teenagers is how fast they change. I regularly watch girls go from bobbing along one week to gunning an outboard motor the next. As Anna Freud noted, "The changeableness of young people is a commonplace. In their handwriting, mode of speech, way of doing their hair, their dress and all sorts of habits they are far more adaptable than at any other period of life." The fact that teenagers transform so quickly caused one of my psychological colleagues to quip that "we get too much credit for our work with adolescents." So how do we know when it's time to worry? We should worry if a girl is so fixated on her future plans that she can't enjoy herself at all, or if a girl is so indifferent to planning that she's closing all sorts of doors.

All Plan and No Play

Some girls can make themselves, and their parents, miserable with their planning for the future. They commit themselves to multiple joyless extracurriculars with the aim of getting into the college of their dreams, practice more than their coaches recommend, or study far beyond what's needed. They are devastated by any grade lower than an A and will stay up late to work and fret, even as their parents exhort them to relax and go to bed.

Parents of girls who are overperforming usually feel as if

they don't know what happened. Typically, they have encouraged success, but they are rarely the taskmasters one would
imagine upon meeting their daughters. Somewhere along the
way, their girl decided to take all of the well-meaning lessons
she'd been taught by adults—to be persistent, careful, and
ambitious—and pursue them to an unhealthy extreme. There
are boys who match this profile, but it's more common among
girls. Research finds that girls are more likely than boys to experience school as intensely stressful (while academically out-
performing boys) and also more likely to become depressed if
they are having academic problems.

When a girl's dedication to her future plans has taken on a
frightening life of its own, parents can feel helpless to convince their daughter to adopt humane standards for herself.
For their part, girls are often surprised when adults encourage
them to take it easy because they feel that they are simply
doing what has been asked of them all along and that *overdo-
ing* it should be praised, not criticized. Girls will sometimes
complain that their efforts aren't sufficiently appreciated or
that the adults have changed their values midstream.

If I'm describing your daughter, she might be able to hear
your suggestion that she ease up when you couch your advice
in forward-looking terms. Acknowledge her impressive efforts
(and the results of those efforts) and that she's doing everything she can to create a terrific array of future options. Next,
consider saying, "We know that this is a demanding time and
understand that it isn't the moment to ease up. Given all that
you are doing now, you can look forward to a less demanding
road ahead. Before the end of school, you should be able to
bring some balance back into your life." Put this way, most
girls can tolerate the suggestion that their current intensity
need not last forever.

Even girls who don't overdo everything can tax themselves

by studying inefficiently. When twenty flash cards would do, they make a hundred. When taking two practice tests would suffice, they take five. Girls who specialize in academic overkill are often reluctant to change tactics that they have seen work, but they can be receptive to advice focused on the next step in their academic success. You might say, "The way you study now has worked well for you. The next step will be to become more efficient in your approach to studying. Soon you'll start to do what the cleverest students do: figure out how to do less while still bringing home the grades you're used to." Girls who overperform and overstudy often lose sight of the possibility that studying smarter might not mean studying harder.

If your daughter's forward drive crowds out all joy in her life, persists beyond any reasonable time frame, or becomes utterly irrational, consider seeking professional support. Let her know that her approach seems to be working insofar as she's enjoying tremendous success, but express concern that she's not able to enjoy anything else. Try to strategize about how she might bring some fun into her life and see if she can follow through on making that happen. If your daughter won't allow herself to relax, tell her she deserves to have some fun and that you want her to talk with someone to figure out why she can't. Consult her primary care provider or another trustworthy source for appropriate mental health referrals.

No Plan in Sight

At the other end of the spectrum, you should worry if your daughter expresses little drive toward anything at all. Occasionally, I'll see teenagers like this in my practice. They're often quite pleasant, but they are totally lacking in a personal plan. They're not serious about school because they don't have any idea what they want to do after leaving. They don't really care if their parents ground them over grades because they feel no burning need to be with their friends on the weekends and are content to watch movies at home. They lack all of the forward thrust and energy that typically characterize adolescence.

Teenagers who lack drive aren't the same as teenagers with plans their parents don't like. A girl who aims to be a punk rock drummer may exasperate her parents, but they can capitalize on her agenda if needed. For example, they could offer to buy some drums or turn their garage over for band practice on the condition that she get reasonable grades. A girl's agenda doesn't need to appeal to her parents, and it doesn't even need to last. In fact, teenagers frequently change their goals but can usually advance their new plans with groundwork laid by their old plans. Long story short, every teenager needs a plan.

Be concerned if your daughter has no goals—not even goals you dislike—and if her failure to think about the future seems to be cutting off options she might, ultimately, want to pursue. Many teenagers who lack a plan find their way to goals once they grow up a bit. Your aim should be to help your daughter develop her interests and to minimize the number of doors she closes while you wait for her to mature. Keep an open mind about what constitutes a reasonable plan, and encourage—or, if necessary, *require*—your daughter to do things she might find appealing. Some parents insist their daughter get a job or volunteer position but remain entirely flexible about where she chooses to work. Others ask their daughter to choose among a number of summer activities while making it clear that hanging out around the house is not one of them.

You can encourage your daughter to keep her options open by helping her to stay on top of her grades. Talk to the adults at her school to see if they have insight into her lack of motivation or ideas about what might inspire her. Know that even the most apathetic teens are usually motivated by something—perhaps money, access to the car, or even access to video games. I appreciate that I'm setting a very low bar here, but desperate times call for desperate measures. The damage done by a failing year of school exceeds the damage done by paying an apathetic teen for good grades. Girls can turn things around quickly when they want to, but it's easier for them to do so if they haven't already shot themselves in the foot academically.

Normally developing teenagers push for independence, look ahead to the next step, and even annoy adults with their vigorous pursuit of their interests. If your daughter is stuck in a state of inertia, consult her doctor about having her evaluated for a mood or substance use disorder. Indeed, if we were to take the totally unscientific approach of asking a group of seasoned clinicians to consider the case of a chronically aimless teenager, I can tell you that they would assume that she has depression, a drug problem, or both until proven otherwise. Don't hesitate to seek support if you see no real evidence that your daughter is planning for the future. Intractable indifference occurs rarely during adolescence and should be taken very seriously.

It's easy to get behind the idea that our daughters should be planning for the future. We *want* them to prepare for what's ahead. Contrast that with entering the romantic world—the developmental strand we'll address next. Most of us feel ambivalent, if not altogether unhappy, when our daughters move into the romantic arena. We remember the intensity of our own teenage crushes, worry about all that can go wrong, and know that the bliss of romance necessarily comes with the misery of heartbreak. When we imagine our daughters' love lives we feel more protective than ever, even as we know that our input has never been less welcome. In the next chapter, we'll consider the nature of girls' romantic lives today and how to make sense of, and perhaps even guide, your daughter's growth along this developmental strand.

SIX

· · · · · · · · · · · ·

Entering the Romantic World

SO FAR, WE'VE FOCUSED ON DEVELOPMENTAL STRANDS WHERE, as parents, we can rely on our observations (such as watching our girls with their friends) and occasional objective evidence (such as grades) to get a feel for how things are going. But when it comes to the strand of entering the romantic world, we're often in the dark about what's happening with our daughters. Girls can be intensely private about their romantic activity and may not talk with their families, or even their friends, about their emerging love lives. Parents who try to dial in to their daughter's romantic world often find that they pick up nothing but static, or that only fleeting signals come through. Accordingly, this chapter will help you make the most of what might be limited opportunities to guide your daughter as she enters the complex world beyond "just friends" and familiarize you with what girls tell me—as someone who is not their parent—about the landscape of teenage relationships.

There's another unique feature of this developmental strand: things change *fast*. Thinking back to the work of harnessing emotions, it's not unusual for girls to start unloading their feelings onto their parents at age twelve and still be doing so, at least from time to time, late into adolescence. In contrast, when it comes to girls' love lives, twelve-year-olds and eighteen-year-olds have little in common. In the USA, 3 percent of girls have had intercourse by age thirteen, but that number jumps to 28 percent by age fifteen, 42 percent by age sixteen, 54 percent by age seventeen, and 63 percent by age eighteen. The progression of this chapter will mirror the rapid evolution of girls' romantic activity, often as it plays out physically. We'll start by addressing young teens' early crushes, then move on to address how girls connect with their partners in increasingly adult ways.

Throughout this chapter we'll take an approach that is radical, but shouldn't be. We'll consider your daughter's entrance into the romantic world from the perspective of helping her focus on *what she wants*. Psychologists Michelle Fine of the City University of New York and Sara McClelland of the University of Michigan are among the smart feminist thinkers who have pointed out that when adults talk with girls about romantic relationships, we almost always focus on risk. Of course the perils that come with girls' love lives are real. Their hearts can be broken, they can be mistreated, and, once sexually active, they need to protect themselves from unplanned pregnancies and sexually transmitted infections. But the hazards that come with romantic activity—be they emotional, physical, or both—are only one part of the picture, and we'll take a deep dive into that topic in chapter 7, "Caring for Herself."

Regardless of how you feel as your daughter embarks on her love life, you likely agree that as she moves along this developmental strand she should come to know what she's hoping for, how to pursue it when ready, and how to make clear what she *doesn't* want. Much of this chapter applies to romances of all flavors, some of the chapter focuses on dynamics that are specific to girls' romantic and physical interactions with boys, and one section considers the experience of girls who identify as lesbian, gay, bisexual, transgender, or questioning (LGBTQ).

But let's start with another critical question that doesn't get asked nearly enough: What inspires girls toward romance in the first place?

A Dream Deferred

It's funny now, but it wasn't at the time. Over dinner one night when I was in Year 7, I casually announced to my parents that I was "going with" a cute classmate of mine named Mike. They were shocked. It had not yet occurred to them to talk with me about romantic relationships and, if asked, they would never have approved of me having one at that age. My parents were (and still are) pretty hip, so I was caught off guard when what I thought was a newsy tidbit dropped like a bomb in the middle of our dinner table. Their backs straightened, their brows furrowed, and they pressed me with questions: What does "going with" mean? Should they call Mike's parents? How were we spending our time together? Were other kids (and by kids, they now meant reprobates) "going with" each other?

I didn't know why they were so freaked out or what I had done wrong. As far as I was concerned, I was getting into the game quite a bit later than several of my girlfriends who had been going with boys since Year 6. And like everyone else's twosomes, mine largely (and merely) consisted of class-wide recognition that Mike and I now formed a couple. That, plus the occasional passing of notes. Well, okay, once we kissed, but only because some Year 8 kids goaded us into it. But that was it. I spent the rest of dinner frantically backpedaling, trying to convince my mom and dad that my "relationship" with Mike was no big deal and that they definitely did *not* need to call his parents.

Things got better the next day when my parents actually called my teacher, who confirmed that "going with" someone meant next to nothing. It was a social distinction, a status update. To the degree that there was any action, it took the form of class gossip about who was going with, or wanted to go with, whom. Ms. Ticer reassured my parents that most couples hardly spoke to each other and often had one of their first conversations when they were breaking up. That is, if they didn't have their friends do the breaking up for them. (If you're out there, Ms. Ticer, please accept, with more than thirty years' interest, my sincere thanks for your able handling of my well-meaning parents.)

At dinner the next night, my folks updated me on their call with my teacher, acknowledged that my account of what it meant to go with someone seemed to be accurate, then took a moment to say their piece about my forward romantic trajectory. They told me that they could live with me going with someone, but they weren't okay with any physical stuff. And, as for actual dating (whatever that meant), I'd have to wait till I was fourteen at least, but we could talk about it then. They probably said other things, but I was too distracted by my own thoughts: "Talk about it then? In what universe do you imagine that I will *ever* raise this topic again given how last night went over?"

Parents are often surprised when their Year 6 or 7 daughter mentions crushes or dating activity. But more than twenty years of research documents that these have long been the ages when chatter about who likes whom starts to dominate the discussion at the lunch table. These early conversations usually involve sharing hot gossip with girlfriends instead of speaking with the boys they talk about. In fact, psychologists

Jennifer Connolly and Adele Goldberg of York University have pointed out the irony that young crushes change how girls interact with other girls long before they have much impact on how girls interact with boys.

When boys and girls do connect, their romantic relationships usually begin when the boy asks, "Can we go out?" or "Do you want to date?" and the girl agrees. It almost always falls to the boy to do the asking, and he usually makes the request after he has employed diplomatic channels to confirm that he will not be turned down. The proposal is more likely to happen by text than in person, and once they are going out, the couple sometimes text back and forth with each other, sit near each other when given the chance at school, and hang out in the same extended tribe.

Looking back, I know my parents couldn't understand why I had a boyfriend, especially once they understood how little there was to the relationship. To add to their confusion, my childhood toys still cluttered our basement playroom and my girlfriends and I still made friendship bracelets during sleepovers. From their perspective, my interest in boys was totally premature; thinking about me going out with boys was like imagining sending me off to college at eleven. Yet from my perspective—and that of most young teenagers—romance was a long time coming.

Though few of us remember this developmental moment, most children go through a phase at around age three or four when they realize that romantic relationships constitute a very special connection and that they don't have a romance of their own. Up until about age three, children see themselves at the hub of all of their important relationships. Each toddler has her connection to her mom and her connection to her dad (presuming, of course, a somewhat traditional family arrangement here). Then somewhere around age four, it dawns on her that her mother and father share an exclusive relationship with each other, an arrangement that has nothing to do with her. To appreciate the emotional impact of this hard news, imagine being a Year 8 girl who has just learned that her best friend from school and her best friend from summer camp get together most weekends but don't invite her. Ouch!

Preschoolers often react to this stunning realization by trying to insert themselves into their parents' relationship. A little girl may be surprised and even offended when a babysitter arrives on a Saturday night and insist that she should be going on her parents' date, too (or, better yet, instead of one of the parents). Some girls beg for a pet so that they can have their own exclusive relationship and, with it, a break from feeling like a third wheel. And, to many parents' surprise, it's not unusual for preschoolers to develop pint-sized crushes. Preschool teachers will tell you that they are often pressed to officiate at pretend weddings during playtime.

Ultimately, little girls come to terms with where they *actually* fit in the family and reconcile themselves to two facts: that being someone's girlfriend or wife is different—and in some ways more significant—than being someone's friend; and that they must wait several years to enjoy the special feeling that comes with a romantic partnership. So while my Year 7 classmates and I were, from our perspective, finally becoming members of the romantic world we'd been hoping to join for so long, my parents saw me as rushing into dangerous adult territory. They might have conjured a dismaying picture of a goofy eleven-year-old boy asking me if I'd like to come up for a nightcap, but I was just trying to tell them that my long-delayed wish had finally been granted and I had a special someone in my life. The complex emotional entanglements and physical sexuality that adults imagine when they think about romance had nothing to do with my "relationship" with Mike. Like most Year 6 and Year 7 kids, I was simply excited by the idea of finally belonging to a couple.

If your daughter has yet to mention that she or her peers are dabbling in romance, prepare yourself for the reality that that day might arrive sooner than you expect. If she shares that kids in her class are dating, going out, talking to each other—or any of the other terms that her group uses to denote a relationship that's more than "just friends"—don't flip out and shut down the lines of communication like my parents did. Temper your reaction and imagine that you are an anthropologist who is studying the romantic rituals of a foreign culture. You will never have a better opportunity to conduct your anthropological research than when your daughter mentions her tribe's romantic practices. Over time, and while paying close attention to your daughter's cues about how much you can ask, make the most of these moments. Pose neutral, genuine questions about the meanings of terms they use to describe relationships, the typical arc of these relationships, what the couples do and don't do, and how much physical activity is involved. Indeed, my parents would have had a different initial reaction—and I would not *still* feel mildly queasy thinking about that particular dinner—if they had asked more questions about what I meant when I said that I was going with Mike.

As you carry out your research, look for opportunities to frame your daughter's approach to romance in the terms we adults seldom consider: what does she *want*? It's easiest to start down this line when romantic activity is at its tamest, when the stakes are as low as they'll ever be, and, especially, when you are given opportunities to talk about girls in general, not your daughter in particular. Without laying it on too thick, ask, "How does a girl let a boy know if she wants to go out with him?" or "What if a girl gets asked out by someone she doesn't want to date?" or "What if a girl wants to do one thing and her friends or her boyfriend want her to do another?" Welcome shrugs and eye rolls as acceptable responses—it's not about the answers, it's about getting her to consider the questions.

A Match Made in a Marketing Meeting

Some girls overflow with romantic thoughts and feelings but don't yet want the relational or physical expectations that come with actually dating. Other girls have crushes on classmates who don't know they exist, and still others are looking for more warmth and charm than they expect to get from the boys they know or are unimpressed by the available options. This is not to say that adolescent boys are, as a group, unappealing. But many girls find that the boys in their class express little interest in girls, focus their interest on only a few girls, or still act too young to be crush worthy. In sum, there are many ways for a teenage girl who knows what she wants to feel hesitant or frustrated when it comes to actually pursuing romance.

Enter the young male star.

Parents can be stupefied by the intensity of their teenage daughter's affections for pop or movie stars. Teenage girls often feel a deep connection to their favorite stars and devote remarkable amounts of time, energy, and even money to following their every move. A girl may feel that a star is her true, if unreachable, soulmate. But their romance isn't a match made in heaven—it's a match made in a marketing meeting. Music, television, and movie industry executives have long known just what many romantically frustrated, not-quite-ready-for-adult-sexuality adolescent girls want, and they are rewarded with billions of dollars in revenue for being attuned to girls' romantic wishes.

The name of the star or band changes from year to year, but the product stays the same. Young male stars are always objectively attractive but lack the markers of male virility that can be threatening to some girls. Their handlers spend as much time ridding the stars of chest hair as they do styling their head hair. In fact, a lot of them look like handsome girls.

When young male pop stars travel in packs, the boy bands invariably feature some version of a lineup including a not-really-dangerous bad boy, a member who's ethnic but not too ethnic, a playful type, a sporty type, and a true romantic. This "diverse" lineup allows girls to feel that they had a say in choosing the object of their affection and lets friends follow the same band without having to share their crush. The carefully crafted visual package sets the stage for the real product—the song lyrics. Listen to any song from any boy band and you'll be struck (and completely creeped out) by how much middle-aged music executives know about the words teenage girls hope to hear: you're beautiful, you're special, you make my knees weak, I'd be lucky to be with you, I wish you were my girlfriend and if you were, all I'd want to do is hold your hand or maybe kiss.

Not all teenage girls fall for stars, but the marketing machine behind young male stars resonates with many girls who are ready for romance, sort of. The beguiling star affords teenage girls an intense, controlled, and sanitized love life that tides them over until they feel the conditions are right to act on their romantic feelings with boys they actually know. Some girls move on from pop stars to local boys by midadolescence. Others are in no rush to trade the stars' crafted, sappy, and transparent communications for the confusing signals they might be receiving from the guys in their own circles.

If your daughter points all of her romantic energy toward a carefully packaged star, consider yourself lucky. Though it may be strange to watch your otherwise rational girl put together an outrageous plan to get tickets and a ride to a concert three states away, enjoy the guarantee that her current "romance" won't end with a painful breakup or an unplanned pregnancy. Proceed into your tough negotiations about what you will and won't allow (star-themed room redecoration, and so on) knowing that your daughter is under the sway of a powerful marketing machine and that she'll soon outgrow its influence. The day will come when she's ready to act on her romantic wishes with someone she actually knows. Save your worries for then.

Offering Some Perspective

As girls age along this developmental strand, they are bombarded by messages about what their romantic and sexual lives should look like, and these messages usually come from sources that don't care one bit about what girls want for themselves. Oddly, the media machines behind young male stars may be among the few voices speaking for what some girls *do* want. The rest of the chorus that tells girls what they should want, how they should look, and how they are viewed includes the mass media, the fashion industry, and, sometimes, blundering adult acquaintances (as in, "Wow, she's a cutie—you're going to have to lock her up!"). Let's consider these messengers and how loving adults can take steps to buffer their impact on girls.

Some of the best minds in my field study the romantic and sexual lives of girls, and they all agree that girls can easily lose sight of their own romantic interests because our culture dictates crazy terms to them. Through magazines, songs, videos, and online content, the popular media tells girls that they should be sexy, but they shouldn't be slutty; that being a prude is bad, but so is having sexual desires; and that having romantic or sexual connections to boys makes a girl cool, but it also exposes her to accusations that she is needy, striving, stupid, or all of the above. Girls become so perplexed by the funhouse mirror images of female sexuality that they can't even begin to reflect on what they want for themselves.

It's bad enough that our culture dictates confusing terms to girls. It's even worse that these messages, especially ones that emphasize the sexual objectification of girls, actually influence girls' thoughts and actions, as well as their mental and physical health. Research finds that the more sexist and sexualized content girls consume as part of their media diet, the more likely they are to hold stereotypical views about gender roles, such as believing that women ensnare men through manipulation. Further, compared to girls who question chauvinism, girls who accept the media's sexist messages are less likely to take necessary steps to prevent pregnancy or sexually transmitted infections and are more likely to suffer from eating disorders, low self-esteem, and depression.

An especially clever research study succeeded in demonstrating that the objectification of women can actually keep a girl from thinking straight. A team of psychologists at the University of Michigan asked undergraduates to participate in what they were told was a study on emotions and consumer behavior. When the subjects arrived at the psychology lab, they were sent into individual dressing rooms with full-length mirrors. Half of the dressing rooms contained bathing suits (one-piece for the women, trunks for the men) and half contained sweaters, all of which were available in a wide range of sizes. Once the subjects put on the assigned clothing, they were told to hang out in the dressing room for fifteen minutes before they filled out a questionnaire about whether or not they would want to purchase the item. While they waited, they were asked, in order to help the researchers use the time efficiently, to complete a math test "for an experimenter in the Department of Education."

As you've already guessed, the psychologists weren't helping their colleagues in the Department of Education. They were measuring whether taking a math test while wearing a bathing suit would affect the women's scores. In keeping with the researchers' predictions, the women wearing bathing suits got lower scores on the math test than the women wearing sweaters. Interestingly, the men's scores were totally unaffected by what they wore. The team conducting the swimsuit study effectively demonstrated that when young women are put in situations where they are made to feel self-conscious about their bodies, they lose focus and intellectual bandwidth. If it's that easy to disrupt the concentration of a college-aged woman sitting alone in a room with a mirror, we can only imagine the distractions girls face when they are peppered by invitations to measure themselves against unrealistic beauty ideals on a daily basis.

There are many excellent books on the impact of sexualized media on girls, and I commend them to you (several suggested titles are listed in the Recommended Resources). Across the board, they encourage parents and other loving adults to talk with teenagers about how our culture views and represents girls and women. When you take up these conversations, help your daughter appreciate how often the *girls'* wishes are left out of media messages and encourage her to take a critical, if not robustly skeptical, view of what drives sexist media content.

For example, if the moment presents itself while you are

with your daughter, you might point to a racy advertisement and ask, "Who is that outfit for? Do you think the girl really *wants* to wear that, or do you think that it's what other people want her to wear?" While listening to music, you might chime in, "I get it that he's the one singing about what he wants, but is that what she wants?" When it comes to raising a healthy cynic, take full advantage of your daughter's growing interest in contending with adult authority. Point out that adults are usually profiting from the sexualized portrayal of girls and young women. Feel free to note that "someone's getting rich by putting that beautiful girl on top of a car in a bikini. And trust me, that someone isn't the girl."

If you find an opening to have a broader conversation about the implications of using images of sexy girls to sell products, go for it, but your daughter doesn't have to be ready to enroll in a home seminar on media literacy for you to make your point. One of my favorite takes on this topic comes from author Marybeth Hicks, who asks her own children to shut down sexualized content by saying, "People are making money off of that girl, and I don't feel comfortable watching this video because I feel as if we're participating in her exploitation."

The cultural messages teens receive around romance and sexuality are further distorted by today's easy access to Internet pornography. Far more than most adults want to acknowledge, pornography now shapes what many teens believe constitutes "normal" courting and sexual behavior. It's not new for teens to seek or to be exposed to pornography, though statistically boys, more than girls, consume pornographic content. What's new is the wide availability of highly explicit sexual material. And I mean *explicit.*

Shortly before I gave a presentation on adolescent sexuality to parents at a local secondary school, a friend whose son attended the school emailed me a link with a note reading, "I think it will be helpful for you see what the Year 10 boys are looking at." I went ahead and loaded the porn website but was not at all prepared for what I saw. If you are not already familiar with the offerings that are available for free online, allow me to inform you that they are vastly more graphic, violent, or downright strange than anything you might be imagining. If you're visualizing tasteful erotica, you're on the wrong track. Like most psychologists, I've become acquainted with the broad range of human sexuality and, on top of that, I consider myself to be pretty progressive thanks to how much time I spend with young people. But what I viewed that day was so raw and overwhelming that I suddenly pictured myself pressing *Playboy* magazines into the hands of thirteen-year-old boys while saying, "Here! This is for you. Just promise for your own sake and the sake of all the girls you will ever know that you will never look at what's out there online!"

But they *do* look, and what they see influences their sexual behavior. Research finds that by fourteen, two-thirds of boys and more than a third of girls report that they've seen sexually explicit material within the last year. With research always lagging behind digital access and portability, we should consider these numbers to be underestimates. Further, studies tell us that teens, especially boys who consume a lot of pornography, become aroused by, fantasize about, and aim to replicate the pornographic acts they've viewed. In other words, teens can come to view pornographic sex as normal and then seek to try out the sexual acts they see online. In fact, for both boys and girls, exposure to pornography before age fourteen has been linked to an increased likelihood of having oral sex or intercourse before age sixteen.

Even if your daughter doesn't look at pornography, by Year 8 the romantic and sexual landscape around her has likely been altered by boys who do (like I said, things on this developmental strand change fast). I routinely hear from girls that boys are now emboldened to expect sexual favors or sexual pictures, both inside and outside of relationships. We already know that digital technology makes it easy for teens to act on impulse and send pictures they shouldn't, but most adults don't know just how much pressure girls can face to participate in sexting.

Demands for illicit pictures usually arrive by text, the practice is typically limited to a subset of boys in any one school, and it often begins in Year 8, peaks in Year 9, and dies down by Year 10. Boys sending the texts seem to think nothing of making repeated requests for nude photos, oral sex, or intercourse. Girls who refuse are usually asked again and, if they persist in their refusal, they are told off for being "boring," or a "prude," or they are called a "bitch" or worse. If your jaw has hit the floor, I understand. Every time I hear these stories from girls I think, "How did we get here?"

Girls who receive such texts face enormous pressure and a terrible dilemma. Turning the boys down invites jabs and harassment and can push a girl to the social margins. Giving in might make a girl popular with the boys, but it still comes at the price of her reputation and may go against her own romantic or sexual wishes. But for the guys, it's "Heads, I win. Tails, I win." Boys who badger girls usually belong to a larger group of guys who are jockeying to prove their masculinity to one another. When a girl acquiesces, the boy has a digital record, and perhaps even a photograph, to share with friends. If a girl refuses and the guy persists to the point of harassment, he has evidence of his aggressive machismo to pass around.

If you're still with me—or if you've come back after stopping to look into technology-free, all-girl cloisters for your daughter—know that there are many ways you can support your daughter should she face digital pressure for sexual favors. First, find an opportunity to say something such as, "I've heard that some boys think it's okay to text a girl, sometimes over and over again, to ask her to send nude photos or do sexual things. This goes without saying, but just to say it, that's *totally* inappropriate behavior on the guy's part. They shouldn't do it at all, and they certainly shouldn't keep doing it once a girl says no." Your daughter might brush you off with, "Geez, of course I know that it's wrong!" but your breath wasn't wasted. Digital harassment and fast-track expectations have become the norm in some circles, and girls who feel uncomfortable sometimes wonder if they're out of step. Your daughter will be glad to hear that she's not the one acting crazy.

The Inner Compass

One afternoon, a Year 10 girl in my private practice brought a predicament to our therapy session. The Year 11 boy she had been dating for several weeks was pressuring her to let him "finger" her, and she wasn't sure what to do. From our previous sessions I knew that she was glad to be dating him, that she didn't want him to see her as a prude, and that she didn't want to lose the relationship and the social status she'd gained with it. The girl continued to talk me through her dilemma. He had been making the request by text, never in person, and had not yet tried to put his hands down her pants when they were making out, but he kept on texting her to ask if they could try it. Further, to point out that "it wasn't a big deal," he had texted her the names of the guys who had already done this with other girls. When she finished describing the situation and her uncertainty about it to me, I asked, as plainly as

I could, "Well, do you want him to put his finger in your vagina?" She looked at me as if I were nuts and firmly said, "No!"
I replied, "Well, I think you *do* know what you want, it's just
hard to focus on that."

In the swirl of messages about what they should want and
how they are supposed to act, we hope girls will heed their
own inner compass. Our daughters should hold the reins of
their romantic and sexual lives and decide for themselves what
they do and don't desire. Once they've done that, they should
feel empowered to express their wishes to their partners.

Some girls have a clear read on their inner compass. I think
here of a Year 11 girl who knew she didn't feel ready to kiss her
boyfriend and welcomed her mother's reassurance that her reluctance was okay. I also think of a sixth former who enjoyed
safe just-for-fun sex with a longtime guy friend. Most girls
need time to get to know what they want, and what they want
isn't always straightforward. When it comes to romance, the
distinction we've already drawn between thinking, feeling, and
doing comes into play. Some girls enjoy thinking about romantic and sexual behavior—ranging from thinking about sitting next to their crush to thinking about having sex—but
don't necessarily want to *do* those things. Other girls experiment first and ask questions later. They figure out what feels
right for them by reflecting, after the fact, on their romantic
or physical activities.

So where do parents fit into the complex and largely hidden
work of helping a girl to know her inner compass? You have
three jobs: to alert your daughter to the fact that she *has* an
inner compass, to support her in asking for what she wants,
and to make sure she knows how to express what she doesn't
want.

With regard to your first job—alerting your daughter to her
inner compass—find ways to let your daughter know that you

want her to *enjoy* her love life. Should your daughter wish to talk with you about her relationships, follow her lead. Otherwise, pick your moments, keep your commentary brief, and capitalize upon the opportunities that present themselves. After watching a movie that features any of the confusing messages we send girls about their place in the romantic world, you could say, "That movie made it seem like guys call all the shots, but I hope you know that what *you* want out of a relationship matters. Anyone worth being with will know that, too." Should she mention that a girl in her class "jacked off" a boy, feel free to muse in a nonjudgmental tone, "I wonder if *she* enjoyed that." Statements like these may send your daughter running from the room, but make them anyway. Our culture doesn't care about girls' inner compasses, so somebody has to encourage girls to tune in to their own wishes.

Carrying out your second job—helping your daughter ask for what she wants—builds on the work of teaching your daughter to be assertive. We want girls to stand up for themselves while respecting the rights of others in their friendships *and* in their romantic and sexual lives. If your daughter confides to you that she has a crush on a boy who is a longtime friend, consider asking her if she'd like to let him know. Over the years, I've often coached girls in this situation to say something such as, "If you wanted to become more than friends, I'd be interested in that, too. If that's not what you want, I'm glad to have you as my friend."

For all the times I've made this suggestion, I doubt that any girl has actually acted on it, yet I keep making it because I want girls to know that they can *ask* for what they want. If your daughter doesn't share her longings with you but tells you about a friend who wants to kiss her boyfriend but is waiting for him to make the first move, you might ask what keeps the friend from making her wishes known.

When it comes to doing your third job—making sure that your daughter knows how to express what she *doesn't* want—find an opening and make your point. You might say something along these lines: "I think that you know this, but I'm going to say it anyway. If someone asks you to do something that you don't want—whether it's holding your hand or having sex—you always have the right to say, 'That's not something I want to do.' You should never have to say it more than once, and you shouldn't be made to feel bad for saying it."

As you offer guidance about your daughter's romantic life, you may feel tempted to encourage her to lay ground rules for any romantic or physical interactions with partners. That advice can sound good in theory, but it's not realistic to expect girls to put it into practice. Few teenagers would say, "Here's the score—I'll allow under the shirt, over the bra, and nothing south of the border. Okay, go!" What a girl wants can depend heavily on the moment and the context, and sometimes a girl learns what she *doesn't* want only through experimentation. You might say, "You'll figure out what feels right for you as you go, but know that just because you've done something once doesn't mean you have to do it again. Anyone who deserves to be with you will respect that."

When adults talk with girls about the place of consent in relationships, we tend to frame the conversation in terms of a girl's right to fend off a boy's aggressive advances. But there are plenty of girls who press their partners to try things their partners might not want, so we need to talk with our daughters about that possibility, too. I often get to have conversations with groups of girls at Laurel and other schools about decision making in romantic relationships. When we turn to the topic of girls knowing their own wishes and respecting their partners', I usually say, "It's important for you to know what you want and to pay attention to what your partner wants. And if you're not in agreement, whoever wants to do less decides for both of you. No pressure, no questions asked."

Girls sometimes need reminders to be kind when turning down romantic invitations. Boys feel as fragile and unsure as girls do when entering the romantic world, but they're given much less room in our culture—where "real men" are full of swagger—to show it. Girls can buy into boys' brash façades and forget that there's a whole and tender human on the other end of any invitation to go out. One terrific girl I know panicked when a guy asked her out in the middle of a phone call. She surprised herself, and undoubtedly hurt the boy, by hanging up on him in response! Your daughter can certainly turn down invitations to spend time with suitors, but you may need to coach her to be polite. Encouraging her to say (or, more likely, text) something such as, "I really appreciate being asked but I'm not looking to move past our friendship right now" gives girls a good place to start.

Girls who come to know, and stick up for, their inner compasses have the happiest romantic lives of all. If they date, they date people they like and who treat them with respect, and they are the girls who are most likely to have gratifying sexual encounters. A teen who knows her inner compass may find herself in a sustaining, long-term relationship—though those are generally rare among today's teenagers—or she may enjoy a series of brief engagements that occur on terms she feels good about. Either way, she's starting her romantic life off on the right foot.

Dating for Credit

Having romantic interactions with boys—be they emotional, physical, or both—changes a girl's social status. Even passing flirtations can draw wide attention and publicly affirm a girl's appeal and success in parting with childhood. You don't necessarily need to worry if your daughter gains social recognition as a side effect of following her inner compass into romance. But when a shift in social status turns out to be the main benefit of a girl's romantic activity, she can find herself in a tricky situation.

A number of years ago I worked with Beth, a witty teen with searching brown eyes and a warm smile, who came to see me midway through Year 11 because her intense anxiety kept her awake late into the night. She talked openly about the worries that ran through her head—about school, her friends, her future—and a few months into our work, her sleep problems yielded. But by then, she had a new topic to bring to therapy: her relationship with Kevin, a fellow lifeguard at the local pool whom she met the summer before she started Year 12. By Beth's description, Kevin was aloof, good-looking, and belonged to a popular crowd of sixth formers at their school. Beth was excited to be connected to him and (peripherally) his heavy-drinking, pot-smoking, high-social-status crowd.

Come autumn, Beth was unhappy with their arrangement. Though teenagers don't often talk frankly about their sexual lives in therapy, Beth and I knew each other well by then, so she spelled it out for me: "The deal with Kevin isn't so good. We got into this thing over the summer where he'd text me late at night to join him at parties and then give him a ride home when he was too high to drive. Somewhere along the way, we'd pull over so I could give him a blow job. It's not something I mind doing, but I'd feel better about it if we spent more time hanging out when he wasn't high. Or if he seemed to be interested in what I'd like. Or if he didn't sometimes ask me to pick him up after the driving curfew. A couple of weeks ago he started bugging me to have sex with him now that we've been hanging out for several months. He says that by Year 13 it's something that everyone does.

"I'm not sure he'll keep hanging out with me if I say no, and there are plenty of other girls who would have sex with him. And I'd like to be okay with ending it . . . but it's complicated. I've talked with some girls in my class about Kevin wanting to have sex, and they know that I leave our parties to hook up with him and drive him home at night. Last week I saw a message in a group text that I wasn't supposed to see. It turns out that some girls I used to be pretty close with now call me Kevin's 'ho' behind my back."

Reports of the death of the sexual double standard have been greatly exaggerated. Today's teens have moved past extreme caricatures of female sexuality (think Rizzo and Sandy from *Grease*), but we've hardly arrived at a moment where girls are admired for adding notches to their headbands. Research finds that girls who are sexually active outside of ongoing relationships, or with multiple partners, are still referred to by classmates as "sluts" or the equivalent. And despite linguistic attempts to level the playing field with terms like "man-whore," boys with multiple sexual partners still gain in social status.

Unfortunately, Beth's connection to Kevin and his popular crowd came at a price to her reputation with her classmates. Girls in Beth's class knew the relationship was essentially a sexual one in which Kevin was dictating the terms and took it upon themselves to police her "slutty" behavior. I see this all the time—situations in which a girl's social position simultaneously rises and falls when she becomes sexually involved with one or more guys. While she often becomes more socially central (invited to parties hosted by boys or referred to as popular), she's looked down upon by girls who may envy her new social cachet and punish her for it.

Entrenched sexual double standards aside, Beth's situation isn't one any of us would want for our daughter. She would like to have a relationship with Kevin that goes beyond the physical but, lacking a social safety net, doesn't feel that she can express what she wants or make clear what she *doesn't* want. Indeed, studies find that girls, much more than boys, engage in oral sex to secure their relationships or because they feel pressured. Further, girls are usually on the giving end of oral sex long before they're on the receiving end. Studies also find that teenage girls, more than boys, are likely to feel used after having oral sex, though girls have explained to me that "going down" on guys allows them to connect to a popular crowd without having vaginal sex. Research suggests that by having oral sex, but not intercourse, girls hope to avoid the risks of pregnancy and sexually transmitted infections while, perhaps, maintaining their reputations.

When it comes to talking with girls about dating for credit—when a girl's romantic or sexual activity changes her social status—adults can feel like part-time firefighters and part-time arsonists. On the one hand, we don't want to reinforce sexist double standards by warning girls (but not boys) to mind their reputations. On the other hand, we want to steer our daughters away from choices that could leave them feeling dependent, like Beth, on an unsatisfying relationship in order to preserve their remaining social ties. Given that many adults struggle to articulate their own position on the topic, it's no surprise that we're often unsure how to guide our daughters. Teenagers themselves can take overly simplified views of the situation. Sometimes they knock girls who become sexually active and sometimes they feel that girls' relationship choices should go unquestioned. In reality, the forces at play when sexual activity changes a girl's social status are extremely complex. The best thing we can do for our girls will be to invite them to give these forces some serious thought.

We already know that teenagers develop an increasingly nuanced view of adults during adolescence. Here's some good news: they also gain an increasingly nuanced view of everything else. They can step back from the concrete explanations they favored when younger (e.g., "Girls who date lots of guys are tramps") and consider how abstract factors—such as cultural pressures or the wish for belonging—might complicate those simplistic views. This is where you come in. If your daughter paints a classmate like Beth in a negative light, consider saying, "I understand that you and your friends don't approve of her relationship, but why don't you talk that way about the guys, too?" or "Maybe she knows how people talk about her. If she wanted to make a change, would she be given a second chance?" or "Where it stands now might not be how it started. I sometimes watch adults get stuck in relationships they don't want and see how that could happen to a smart girl like Beth."

How might Beth's parents weigh in if they became worried about her arrangement with Kevin? They might say, "It seems as if he's only reaching out to you on the weekends. If that's what you want and you're happy with that, then that sounds fine. If you want something more, do you feel you can ask him for it?" or "You don't hang out with your classmates as much as you used to—is that okay with you?" If the topic felt too delicate to address directly, they might wait for an opening and say, "Sometimes girls lose sight of what they want because they are so good at paying attention to what everyone else wants. It's okay to make sacrifices in relationships so long as what you're giving up feels worth what you're getting."

Having a teenager in your home can inspire the discussion of deep political and philosophical topics, such as how our culture views women and what sacrifices should, or shouldn't, be made in the name of relationships. Let go of any hopes that you have all the answers all the time because you don't, and needn't. As one especially wise mother of three teenagers once told me, "The best conversations I've ever had with my kids always started when I said, 'Wow, that's a really complicated situation. I don't know what to say. What do *you* think?'"

Being Gay: The Slur and the Reality

By Year 8, at least, teenagers start to call each other "gay"—a term they wield as a potent insult. Boys are more likely than girls to tease peers this way, but girls sometimes throw the terms "gay" and "lesbian" around, too. The use of homophobic slurs occurs in almost all communities and schools, regardless of how progressive or accepting the families in that community may be. Indeed, teens who have beloved relatives or close family friends who are gay sometimes accuse classmates of homosexuality without considering their contradictory behavior.

It can come as a surprise to learn that teens still employ homophobic language at a time when our society is making dramatic strides toward equity and inclusion. There are several (indefensible) reasons that teens use "gay" as an insult. As we know, teens are working hard to gain membership in a tribe, and they sometimes establish their in-group status by accusing others of belonging to an out-group. Anyone can accuse anyone else of being gay, and doing so instantly reinforces the accuser's in-group status. Teens are most likely to accuse a peer of being gay if the peer drifts, sometimes even slightly, from cultural stereotypes of masculinity and femininity. Indeed, boys' painfully narrow definition of masculine behavior drives their dogged gender policing of one another. That said, teens seem to be able to turn almost any behavior into grounds for a homophobic insult—from how a boy zips his backpack to how a girl wears her socks.

Adolescents who are struggling with questions about their own sexual orientation sometimes call peers gay. Psychologists have long known that people occasionally deal with uncomfortable feelings by projecting them onto someone else: "*I'm* not attracted to the girls in my class, but I think *she* is." This process occurs outside our awareness and shows up in situations when we wish to get rid of an unwanted feeling. Teens who have sexual feelings while in the company of a same-sex peer may not be able to accept—or even admit to themselves—the possibility that they're attracted to that person. They accuse others of being gay and, by hostilely projecting the feeling onto someone else, reassure themselves (and perhaps their classmates) of their own heterosexuality. In fact, research finds that people who are uncomfortable with their own same-sex attractions may be the *most* likely to engage in homophobic behavior.

LGBTQ girls often hide their sexual orientation or gender identity throughout adolescence (or longer), a fact that comes as no surprise given how routinely teens use homophobic insults. And teens with questions about their sexual identity may need time to get in touch with their feelings and figure out what they want. Unlike their peers in the sexual majority, they can't always explore their questions openly, especially if they live in communities where being LGBTQ might be grounds for social shunning or outright physical attack.

How girls feel about coming out to their parents depends on many things. Not surprisingly, some research finds that

LGBTQ teens are more likely to come out to parents who generally support their choices and are less likely to come out to parents who are domineering. Paradoxically, some research shows that teenagers with stronger ties to their family may be reluctant to come out to their parents for fear of disappointing them or jeopardizing their close bond. In other words, teens are more likely to come out to their parents when the benefits of doing so seem to outweigh the costs. The same research finds that teens who have access to positive, supportive resources outside of the family—such as LGBTQ organizations, a supportive school environment, or accepting peers— may feel that they can better afford the potential downsides of coming out at home.

There are two different issues on the table when it comes to where the adults enter into this picture. The first has to do with teens' use of the terms "gay" and "lesbian" as insults, the second with the possibility that your daughter may identify as LGBTQ. Though we'll address each issue separately, they obviously overlap. When you take time to talk with your daughter about the fact that she should not allow herself or her peers to use homophobic language, you are sending a strong message about your wish to support and protect members of the LGBTQ community. If your daughter happens to identify as LGBTQ, this is a message she'll be glad to hear and one that may help her feel more comfortable coming out at home.

Should you learn from your teenager that her peers use "gay" or "lesbian" as an insult, or if you have reason to believe that she herself uses these terms as put-downs, you'll want to think about this behavior from the standpoint of bullying. We know from chapter 2 that bullying occurs when a person is repeatedly exposed, over time, to negative actions by one or more peers and has difficulty defending himself or herself. With this definition in mind, it's not clear that every use of "gay" or "lesbian" as an insult constitutes bullying—indeed, adolescent boys often volley homophobic terms back and forth without even flinching. Nonetheless, these slurs belong on a continuum of homophobic aggression that includes violent hate crimes. It falls to adults to help teens make that connection.

What should you do if you wonder if your daughter might identify as LGBTQ or if she comes out to you? Teens are often fearful of what will happen when they share their sexual orientation or gender identity with their parents. If your daughter comes out to you, or if you suspect that she might wish to, make every effort to let her know that you support and accept her, regardless of who she loves or how she identifies. Not surprisingly, research on LGBTQ teenagers finds that being a member of a stigmatized group adds a whole layer of stress to the already taxing adolescent experience. Half of the LGBTQ adolescents in one study worried that their sexual orientation would be an obstacle in life, and roughly two-thirds had entertained suicidal thoughts. Indeed, studies consistently find elevated alcohol and drug use among LGBTQ teens who may turn to substances to manage the hardship of being a sexual minority. Yet research also finds that parental acceptance reduces stress for LGBTQ teens and, accordingly, reduces drug use, depression, and suicidal thoughts and actions, while increasing self-esteem.

Obviously, the response to a daughter's expression of an LGBTQ identity is an extremely delicate moment for parents. Correspondingly, any girl who is coming out will be highly attuned to indications that her parents are less than accepting. Indeed, teenagers often share the news with their peers first and tell their folks—or just let them figure it out—once they've already tested the waters elsewhere.

Late on a Wednesday evening in my private practice I met

with Ted and Melissa, the parents of Paige, a Year 11 girl at a local school. Ted called me to make an appointment when he saw a long chain of group texts on Paige's phone in which she had written openly to several friends about being a lesbian. Sitting next to each other on my office couch, Ted and Melissa expressed their double surprise: they didn't know that Paige was gay, and they didn't know what to do with the fact that she was broadcasting the news quite comfortably to several classmates.

"Don't get us wrong," Ted said while shrugging his shoulders and holding out his large hands. "We don't mind if she's gay . . . I mean, it's complicated, but we'd always support her."

"What bugs us," Melissa added, "is that she doesn't seem to get that it's a big deal to tell everyone. And she's only fifteen, so how can she be so sure? I *will* say that her friends don't seem to think much about it, which is good, I guess. But we don't know who else she's told, and she doesn't know we know."

Curious, I asked, "What keeps you from telling her that you read her texts?"

Melissa replied, "She knows that what happens on her phone isn't private—we've reserved the right to look at her texts. And we didn't really go looking. Paige left the phone on the counter and a new text in the thread came in when Ted was standing right there. Then he read the whole conversation."

Ted sighed before saying, "We're just not quite sure what to say. We want her to understand that we're on her side, but, to be honest, we're also wondering if she might change her mind at some point."

Melissa nodded before adding, "Last summer she had a huge crush on a boy who lives down the street, so we don't know what to do with that."

"Have you given some thought to what you *might* say to Paige?" I asked.

Melissa nervously tucked her graying hair behind her ear before responding, "We thought we'd tell her that we saw the texts, that we love her, and that who she likes doesn't matter to us. We just want for her to have good relationships." Ted nodded as Melissa continued, "We're wondering if it's okay to tell her that how she feels right now might not be how she feels later on, but that no matter where she ends up, we're on her side."

"The first part sounds good," I said, "but I wonder if mentioning that she might change her mind could feel invalidating. Even if her feelings do change, Paige's current interest in girls will still be part of her evolving sexual identity. What if you asked her what term she'd like for you to use to describe her sexual orientation and let her know that she should keep you posted if there are other terms that would work better as she figures out what makes sense for her?"

Melissa and Ted looked at each other, then at me. Ted said, "We'll think about that."

I asked, "What about your worries about the kids she has already told?"

"Yeah, that's a tough one," said Melissa. "We don't want to seem critical, but we're not sure she understands that she might not want to shout this from the rooftops. And there's something else. She has a best friend, Monica, who comes over a lot and they go in Paige's room, close the door, and hang out for hours. Now we're wondering if we should say something to Paige about that."

I thought a moment before saying, "My hunch is that you're starting what will be a long series of conversations. What if you begin with what you already have in mind—about being supportive—and add that you worry that not everyone will be so supportive?"

"We can do that," Ted said, "but what about when Monica comes over?"

"I think that's a question you should consider with Paige. How do you think she'll react if you bring it up?"

Melissa jumped in. "She'll be pissed."

"Okay," I responded, "well then maybe you could say something along the lines of, 'We're feeling our way here and don't want to hurt you. As far as we know, you and Monica are just friends, but we wouldn't be okay with you having a guy friend over and closing the door to your room, so we're not really sure what to do when Monica comes over.'"

Ted chimed in, "I can tell you right now that Paige will say that we're invading her privacy if we tell her she can't close the door when Monica comes over."

"Fair enough," I said, "and I doubt you'll be able to wrap this up in a tidy bow anytime soon. Just because you support Paige's romantic choices doesn't mean that all the rules go out the window. You could ask her to propose a way forward that allows for privacy without opening up the possibility of turning your house into make-out central. Of course she'll have platonic friendships with girls going forward, but you're still within your rights to discuss when some rules might be in order."

From there I talked with Ted and Melissa about my experience that teens really *want* grown-ups to act like grown-ups around their love lives, even if they complain about the rules we make. In my private practice, I've had girls tell me how unsettled they are by parents who host coed sleepovers. One particularly well-spoken client of mine felt as if she'd been "fed to the wolves" when her parents left the house for hours while knowing that she and her boyfriend were holed up in her bedroom. Teens can find plenty of places to make out with each other. And they do. Your daughter will feel better (and you probably will, too) if you don't condone the use of your home for sexual activity, regardless of her sexual orientation.

Our appointment came to an end, and we reached the understanding that Ted and Melissa would be having many conversations with Paige in the weeks, and perhaps years, to come. They resolved to approach their talks with several guidelines in mind: that they wished to support Paige in pursuing what she truly wanted for herself; that their primary goal was for Paige to have warm, healthy romances and to be protected from homophobic bias; and that they would work with Paige to figure out some appropriate rules for her romantic and social life while she lived at home.

If your daughter comes out to you, you'll filter your reaction through your own feelings and your knowledge of your girl. Many parents feel as Ted and Melissa do. They are open to what works for their daughter but surprised by the news and full of questions about what's behind it. Other parents have been wondering about their daughter's sexual orientation or gender identity for years before she shares her LGBTQ status, and they may feel relieved when she comes out to them and glad that she's no longer harboring a secret.

Some parents feel that they can only accept their daughter if she is heterosexual. Given that our girls often know us as well as we know ourselves (if not better), parents who don't feel ready to support their daughter's LGBTQ identity may not learn of it until well past her adolescence. Ultimately, if they wish to maintain their relationship with their daughter, they may need to seek guidance as they work to reconcile their personal views with their love for their girl.

Girls can have questions about their sexual orientation, their gender identity, or both. Gender identity (how much a girl *feels* herself to be female or male) operates independently of sexual orientation (whom she's attracted to), though the two are often, and wrongly, conflated. Put another way, girls who adopt a masculine identity might feel attracted to guys only, girls only, or be bisexual. Separating sexual orientation from gender identity, as we should, points our attention to what gender questions are really about: *identity*.

Today's culture, especially its younger segment, accepts more fluid expressions of gender identity than the rigid male/female binary most of us grew up with. Male athletes now routinely hold back their flowing locks with what have, up until recently, been seen as girls' headbands. And though girls have long enjoyed more latitude in their gender expression than boys ("tomboys" are cool, "sissies" aren't), you may have noticed that your local female barista is finding new ways to push the bounds of gender expression. That said, girls are still bombarded by pink princess models of femininity. These trends are changing, but not fast enough for most girls and certainly too slowly for girls on the masculine side of gender identity.

However your daughter presents her gender, you'll want to remember that it's about her identity, not yours. Though it would certainly be easier on everyone involved if your daughter's nontraditional identity expression took the form of wanting to be a football player instead of wanting to be recognized as a boy, put yourself in the role of pragmatic advocate regarding any identity she considers. What barriers will she run into? How will she address them? What support does she need? Who will be against her? And addressing these concerns does not preclude the possibility of entering into some heady arbitration: Should she really wear a suit to her cousin's bar mitzvah? Should you honor your daughter's request to call her by a new name or refer to her with masculine or gender neutral pronouns? (Obviously, I've stuck with feminine pronouns here; your daughter may prefer something different.)

Being LGBTQ is stressful for teenagers and the parents who are trying to support them, even at a moment when mainstream culture has begun to welcome the full range of sexual orientations and gender identities. Many communities have local chapters of organizations such as Parents, Families and Friends of Lesbians and Gays (PFLAG) where families who are facing similar challenges can learn from one another's experiences. Such groups include families who are at every point along the way, and veteran members can provide seasoned, tested guidance to parents who are still finding their feet. It's tricky enough to help our daughters navigate their entry into the romantic world. It's that much more difficult when girls enter the romantic world as a sexual minority or bearing an unconventional gender identity.

Entering the Romantic World: When to Worry

Let's start with a common scenario that is *not* grounds for concern: the girl who seems to be making no attempt to enter the romantic world. Many girls move happily through their teenage years without seeming to engage in a love life. So if your daughter expresses zero interest in romance and would prefer to do anything but gossip about boys or dress to get their attention, go with it. If she's comfortable with setting romance aside during her teenage years, you should be comfortable with that, too. Even if she's not acting on her amorous wishes, chances are she's becoming familiar with what she wants for herself. And when it comes to getting her sex life off the ground, research consistently shows that girls who hold off on having sex until their late teens or thereafter feel better about the experience than girls who become sexually active in early adolescence.

Sometimes, the heavy emphasis that teenagers place on romantic activity can cause girls who want no part of it to feel left out or, worse, to worry that there's something wrong with them. If necessary, reassure your daughter that having a romantic life as an adult does not depend on having a romantic life as a teenager and support her as she devotes her time and energy to doing other things that she enjoys. Indeed, a girl who has many sources of self-esteem *besides* romantic activity is a girl who's positioned to have a healthy romantic life when the time is right. In contrast, girls who derive their self-esteem entirely from their romantic relationships give us a reason to worry.

The Tributaries and the Lake

People feel good about themselves for the things they do well; actual accomplishments are life's most reliable source of self-worth. When I think of girls and self-esteem, I picture a lake that, ideally, has many tributaries keeping it full. These tributaries will differ from girl to girl and may include their successful efforts as a serious student, a dedicated athlete, a dependable friend, an animal shelter volunteer, a budding inventor, an amazing big sister, or a reliable employee, just to name a few. Teenagers can be fragile and easily lose a sense of their value, so it's best if they have more than one way to feel good. A girl who is flattened by a low grade can be restored later the same day when she picks up her paycheck at the store where she bags groceries. A girl who gets cut from the basketball team might find she feels better after she's spent a Saturday afternoon tutoring kids at the local primary school.

We should worry about girls whose capacity to attract romantic or sexual attention is the only tributary feeding their lake. Unfortunately, girls sometimes organize themselves around getting boys' attention when they have little else to feel good about. They focus heavily on how they look, put romantic opportunities ahead of their friendships, treat guys poorly with an eye toward trading up, and may totally disregard their own inner compasses because they are entirely focused on giving boys what they want.

In the long term, we're not looking to raise women who pin their self-esteem on their romantic or sexual appeal. In the short term, the worst decisions I've ever known teenage girls to make have resulted from desperate efforts to keep the romantic waters flowing. Over the years, I've worked with girls who have walked through unsafe neighborhoods at night because they couldn't get a ride to a party hosted by popular boys. I've helped to pick up the pieces when girls invite guys they hardly know to stop by when their parents aren't home. And I've counseled girls who provided sexual favors they later regret because they were desperate to maintain a boy's attention.

Should your daughter rely on her allure to keep her self-esteem intact, help her develop new tributaries. If she's not proud of how she's doing in school, take steps to address any academic difficulties she may be having. If she has few interests besides guys, ask—or require—her to take on some extracurricular activities, find a volunteer opportunity, get a job, or all of the above. Sometimes girls turn to boys when they have a hard time maintaining friendships with other girls. If this is true of your daughter, get advice from trusted sources about any changes that can be made to improve her platonic social connections. Filling up your daughter's schedule will give her more ways to build self-esteem and less time to seek attention, and a sense of personal worth, from boys.

April–June Romances

If you spend any time around students in years 7 to 9 it becomes pretty obvious that girls, on average, hit puberty at least two years before boys do. The developmental discrepancies sometimes border on the comical as Year 7 girls who look as though they could be in Year 11 tower over boys in their class who could easily be mistaken for kids in Year 5. If we were to go strictly by biological indicators of sexual maturity, most Year 8 girls find their match in Year 10 or 11 boys. Yet if we go by everything I know about girls, good things rarely come of girls dating boys who are more than a year their senior.

Studies find that, compared to girls who are dating age-mates, girls who date boys two or more years older have sex at younger ages, are more likely to contract a sexually transmitted infection, and are less likely to use condoms or other forms of contraception. Further, dating older guys increases the chances that a girl will use drugs and show signs of depression. There are two ways to consider these findings. First, older teens tend to do riskier things than younger teens, and that likely extends to anyone who hangs out with them. Second, and to put a fine point on it, show me a Year 11 boy who pursues Year 8 girls and I'll show you a boy you probably don't want hanging around your daughter.

The "not more than a year older" rule is hardly universal; there are certainly Year 13 boys who treat their Year 11 girl-friends as respected equals. But if your daughter dates someone more than one year ahead, or if she's hanging out with a sixth-form boy while she's still in lower secondary school, you should wonder, "Is she truly an equal partner in this relationship?" If you suspect she isn't, consider taking the same steps recommended for girls who rely on boys to maintain their self-esteem. It's nearly impossible to control your daughter's romantic life, however much you may want to, but you can work to keep her busy with activities that will fill her time and offer her reliable sources of self-worth.

Of course, the bigger the age gap, the more grounds for concern. Thanks to the seedy world of hook-up apps and on-line dating, teenage girls can easily meet men who are nothing but bad news. While on a family vacation, a frighteningly impulsive sixteen-year-old client of mine lied about her age on an app designed to connect people looking for geographically convenient sexual partners. My client asked her twelve-year-old sister to help her keep her plans secret from her parents so she could meet up with a twenty-three-year-old man. Luckily, the little sister broke down and told their parents what was happening. The parents tracked their teenager down quickly, interrupted the "date" before it took a disastrous turn, and let the man know they'd call the police if he contacted their daughter again. Needless to say, it's time to worry if your teen-age daughter is pursuing or hanging out with adults. If this happens, let your daughter know that you are stepping in to protect her, strictly limit her online access, and work with trusted mental health professionals and, perhaps, your local law enforcement to make things right.

Once we're talking about girls dating older guys we are out of the realm of focusing on what your daughter wants and squarely in the world of talking with your daughter about what girls need to do to care for themselves effectively. Next, we'll turn our attention to the all-important conversations you'll be having with your daughter as she takes over the work of looking after herself.

SEVEN

. . . .

Caring for Herself

WE'VE ARRIVED AT THE FINAL STRAND OF ADOLESCENCE—THE one where your daughter learns to make wise, independent decisions about her own health and safety. Of course she has been taking care of herself in many ways since she was young. She looks both ways before crossing the street, bundles up on cold days, packs her own lunch, and so on. Anna Freud described the "slow and gradual manner in which children assume responsibility for the care of their own body and its protection from harm," and in this chapter, we'll consider how that work extends into the teenage years. We'll start by addressing how your daughter eats and sleeps, the two basic aspects of self-care that she will begin to manage independently as a young teenager. From there, we'll consider the dicey choices and adult scenarios that girls encounter as they move into later adolescence.

It would be really easy to teach girls how to care for themselves if we could simply tell them what to do. Our advice would be predictable and straightforward: eat a healthy diet; get a good night's sleep; when you have sex, make sure it's safe; be careful about drinking; and don't do drugs. There's nothing wrong with offering advice, but it's just not that simple. When it comes to taking care of themselves, most girls are resistant to adult input—even thoughtful, loving input—especially if it comes from their parents. As we know from chapter 5, there's no more powerful force in your home than your teenager's drive toward autonomy. Telling your daughter how to manage some of the most personal aspects of her life can inspire, if not provoke, her to want to do the opposite. And that's if she doesn't tune you out altogether.

Nodding Without Listening

Girls can excel at seeming to soak up our wisdom while they're actually ignoring us. When I meet with groups of teenage girls to talk about their health and safety, I always begin by warmly saying, "You know that thing you guys do when an adult is giving you advice and you don't agree or you've stopped listening, but you just keep nodding anyway?" In response, they beam at me with glittering recognition; some girls even say, "Oh yeah, we *totally* do that." Then I add, "I call that your 'veil of obedience,' and you get behind it when an adult says something that doesn't fit with your experience and you check out." They inevitably greet this with knowing smiles and unveiled nods of agreement.

Boys sometimes hide behind their veils of obedience, too, but they differ from girls in that they're more inclined to disagree openly, or look away, when they've fallen out of step with us. Girls, on the other hand, give us what we think we want: a teenager who at least appears to be paying attention. If your daughter exhausts you with her willingness to disagree, consider yourself lucky. At least you *know* when she's not going along with you.

Before you even consider how to help your daughter take over the work of caring for herself, you'll need to account for her veil of obedience. Over the years, I've asked girls to share with me what adults do or say that gets them to disregard our advice. Here is what they tell me.

Girls stop listening to us when we lecture. If you find yourself talking *at* your daughter or pressing any point at length, know that she has likely put on her veil and you are almost certainly wasting your breath. The wisdom and accuracy of your advice are inconsequential. It's almost impossible for any human being to endure a lecture without feeling defensive in response, and the longer the lecture goes on, the more defensive we become. People don't like being told what to do and this goes double (at least!) for teenagers.

Girls don their veils of obedience when we take a suspicious tone. As soon as we ask, "Will there be drinking at that party?" they start assuring us that the party will be alcohol-free and figuring out how to keep us from learning otherwise. This is true even for teens who were already worried that the party might be bad news. Girls tell me that when their parents come at them with what feel like accusatory questions, they'll aim to end the conversation as fast as possible, even if they have nothing to hide. As one Year 13 girl put it, "If I was just watching TV over at a friend's house I'll shut down if my mom starts with, 'Who was there? What did you do? Did boys come over?' I'll say as little as possible and try to get out of the room."

Girls brush us off when we level moral judgments. Feel free to embrace your beliefs (e.g., breaking the law is "wrong," only married sex is "right"), but don't expect your daughter to share your perspective. Morals are always relative and highly personal, so foisting your principles on an authority-questioning teenager will only invite her to look for holes in your argument, even if she actually shares your views. When talking with your daughter about how she cares for herself, it's better to set the moralizing aside.

And girls discount what we have to say when we overstate risks. Loving parents sometimes try to scare their daughters safe by exaggerating. When we say, "Alcohol is poison!" girls put on their veils and nod at us while thinking, "Sure. Except for all the kids who showed up safely at school on Monday after getting really drunk and, by the way, seeming to have an excellent time over the weekend." When we say, "Stay away from drugs. They're bad!" girls nod while thinking, "Um, hello? Marijuana is legal in some states. Clearly, you have no idea what you are talking about."

So how do you talk with your daughter about caring for herself without causing her to glaze over? It's not easy, and sometimes she'll hide behind her veil no matter what you do. But if you are to guide her successfully at all, you'll need to account for her predictable reluctance to accept your advice. You *can* communicate effectively with your daughter about her health and well-being, and throughout this chapter we'll consider the tactics that make for real conversations.

Girls, Food, and Weight

It's especially tricky to talk with girls about food and weight. We don't want them to face the health consequences that come with poor nutrition or obesity, but we don't want to say things that might trigger an eating disorder. While parents fret over how to communicate with their daughters about nutrition, girls encounter a world of toxic messages about their size and shape.

Experts have questioned whether the barrage of media images of unusually slim women causes girls to feel unhappy with their bodies or whether the media simply portrays unrealistic ideals girls already buy into anyway. Amazingly, a group of Harvard researchers found a way to address this question— "Which came first, unrealistic media images or body dissatisfaction?"—by studying the inhabitants of Fiji, a South Pacific island where a healthy appetite and full-bodied female figure have long been seen as signs of psychological and physical health. Shortly before the island started receiving American television programs in 1995, the research team had the foresight to record the island's expectedly low rates of disordered eating in teenage girls. After just three years of watching American television, the rates of dieting and body dissatisfaction soared. In a culture where dieting had been virtually nonexistent before the arrival of Western television, 69 percent of teenage girls reported that they limited what they ate in order to lose weight and 74 percent said they sometimes felt that they were overweight.

In sharing their findings, the researchers noted that Fijian islanders faced a number of modernizations, which may have contributed to their results, around the same time that Western programming arrived. Yet during research interviews, the Fijian teenagers talked in specific terms about what they saw on TV, saying, "The actresses and all those girls . . . I just admire them and want to be like them. I want their body, I want their size" and "When I see the sexy ladies on the television, well, I want to be like them, too."

Studies of American girls support the Fijian findings. The more girls are exposed to images that celebrate the "thin-ideal" female form, the more likely they are to be dissatisfied with their own bodies. A particularly fascinating study of the effects of visual media on body image compared body dissatisfaction in women who were blind at birth, women who became blind as adults, and sighted women. Not surprisingly, the study found that the congenitally blind women felt best about their bodies while the women who had spent a lifetime exposed to visual media felt the worst.

Where visual media leaves off, peer culture kicks in. Girls talk with one another about weight, dieting, and appearance, and research tells us that they are more likely to feel dissatisfied with their bodies and flirt with eating disorders if they have these conversations frequently. Given the troublesome messages that girls inevitably receive from the media and some peers about eating and weight, you'll want to be mindful of any judgmental comments you might make about appearance and weight and, instead, find a helpful way to chime in.

A research study with one of my favorite titles—"Adolescent girls with high body satisfaction: Who are they and what can they teach us?"—found that girls feel good about their bodies when their parents focus on *positive* ways to maintain a healthy weight, as opposed to encouraging dieting. Specifically, the girls in the study who reported high levels of body satisfaction had parents who exercised, encouraged their daughters to be fit, and emphasized healthy eating. So make physical activity a part of your life as a family and focus on the sustaining foods you *should* eat, not on counting calories or restricting certain foods.

And try to steer clear of value judgments when it comes to food. Labeling foods as good or bad can make "bad" foods (or worse, forbidden foods) particularly alluring for some girls and can contribute to eating disorders in perfectionistic girls who refuse to eat anything but "good" foods. The terms *healthy* and *unhealthy* can have the same effect. The best take I've heard on this topic comes from the geniuses at *Sesame Street*, who describe foods as being "anytime foods" or "sometime foods." When you define these categories for your daughter, explain that anytime foods are unprocessed (and are the foods that take the best care of her body) and sometime foods are the heavily processed. If necessary, educate your daughter about how to identify a sometime food: it's made in a factory, it comes in a package, it usually has more than five ingredients, and it contains things she can't pronounce.

When talking with your daughter about how *much* she should eat, encourage her to pay attention to the cues her body sends. We are all equipped with a finely calibrated system that helps us take care of ourselves by reminding us to eat when we are hungry, telling us how hungry we are, and signaling when we are full. Ideally, your daughter will use her internal system—not external markers such as a clock or portion size—to dictate when and how much she should eat. Most girls do this naturally, but if your daughter seems unsure, ask her, "Are you hungry?" "How hungry are you?" "Do you feel full, or do you want more to eat?" and matter-of-factly commend her for taking good care of herself when she's listening to her body's signals.

If you hear your daughter commenting unfavorably on her own size or shape, say something. Assuming she's at a healthy weight, you might note that she is strong and vibrant and doing a great job of taking care of herself. When I was a teenager I happened to be looking at a beauty magazine when Diane, a trusted family friend, pointed to a model in one of the ads and said to me, "You know—that's her *job*." Of course the model in the photograph was playing at having some other job—dressed for the office and looking fabulous—but as soon as Diane weighed in I thought, "Right! That woman doesn't have an office job. Looking good *is* her job." At least for the moment I felt that if I went about my regular busy day looking even halfway decent, I was doing very well for myself.

We know that it's wise to stay out of conflicts in domains where your daughter holds all the power. Food, like school-work, is one of them. Parents who wield their authority around what their daughter eats or how much she exercises can find themselves faced with a teen who puts on her veil and does the opposite of what they ask, just to prove her independence. I think here of an overweight girl whose parents wanted her to get more exercise and, before the dawn of smart technologies, had her wear a pedometer so they could track her daily steps. In my office, she explained to me that she got her steps by stuffing the pedometer in a pair of balled-up socks that she put in the dryer (on the no-heat cycle) while she did her homework. At the opposite, frightening extreme I've worked with underweight girls who secretly do calisthenics in their bedrooms against their parents' wishes and doctors' orders. To stay out of a fruitless—even dangerous—power struggle with your daughter about food and weight, frame your commentary on nutrition, weight, and exercise *entirely* in terms of your daughter's developing ability to care for herself.

Joan and Eric, the parents of sixteen-year-old Haley, made an appointment with me because they were at odds about how to handle their daughter's recent weight gain. When we met, Eric, an even-tempered stay-at-home dad, explained to me that Haley had a ravenous sweet tooth and would nosh on piles of candy while studying. Joan, the affable owner of a local daycare, added that Haley had stopped fitting comfortably into her clothes but hadn't asked to go shopping for new ones. In fact, she hadn't said anything about her rapid weight gain and seemed to be managing it by limiting herself to clothes that still fit. Eric, who was around when she got home from school, wanted to ban candy from the house and encourage Haley to start working out. Joan, whose sister had been hospitalized for anorexia as a teenager, didn't want to do or say anything that might hurt their daughter's feelings or, worse, inspire her to starve herself.

I acknowledged that both parents had valid points and suggested that they could take up their concerns from the side of how well (or not) Haley was looking after herself. We agreed that without any fanfare, Eric would say something along the lines of, "It seems as though you want some sugar to keep you going while you do your homework. All that candy won't give you the energy you really need. Would it help if we put together some fresh fruit at homework time so that you can snack on something sweet while taking better care of yourself?" I discouraged banning candy, as I've had overweight teenagers who want to lose weight tell me that they sneak sweets when they're out of the house because their parents have forbidden desserts at home.

Joan rightly asked, "What do we do if Haley stops eating candy at home but keeps eating lots of junk food when she's on her own?"

"That could certainly happen," I answered. "If it does, let's treat her weight gain as the health concern it is and involve your pediatrician. If we get there, you can say, 'We've noticed that you've gained some weight and we're concerned that your weight is unhealthy. We've made an appointment with your pediatrician—we'll leave it to the two of you to determine what's a good weight for you.' More than anything, we want to keep the issue of Haley's size as neutral as possible, making sure it's about how she's caring for herself and her physical well-being. Getting your pediatrician on board will put the emphasis where it belongs and keep you out of a fight about food."

Eric asked, "But what if she takes things too far in the other direction? What if she starts eating ultrahealthy and loses too much weight?"

I reassured Eric and Joan that we would keep a close eye on Haley's weight and, if Eric's fears were realized, they could point out that by eating an overly restricted diet, Haley was still failing to take good care of herself. Haley's pediatrician could, again, be brought into the picture if Haley found a new way to have an unhealthy relationship with food. Given that girls sometimes try to turn internal conflicts into external ones, Eric and Joan should frame their daughter's struggle in terms of a fight between the part of Haley that knows how to take good care of herself and the part that's falling down on the job.

Girls often experiment with dieting during adolescence or talk about wishing to lose weight. Teenage girls are a high-risk population for eating disorders, and not just the upper-middle-class white girls who might be the first to come to mind. In fact, recent research evidence finds that African-American, Hispanic, Asian American, and Native American girls are as likely as white girls to have experimented with unhealthy tactics for controlling their weight. We'll return to the importance of recognizing and treating disordered eating in the "When to Worry" section at the end of this chapter.

Food is one of many domains where you will want to frame your daughter's choices in terms of the care she takes of herself, not in terms of the rules you are telling her to follow. Even if you could enforce your rules in the short term—which is highly unlikely—you're setting up a situation in which your daughter gets behind her veil of obedience and goes along with your guidelines about food (or drinking, drugs, or sex) while she lives with you but then breaks those rules as soon as she's on her own. Instead, admire the smart choices your daughter makes and offer support when she's failing to care for herself effectively.

Sleep vs. Technology

Girls can't stand it when we come at them with judgments about "typical teenage" behavior and will put on their veils of obedience faster than you can say, "Your phone is disrupting your sleep." By early adolescence, many girls have attached themselves to digital technology and don't give a second thought to treating their phones like the blankets or stuffed animals they carried around everywhere when they were little. But if your daughter's teddy helped her sleep as a toddler, we now know that her phone—and computer, and all other forms of technology—has the opposite effect.

To have a constructive conversation with your daughter about how digital technology interferes with sleep, don't play the role of a high-handed adult who has come to criticize how today's teens use technology. Instead, focus on the behavioral and biological underpinnings of sleep that apply to everyone, regardless of age, when encouraging your daughter to get her recommended nine hours of sleep each night. And yes, you read that right: teenagers need about *nine* hours, but almost half sleep fewer than seven.

Here's the science that you, and your daughter, need to know about how technology undermines sleep.

For starters, experimental psychology has taught us that we're not nearly as in charge of our routines as we'd like to think we are. Our bodies learn the patterns of what we do—the when and where—and these patterns shape our behavior. The best example to bring this theory home has to do with the impulse to urinate. We have all had the experience of feeling the urge to go to the bathroom while we're out and about running errands. On a scale of one to ten, your need to urinate might hover around a three; if necessary, you could probably throw in an extra errand without having to make a pit stop. But when you walk into your home your bladder suddenly howls, "TEN, TEN, TEN!" Why does this happen? Because your body knows that it doesn't usually urinate at the grocery store or the dry cleaners or (giving you the benefit of the doubt) in your car. But it does know that you relieve yourself at home, and when you walk in your door, your urges take over.

What does this have to do with teens, technology, and sleep? Unfortunately, many girls treat their beds like offices. In cozy comfort, they do their homework, post online, watch shows, and communicate with their friends. While sprawled out over their cushioned workstations, girls gradually sever the association their bodies have built between being in bed and falling asleep. Before long, your daughter's body stops recognizing the bed as a "ten" for sleeping. When your girl tries to fall asleep, her body wonders, "Why are we trying to crash at the office?" and stays awake out of sheer bewilderment.

To make matters worse, the light emitted by digital technology disrupts melatonin, the natural hormone that causes drowsiness when it gets dark. Artificial light drives down melatonin levels, and research indicates that the blue-spectrum light emitted by digital technology may be particularly effective at undermining healthy fatigue. Perhaps you've checked email one last time on your way to bed and experienced a small burst of energy followed by trouble sleeping; despite what I know about the science of sleep, I stupidly conduct this experiment on myself at least twice a week.

Here's a scene played out nightly by technology-using teens

everywhere. After a long day at school, the teenager retires to her bed to begin her homework and spends the next several hours working, and sometimes playing, on her computer. Finally, she decides to hit the hay. She powers down, brushes her teeth, and calls it a night. Or so she thinks. Unable to sleep, she returns to her technology to entertain or distract herself some more. I've often thought that if an evil genius crafted a diabolical blueprint for causing chronic sleep disruption, it would be the all-too-common scenario described here.

In sum, digital technology should never find its way into anyone's bed, and everyone in the family should step away from his or her devices *at least* a half hour before trying to go to sleep. But how do we implement such policies with real live teenagers? Once you've educated your daughter about the science of sleep, ask her to do her homework anywhere but on her bed. A desk or the bedroom floor are great alternatives if she insists on being in her room, or ask her to use another bed in your home—perhaps your bed or a guest bed if you happen to have one—to help preserve the link between the sensory experience of being in her own bed and her body's impulse to sleep.

If your daughter needs to use a computer to do her schoolwork, as is true for most teenagers, encourage her to manage her melatonin levels by doing work that requires a computer early in the evening and leaving reading or reviewing notes to last. If she finishes her homework before bedtime and wants to use digital technology for fun, suggest other forms of leisure (reading, watching television) in the half hour before bed. Many parents find it helpful to make a rule that all of the family's portable digital devices are turned off and charged overnight in the parents' bedroom. This removes the powerful temptation to engage with a laptop or phone late into the night—for everyone, of course, except the parents—and keeps digital alert noises from interfering with a teenager's sleep.

Perhaps your daughter has already established her bed as her command deck and you feel understandably reluctant to ask her to change her habits now. If she's falling asleep quickly and getting enough sleep, consider leaving well enough alone. Otherwise, talk with her about the impact of technology on sleep and help her try out new habits. Families that start off with firm rules about the when and where of using technology often give girls more slack over time. This makes sense. When your daughter leaves home, she'll need to regulate her technology use on her own; as we know, it's better for her to practice doing so at home than to feel that the best part about moving out will be that she can play on her phone all night.

In sharing these rules with your daughter, be clear that you are setting these limits because sleep acts as the glue that holds each one of us together, regardless of age. When we get adequate sleep, we feel better physically and emotionally, work faster, remember more, have better focus, feel less stressed, and are far less likely to get sick. Girls usually resist when their parents try to restrict nighttime use of digital technology, especially if they've had unfettered use of it in the past. But if your daughter is still forming her technology habits or if she's having trouble sleeping, stick to your guns on this one and show her that, as part of taking good care of *yourself,* you follow the same guidelines.

Getting Real About Drinking

As girls advance along this developmental strand they move quickly into the self-care big leagues of managing themselves around teenage drinking. It would be convenient for adults if we could simply fall back on the law and say, "Don't drink until you're twenty-one" or "Don't go to parties where teens are drinking," but the reality is this: by the time they leave school, roughly 80 percent of adolescents have tried alcohol. Breaking that number down, we find that by age fourteen, 43 percent of teenagers have experimented with drinking, and that number jumps to 65 percent for sixteen-year-olds. White teens are significantly more likely to drink than African-American or Hispanic adolescents and, contrary to negative stereotypes about substance use in impoverished communities, affluent teens are more likely to drink, smoke, and try drugs. Across all groups, teens are (not surprisingly) more likely to drink if their friends do. While there are certainly some teenagers who fall in with a teetotaling crowd that finds its own fun each weekend, by the sixth form, if not sooner, a girl's social life might be highly limited if she can only attend alcohol-free parties, especially in some communities.

When we tell teenagers not to drink and to stay away from peers who are drinking, we are parenting for the social options we *wish* our daughters had, not the options most girls *actually* have. This puts girls in an impossible position: they can give up their social lives and stay home with us or they can sneak around and lie to us about what's happening at the parties they're attending. Most healthy tribe-seeking teenagers would, often reluctantly, pick the second option. To make matters worse, girls who choose door number two are unlikely to ask their parents for help if things go sideways at a party they're not supposed to be attending in the first place.

Until we have some iron-clad way to prevent teens from drinking or to guarantee that all teen drinking is safe, it's best to recognize the reality that most adolescents drink. Doing so when discussing this topic with your daughter will help to keep her from getting behind her veil of obedience and will increase the chances that she'll take you, and your expectations for how she'll handle herself around alcohol, seriously. There aren't firm guidelines for when you should first broach the topic of teen drinking—you know your daughter best—but don't expect to have a single sit-down to say your piece. Over time, you'll be having many conversations on this topic as your daughter ages and as her views, and social encounters, evolve.

To get the conversation started, perhaps when your daughter is still an early adolescent, you might begin by discussing how adult drinking often differs from teenage drinking. Naturally, our daughters notice that many of us drink, and we look like hypocrites when we don't acknowledge this. (In other words, cue the veil.) When I talk with girls about alcohol, I always note that some adults do dumb or dangerous things when drunk, but we like to think that, more than teens, adults drink in situations where key variables are under control: we're surrounded by responsible companions, we're in the safety of our own homes, we know how much we can drink while remaining well under control, and so on.

Parents are often surprised to learn that it's legal in most American states for teens to consume alcohol in private settings with their parents' presence and consent. Indeed, the law recognizes that alcohol safety is often less about the alcohol and more about the context in which it is consumed. You can readily look up the exceptions to the minimum legal drinking age; if you want to let your daughter taste alcohol at home under your supervision in order to take some of the mystique out of drinking and underline the critical importance of context, chances are you can do so legally. That said, research suggests that the neural structures associated with feelings of reward can be altered during adolescence by the enjoyable buzz of intoxication. Because the adolescent brain reacts to alcohol and drugs differently than the adult brain does, teenage substance use can shape what the brain deems pleasurable and lay the groundwork for addiction.

As your daughter ages, you should continue to talk with her about the contextual factors that make teen drinking especially risky. Make it clear that alcohol impairs the judgment of anyone who drinks it and that teens often drink in situations where they need every ounce of good judgment they've got. In my conversations with girls, I always invoke an equation with many factors that determine the ultimate outcome. I say, "Consider a situation with the following variables: you go to a party, your friends ditch you, and there are some guys at the party who seem pretty creepy. To that equation, let's add one more variable: whether you are totally sober, or whether you've had a few drinks." From there, girls can readily imagine any number of bad scenarios if they've been drinking. And they can strategize about how they would keep themselves safe if they were sober.

Never miss an opportunity to frame your expectations for how your daughter will deal with drinking in terms of her responsibility to care for herself. If you know that your daughter will be going to a party where there will be alcohol, you might say, "Parties where teenagers are drinking make us nervous because things can easily get out of control." From there you could add, "We are counting on you to take great care of yourself. That means keeping your wits about you when you are in a situation that could get out of hand."

When the right moment comes along, you'll also want to talk with your daughter about the *quantity* of alcohol some teens consume. There's now ample evidence that alcohol abuse during adolescence, whether it takes the form of chronic alcohol abuse or periodic bingeing, harms the developing brain. We know that heavy drinking can damage the brain's frontal networks and hippocampus—the parts of the brain associated with learning and memory—and lead to long-term neurological impairment. Brain damage aside, alcohol is a major player in most adolescent fatalities, whether due to impaired driving or drinking to the point of death.

To address these concerns with your daughter you might say, "Drinking too much is a bad idea at any age, but it turns out that the developing teenage brain can be especially vulnerable to long-term damage from alcohol and other substances. You've got a lot to look forward to; I'm trusting that you want to face what's ahead with as many IQ points as possible and that you won't put yourself in a position where you could be hurt or killed by drinking."

Of course, you are well within your rights to ask your daughter to join the 20 percent of teens who conform to the legal drinking age. But don't hand this expectation down in the absence of a broader conversation. Talk with your daughter about the safety and neurological reasons behind your expectation that she won't drink and help her develop strategies for managing peer pressure and turning down the drinks she will almost certainly encounter at some point during her teenage years.

I've heard of parents who encourage their daughters to tell partygoers that they have a potent family history of alcoholism (true or not) that makes drinking too risky. Or, as already suggested, make it easy for your daughter to blame her good behavior on you by making an advance call to confirm that there will be adults supervising any party she attends. Alternatively, you can encourage your daughter to explain to her friends that you have a sixth sense for when she's been drinking. You can also offer that your daughter might hold, but hold back from, alcohol when she's at parties. Never much of a drinker myself, I spent most college parties clutching a half-filled cup of warm beer. I'd like to say that I had the where-withal to brush off peer pressure to drink, but school and college drinkers feel judged by nondrinkers and urge them to join in. Holding, even nursing beer made parties more fun for me.

Finally, in the spirit of not painting your daughter into a dangerous corner, let's revisit another key point: make sure that your daughter knows that her safety comes before any of your disciplinary policies. Regardless of the rules you make about drinking at home or elsewhere, really mean it when you tell her that you know that good teens can find themselves in bad situations and that you will *never* make her sorry she asked for your help. And, as already addressed, you must step in if your daughter becomes involved with drinking early in adolescence or gets drunk to numb painful feelings. If at any point in your daughter's life you worry that her drinking seems uncontrolled, seek professional help.

It had been a long time since I heard from Maya about her daughter, Camille. When I answered her phone call one December morning I quickly calculated that Camille must now be in her final year. Maya gave me an update. On the whole, things were going really well. More pleasant around the house than not, Camille had pulled excellent grades in Year 12 and set her heart on majoring in engineering in college. She had been dating a sweet, studious classmate for six months and was waiting to hear back on her applications to several in-state universities. Maya explained that she was calling now because Camille had done something totally uncharacteristic the previous weekend: she had gotten extremely drunk at a party, a fact that came to light when three friends tried, un-successfully, to sneak Camille into her bed without waking Maya.

After a scary night in which they seriously contemplated taking their daughter to the emergency room to have her stomach pumped, Maya and her husband tried to talk with Camille the next day. She was tearful, testy, and unwilling to discuss the events of the night before. Exasperated, her mom suggested that perhaps Camille should get some help and, to Maya's surprise, she agreed.

Maya told me that Camille was open to meeting with me or to seeing a clinician I suggested. I explained that as long as Camille knew that Maya had talked to me about her over the years, I was okay with setting up an appointment. Maya understood that I wouldn't be able to share anything her daughter told me and said that she'd prefer to have Camille meet with me rather than with an unfamiliar clinician.

When I went to find Camille in my waiting room, she only partially fit the picture I'd built of her in my mind. Like her mother, she was tall with dark hair, but Camille's was much longer and pulled into a ponytail that fell over one shoulder. In contrast to Maya's poise and reflective demeanor, Camille was bouncy and outgoing. When I introduced myself she stood quickly and, with surprising warmth and composure for an eighteen-year-old, said, "Hi, yeah, thank you for meeting with me."

Once we settled into my office, I began. "So, your mom and I have touched base over the years and she has told me a lot about you."

Camille nodded.

"Do you want for me to give you a quick summary of what I know, or do you want to start with what brought you my way?"

"I feel like I know what I need to," she said. "My mom told me that you've been like a sounding board for her over the years." She paused. "Will you tell her what *we* talk about?"

"No," I said, "your mom knows that our meeting will be confidential unless there's some reason to worry about your safety or someone else's."

Camille waved her hand. "Oh, no. It's not like that, but something happened last week that wasn't good."

"Yeah," I replied, trying to drain all judgment from my voice. "Your mom mentioned on the phone that you got really drunk."

Camille shifted in her seat before saying flatly, "It was bad." She stopped for a moment, then continued. "Someone brought vodka to a party at my friend's house and thought it would be fun if we did shots. I don't know what we were thinking. I feel like I usually handle myself really well, so I was pretty freaked out when I sobered up and realized how crazy things got."

I asked, "Do you feel that you now understand what happened?"

"Kind of. I've never had hard alcohol before, just beer, and we were running around all afternoon so I only had snacks, no dinner." She shook her head while saying, "I think I drank more and faster than I realized. But it makes me worried about next year because you hear all these stories about college drinking . . ." Her voice trailed off and she looked down at the floor between us.

When I was in training to become a psychologist, I was taught to ask a specific series of questions to diagnose alcohol abuse: How much do you drink? What are you drinking? How often? Are you blacking out? And so on. I dumped this approach ages ago, especially with teenagers, because I felt as though I might as well be saying, "Now, lie to me about this. And now this. And also this." Instead, I asked Camille a question that has served me very well over the years.

"Are *you* worried about your drinking?"

With practice I've found a tone that communicates that I'm neither critic nor judge; I'm just interested in siding with the teenager's wise, mature side to see if we have any reason to be concerned about her ability to take care of herself.

Camille thought for a moment before saying, "Actually, I'm not. I think that it was just a weird night and I've never had any trouble with drinking up till now. I'd be worried if it had happened before and, honestly, I'd be worried if I felt like I couldn't tell you the truth about it."

This is why I love working with teenagers. When you ask straight questions, they almost always give straight answers. I've had other teenagers answer this question, "I'm not sure . . . I don't know . . . yeah, maybe," and some say, "Yes. I think I am." From there, we can proceed as partners in the work of figuring out what kind of help might be in order.

Of course I've occasionally had teenagers (and adults!) give crooked answers to my straight question. They abruptly say no or defensively lay out all the reasons why they're not worried, often while pointing to other people's problems or questioning the motives of anyone who has expressed concern. When this happens, I play my cards faceup and say, "Okay, I hear you. But for me, the jury is still out. I'm not sure if your drinking is worrisome or not. If I start to think it's a problem, I'll tell you." This is not, I'm sure, what any client hopes to hear me say. But in my experience, teenagers respect honesty and are surprisingly receptive to direct feedback. They only put on their veils of obedience when they feel that an adult has an angle or a hidden agenda.

I said to Camille, "That makes sense to me. And I agree that the fact that you wanted to come in to talk about what happened tells us that you are willing to look at it head-on. Where do you want to go from here?"

She tilted her head to the side and said, "I guess I don't

know. Everything else seems to be going pretty well." Camille then shared how hard it was to wait to hear back from colleges, her questions about how she would spend her last summer before leaving home, and her excitement about being in her last year of school and not having to worry quite so much about how every test grade could affect her future plans. When we came to the end of our hour I asked, "Do you want to make a plan to come back, or do you want to just keep in touch as needed?"

Camille said, "I think that I'll just let you know."

"That sounds fine. And if something changes and you do start to have questions about your drinking, would you feel okay about meeting again?"

"Yes," she said, "I don't think that it's going to be a problem, but I'll keep an eye on it." Then smiling to herself she said, "And believe me, I'm ready to swear off drinking for a while."

I did see Camille again, twice, but not for anything to do with alcohol. We met in July shortly before she left for college because she wasn't sure what to do with her school romance that was still going strong; Camille was headed to a school in southern Ohio and her boyfriend was going to college in California. I shared my observation that there are really no good solutions to this dilemma. It's difficult to end a thriving romance, and trying to start college while tending to a long-distance relationship is very hard, too. Ultimately, Camille and her boyfriend decided that they'd try to just be friends while staying in close touch. But the outcome of her romance didn't matter so much to me. What impressed me was Camille's robust capacity for self-care. She had become a young woman who so fully understood her obligation to protect and advocate for herself that she could comfortably seek consultation from me and, I imagined, other trustworthy sources along the way.

Straight Talk About Drugs

At some point in your daughter's adolescence, she'll have access to illegal drugs or at least be in contact with other teenagers who are using them. Needless to say, she will need to take her responsibility to care for herself very seriously when that time comes. The conversations you have with your daughter about keeping herself safe from illegal substances are critically important because with drugs, the margin for error is frighteningly small. Though some teens experiment with substances without incurring obvious damage, others face lasting legal or physical consequences, including death, even from onetime use. So how do you talk about drugs with your daughter without bringing down her veil of obedience?

Don't be the bad guy. Make drugs the bad guy.

To do this effectively, skip any threats you may be tempted to level (as in, "If I catch you with dope I'll call the cops myself!") and get ready to discuss the actual impact of substances on adolescent brains and bodies, as well as the legal implications of tangling with drugs. We have already seen that your daughter is more likely to act responsibly when she focuses on the risks that rules are designed to minimize. When it comes to talking with your daughter about drugs, play the role of the dispassionate purveyor of reliable information and let the facts about illegal substances do all the work for you. Trust me, they are terrifying enough.

Embrace any curiosity your daughter shares about drugs and how they work. Asking you about substances doesn't mean that she is experimenting with them. Even if her questions come across as provocative, welcome them as opportunities to give her solid, unbiased information. If she doesn't raise the topic by the time she's fourteen or so, you should. Find an opening and say (as impartially as possible), "I heard something on the radio about teens and drug use. It reminded me that there are some things I want to be sure you know. I'm not suggesting that you are doing or will try drugs. But you'll certainly know kids who do, and I want you to make sure you've got good information."

Some of the trickiest questions you'll face will be about marijuana. With the medicinal use of marijuana and the legalization of pot for adult recreational use in a few American states, many teens wonder why they shouldn't smoke it. And smoke it they do. Recent large-scale surveys show that 41 percent of teenage girls (compared to 49 percent of boys) try marijuana while at school, and that the overwhelming majority of sixth formers do not see occasional marijuana use as harmful.

To address the recent legalization of marijuana in some states, don't hesitate to point out that legal isn't the same as safe. Lots of dangerous things are legal (cigarettes, tanning beds, alcohol) and we count on consumers to make informed decisions about their own health and safety. Adults who use alcohol legally can still become alcoholics or make bad decisions when drunk. Similarly, getting high on marijuana impairs judgment and can lead to regular use that can be especially detrimental to teenagers. Though the available evidence suggests that marijuana causes much less societal harm than alcohol, there's a big fat asterisk in the data when it comes to teenage pot smoking. Indeed, studies show that, like alcohol, marijuana is toxic to the maturing adolescent brain.

An extraordinary research program, under way for more

than forty years, has tracked the health and behavior of everyone born in one calendar year, beginning in 1972, in the town of Dunedin, New Zealand. Over time, the research team has measured, among many other things, the participants' intelligence and marijuana use. With their comprehensive data set—96 percent of the study's 1,004 living participants still remain involved with the research program—the investigators found that people who were using pot regularly by age eighteen saw significant drops in their IQ from the time they were children to the time they were adults, but the same result was not found for people who didn't become regular marijuana users until adulthood (in this study, by age twenty-one). The researchers used statistical techniques to account for the participants' years of education and overall drug and alcohol habits and *still* found that marijuana stole IQ points from teenage users but not adult users.

Further, the investigators tracked the intelligence of participants who lost IQ points as teenagers and found that their IQ scores never recovered, even years after their marijuana habit ended. Sadly, their brain damage was permanent. Specifically, using pot regularly as a teenager has been connected to changes in the brain's structure and the impairment of learning, reasoning, and the ability to focus and sustain attention.

As you read this, you might find yourself thinking, "Now wait a minute, I smoked some pot in my day and I came out just fine." Before you put on your own veil of obedience, allow me to share two things: first, I don't doubt for a minute that you came out great; second, the pot teens smoke today is up to *seven* times more potent than what was available twenty or more years ago. And that's before we consider new forms of concentrated marijuana known as "wax" or "butter" that contain almost pure THC (the active ingredient in marijuana) and are wildly dangerous to prepare or consume. So let's keep this new potency in mind as we think about what regular use of today's highly cultivated marijuana can do to a girl's brain.

Once you get past marijuana, conversations with your daughter about illegal drugs become more straightforward. In general, it's wise to point out to teenagers that the government doesn't outlaw substances because it hates fun or needs to find a way to occupy its drug enforcement officers. Drugs are banned when their molecular properties are known to make them highly addictive and incredibly hazardous. Teens who are contending with adult authority can be so busy trying to break the law without getting caught that they forget about the science behind drug regulations.

The available substances—and their names—change constantly, so you and your daughter may be learning together about what's out there and how it works on the brain and body. When the topic of drugs comes up, hop online with her to look for information on the effects of the substance of the moment: spice (a synthetic marijuana) has been found to cause psychosis and seizures, MDMA (ecstasy) often leads to chronic depression, cocaine can stop your heart, and so on. The opiates, a category that includes heroin as well as prescription drugs such as Vicodin and Percocet, hijack the brain's pleasure centers and cause cravings even years after a person stops using them. While you're surfing online, don't hesitate to point out that we have no way to regulate illegal drugs. We don't know the dosages or even what the substances actually contain. When I have opportunities to talk with girls about drugs I often ask matter-of-factly, "Why would you put the *only* brain you will *ever* have in the hands of some sketchy guy making money as a dealer?"

And take time to address the legal implications of messing with drugs. A drug arrest (with or without a conviction) has the potential to limit educational, travel, or job options indefinitely. Disgracefully, being caught with substances in the United States is especially dangerous for minority teens: though African-American and white teens use pot at similar rates, African Americans are nearly four times more likely to be arrested on marijuana charges.

Teenagers sometimes seek or share prescription drugs for illegal uses. Adolescents who become addicted to opiates often start by experimenting with the prescription painkillers that languish in many people's medicine cabinets. Once addicted, teens move on to heroin, a narcotic that can be easier to obtain than ongoing access to prescription medication. Less disturbing, but still concerning enough, are teens who abuse stimulant medications—drugs that are typically prescribed for the treatment of ADHD. Taking unprescribed stimulants can lead to an energetic, euphoric feeling, but girls, more than boys, report using stimulants not for the high but as a study aid that effectively increases concentration and alertness. ADHD medications are considered to be quite safe when taken as prescribed, but unmonitored use of stimulant medication has been associated with alarming psychiatric symptoms such as disorientation, hallucinations, and paranoia; stimulant misuse can also increase the risk of cardiac complications in people with heart conditions.

On an unseasonably warm evening in early March I sat in my office with Bill, a physician, Wendy, an attorney, and Zooey, their tearful Year 12 daughter. Bill had called me after several orange tablets fell out of Zooey's backpack when he moved it off the kitchen table. Knowing that she wasn't taking any prescriptions, he presumed that she had obtained Adderall from a classmate and confronted her with his suspicions. Zooey confirmed that she was using the stimulant to get through her piles of homework, refused to say who had given her the drug, and insisted that she only took the pills to keep up with the crushing Year 12 workload.

Bill and Wendy had already talked with Zooey about the physical dangers of taking unprescribed medication and wanted to use our appointment to figure out what to do next. In our meeting, Zooey was, in equal measure, genuinely contrite about taking the pills and unsure how she'd stay on top of her work without them. Tears streamed down her face throughout our meeting but she refused the tissues I offered. Instead, she used her fingers to wipe her tears across her cheek as she described the tremendous pressure she felt to stay in the top level at school, especially as the only child of two obviously successful African-American professionals.

Her parents were sympathetic but pointed out that she had always done well and asked why she had started using Adderall now. Zooey walked them through the time demands of her three AP classes, her lengthy swim practice, and their expectation that she join them for a family dinner several nights a week. Her math was correct. It was not actually possible for her to meet all of the demands of her schedule unless she worked at a breakneck speed most nights.

Bill and Wendy were quick to reassure Zooey that they cared much more about her well-being than they did about her grades or college prospects. When they stressed that they truly did not expect Zooey to get straight A's, she bristled and pointed out that she had her own reasons for wanting to attend a top-level college. Wendy expressed warm support for her daughter's ambitions before cutting to the chase: they would not even consider sending her off to college if they had any reason to think she was using unprescribed or illegal drugs. We spent the remainder of the appointment arriving at a solution to get Zooey through the rest of the year. Her parents agreed that she should replace one of her optional courses with a daily study period so that she'd have more time during the school day to get her work done and that, on her busiest nights, they could touch base briefly before she started her homework while eating dinner.

I encouraged them to be in touch if needed and did not hear from them again until I ran into Bill at the grocery store a couple of years later. I never acknowledge clients when I see them out in public (out of respect for their confidentiality), but I'm always happy to catch up if they take the lead. Standing between the broccoli and potatoes, Bill let me know that Zooey had been admitted off the wait list at one of her top-choice universities and made a happy, healthy adjustment to college.

Not all stories end as well as Zooey's. As already discussed, if you have any reason to suspect that your daughter might be experimenting with drugs, don't delay in reaching out to her primary care provider or a trusted mental health professional. Adults, especially those who experimented with drugs without consequence when they were teenagers, sometimes take a casual view of adolescent substance use. I'm not one of those adults because the most devastating outcomes I witness invariably involve drugs.

Substance use robs teens of their futures by making a mess of the day-to-day. Often, things start small. I've seen girls who smoke pot on a regular basis slowly lose ground at school, drift away from their principled friends, or distance themselves from helpful adults. When a girl gets upset about the troubles caused by her drug problem, she often soothes herself by using more, and harder, drugs. From there, you can easily imagine how this terrible story unfolds as her escalating substance use only makes matters worse. Drug and alcohol abuse becomes exponentially more difficult to treat the longer it persists; the sooner girls get help for substance abuse problems, the more likely they are to recover fully.

Sex and Its Risks

Awkward city: that's how most parents feel about talking with our daughters about their sex lives. But you'll find it a lot easier if you remember that everything we already know about addressing delicate subjects with teenagers applies here. Don't expect to have "the talk"; instead, plan on a series of conversations. Capitalize on news your daughter offers about her peers to ask a few questions and make a few (nonjudgmental) points. Focus on the risks that come with intercourse instead of rules you can't enforce anyway. If she has questions about sex, answer only what you've been asked instead of telling her everything you've ever wanted her to know on the subject. And when you have something to say, make sure to look for moments that will be relatively comfortable for your daughter. This may be in a conversation with just one parent (often mom), possibly while riding in the car or out on a walk so nobody has to make eye contact, and maybe when you're five minutes from home and can offer her a quick escape.

With these ground rules in mind, let's consider several sex-talk specific questions: What's the most useful stance for a parent to take in these conversations? How do we effectively communicate our own principles regarding intercourse? And what do we say, when?

In terms of your stance, we already know that girls live up to expectations and live down to them, too. We want our daughters to handle themselves maturely around the risks that come with sex, so we should address them as the thoughtful young women we expect them to be. If you approach the topic from the standpoint of, "Sex is for grown-ups, you're still a kid, stay away from it," your daughter will simply nod at you from behind her veil. Worse, she might be inclined to *prove* her maturity by becoming sexually active.

When I meet with groups of girls to talk about how they'll take good care of themselves when they decide to have sex, I usually say, "The risks that come with sex have almost nothing to do with how old you are. Whenever you decide to have sex, you'll need to manage these risks. I know thirty-five-year-olds who are having sex and not taking care of themselves appropriately. So I don't think they should be having sex." By talking about irresponsible thirty-five-year-olds, I try to make it clear that I am not an adult who has swooped in to give teenagers a lecture. I've come to talk woman-to-women. Should you decide to take this approach with your daughter, I owe you a warning: teenage girls are completely grossed out by the idea of thirty-five-year-olds having sex, and they don't even try to hide their disgust. It's pretty amusing.

Different adults might point to different risks when talking with teens about sex, but here's a short list to consider: unwanted pregnancy (in heterosexual relationships), sexually transmitted infections, a misunderstanding about what sex means to each partner, and the potential for the encounter to go past the point of consent. In my discussions with girls I note that these risks are best managed in mature relationships where the partners are communicating clearly about contraception (for heterosexual sex), their sexual histories and physical health, the impact on the relationship of deciding to have intercourse, and their wishes for what they do—and don't—want to have happen as part of the sexual encounter.

Evidence that girls should be treated as an intelligent audience on the topic of sex comes from one of the most compelling and inventive research studies I've ever encountered. The birth rate for American teenagers had been dropping steadily since 1991, but suddenly, in 2009, the rates fell off a statistical cliff. After declining by about 2.5 percent for many years, teen births fell at a rate of 7.5 percent from 2009 to 2012, and economists and teen pregnancy experts Melissa Kearney of the University of Maryland and Phillip Levine of Wellesley College wanted to know why. To the surprise of many, Kearney and Levine wondered if the reality show *16 and Pregnant* should get the credit.

When *16 and Pregnant* first aired on MTV in June 2009, it was an instant hit. While the show was criticized for glamorizing teen pregnancy, it actually depicted girls from around the country as they faced the realities of childbirth and motherhood: long labors, C-sections, health complications, sleep deprivation, and, for most, strained or collapsing relationships with their baby's father. Kearney and Levine discovered spikes in Google searches and Twitter mentions about the show when new episodes were released, and those spikes were associated with jumps in searches and tweets containing the terms *birth control* and *abortion*. The sample tweets included in the research report range from humorous ("Still not overly impressed with my decision to take a spring class. I've seen better choices on *16 and Pregnant*") to blunt ("Seriously, watching #16andPregnant is birth control itself").

Here's where things get interesting: using television ratings data, Kearney and Levine found that teen births dropped most precipitously in the geographical areas with the largest *16 and Pregnant* audiences. Of note, abortion rates also declined in the same period, suggesting that the birth rate went down due to fewer pregnancies, not more abortions. Ultimately, they concluded that the show accounted for a staggering *one-third* of the overall decline in teen births in the entire United States in the eighteen months after it first aired.

The *16 and Pregnant* study shows that teenage girls aren't dumb. Given a relatively objective picture of the consequences of unprotected sex, girls changed their behavior. To take a page out of MTV's book, have matter-of-fact conversations with your daughter about the dangers that come with sex and how they are best managed. If she says, "So I heard that Amy had sex with a guy she barely knows and got an infection from him," you could say, "Gosh, I'm sorry to hear that. If she could push a reset button, what do you think she'd do differently?" Engage your daughter as an equal and invite her to think with you about how she'll be her own best advocate when she decides to have sex.

You can speak to your daughter as an adult *and* share your own views and values at the same time. For most families, there's no precise measure of when certain sexual behaviors should occur, but if you do have an opinion, share it. You won't necessarily be able to enforce what you recommend, but research shows that teens care about their parents' opinions and change their attitudes in response to their parents' input. If you feel that intercourse (or the behaviors that lead up to it) should only happen in the context of a long-standing relationship, mutual love, adulthood, marriage, or some or all of the above, let your daughter know.

As you have these conversations, know that research consistently suggests that the older girls are when they start having sex, the better they are at talking with their partners about its risks. For example, you might say, "Your dad and I feel that sex is something that should only happen as part of a loving, adult relationship because grown-ups who really care about each other are likely to do the best job of addressing the complications that come with sex." Or, "The age at which you have sex and the nature of the relationship isn't what matters most to us; our expectation is that you won't have sex until you are responsible enough to work with your partner to make sure nothing goes wrong." Or, "Making love is supposed to be a good thing, and it's not much fun if you are worrying about getting pregnant or getting an infection. We hope that you won't have sex until you're ready to manage those risks."

You may have religious views about when sex is, and isn't, appropriate. If so, take advantage of your daughter's teenage ability to think in abstract terms and invite her into conversations about *why* your religion dictates what it does. Again, your best chance for a successful conversation will be to talk to your daughter on the level, not to lay down rules. After you've offered your perspective, settle in for an open discussion of why you'd like for her to share your beliefs.

Finally, when should these conversations happen? There's no universal standard, but here are a few guidelines. Starting these conversations by Year 9 or Year 10, when sex isn't yet prevalent among teenagers in most communities, should give you time to talk about girls in general and keep your daughter from feeling that she's in the hot seat. Many parents address pregnancy, and its prevention, with their young teen before moving on to more complex topics over time (such as preventing sexually transmitted infections, granting consent, what sex means in a relationship, and so on).

As your daughter ages, you may want to make sure she knows how to access contraception, with or without your help. If you have open channels of communication about sex, make good use of them to help her obtain contraception should she need it. If you don't have open channels, an indirect approach can also work. When the topic of pregnancy comes up consider saying, "I wish teen girls knew that they could get contraception without their parents' knowledge. They can buy condoms at any drugstore and they can have private conversations with their doctors. When doctors can't connect girls with free birth control, they can direct them to low or no-cost clinics." The same tactic can work for talking about preventing sexually transmitted infections. Returning to our fictional conversation around Amy (who contracted one) you could chime in with, "Not all girls know that there are inexpensive or free clinics where they can go with their partners to check for infections or get help if they catch one." Should you want to be more specific, look into the options that family planning clinics make available in your community.

Conversations about sex can be driven by discussions of the other risky things girls do. If you have reason to think that drinking plays a role in your daughter's social life, you could note that sex and substances form a dangerous combination. You might say, "When I was growing up, I knew that some girls were getting drunk to have sex. That's not good. First of all, it raises serious questions about any partner who would have sex with someone who's drunk and it meant that the girls weren't able to look out for their own interests and probably weren't comfortable having sex in the first place."

Don't worry that talking with your daughter about intercourse will come across as encouraging or endorsing teenage sex. You may not be in a big rush to have these conversations with your daughter—and she may be in even less of a rush than you are—but teen sex is part of her world. In fact, one survey one carried out across the USA found that a full 71 percent of twelve- to nineteen-year-olds had seen at least one episode of *16 and Pregnant* and this, of course, doesn't account for viewership of its popular *Teen Mom* spin-off shows. Your daughter gets input from many sources on the topic of sex. You should be one of them.

Caring for Herself: When to Worry

Throughout this book we have considered many of the self-destructive things girls sometimes do when trying to numb emotional pain (such as heavy drinking, drug use, self-harm, and other dangerous behaviors). But there are still two categories of concern for us to consider: girls who develop eating disorders and girls who aren't ready to take care of themselves, even when they come to the end of school.

Eating Disorders

Among girls, eating disorders usually start during adolescence, and recovery rates for these disorders are alarmingly low. Nearly a third of people who develop an eating disorder continue to suffer from the disorder for *at least* ten to twenty years after being diagnosed. Further, eating disorders have the highest death rate of all mental health disorders. For roughly every twenty people who develop an eating disorder, one dies from suicide or the physical effects of the eating disorder itself.

Pay attention if your daughter starts dieting, "eating healthy," or limiting her food choices (such as becoming a vegetarian or vegan). Not all girls who diet develop eating disorders, but girls who develop eating disorders *always* start by restricting certain food categories or changing their food habits. Eating disorders progress slowly, and girls will go to great lengths to hide their troubling behavior as it develops. They skip meals or tell adults that they've already eaten or will eat later. They exercise excessively or vomit or abuse laxatives to rid themselves of unwanted calories. And girls will put their food rules ahead of everything else, even refusing to share friends' birthday cakes or go out to restaurants with their parents.

If you have any reason to suspect that your daughter might have an eating disorder or be flirting with one, make an appointment with a doctor who specializes in assessing eating concerns. It is not my aim to inspire fear or paranoia in parents when it comes to their daughter's eating habits. That said, eating disorders are a lot like substance abuse disorders. When caught early, they are often successfully treated. But those that are allowed to take hold over a long period of time become extremely difficult to treat and, as is also true for substance use disorders, many people who recover from a full-blown eating disorder spend the rest of their lives trying not to return to that behavior when they're stressed. Waste no time in seeking help if you think your daughter might be struggling to care for herself when it comes to eating. No one should spend her life at war with her body.

Not Ready to Launch

As a culture we do a surprisingly bad job of drawing a distinction between leaving school and being ready to care for oneself. Too often in my practice I find myself sitting with teenage girls who are reeling from a disastrous departure from home. Despite the fact that they often spent their last few years of school all but announcing that they weren't ready to be on their own (by drinking too much, missing due dates, or failing to care for themselves in other ways) they moved out without much of a plan or headed off to college. By the time we're meeting, things are bad: they're struggling at university because they're sleeping through classes, they're making stupid or dangerous choices and may already have had a run-in with the local police, and so on. Getting themselves back on track isn't easy, and I always leave these meetings wishing that the young woman hadn't been sent out into the world before she was ready.

All of these examples rushed to mind when I got a call at home one January evening from Mary, a mom in my neighborhood, who was seeking advice about her daughter, who used to babysit for my two girls. After a few pleasantries, Mary told me that Jeanie was now in her final year at school and that the last few years had been rough ones. I had fallen out of touch when Jeanie moved on from babysitting, but I was fond of her and glad to try to be of help. Mary explained that Jeanie had started to sneak around with some guys from a nearby college during Year 11. They only found out what was going on when Jeanie came to them with fears about a pregnancy that turned out, luckily, to be a false alarm. In the wake of that scare, Jeanie's parents required her to cut off contact with the college boys and kept a close watch on her socializing.

Matters seemed to settle down until midway through Year 12, when Mary found pot in Jeanie's bureau. When confronted, Jeanie insisted that she was holding it for a friend, but a drug test run by the family pediatrician revealed that she was not only smoking pot but had tried cocaine as well. Mary and her husband promptly enrolled their daughter in a drug counseling program that included routine urine tests. For several months, the results had been coming back clean.

Mary was calling now because in the past week Jeanie had tested positive for marijuana and they had received a notice from school that she was missing a handful of critical assignments. Mary explained, "Here's the thing we don't understand: even with all this going on, Jeanie is talking about heading off to college in Cincinnati like it's no big deal. Should we let her go and just cross our fingers, or should we make an issue of it?"

I strongly encouraged Mary to make an issue of it. We agreed they would let Jeanie know that college wouldn't be an option for the autumn if she tested positive for drugs again or if she got lower than a C in any of her classes. Mary and her husband worried that Jeanie might feel they were too much in her business, given that she had been drug-free for so long and the academic problems were new ones. Over the phone I said, "If Jeanie complains that you are being intrusive, feel free to say, 'We want nothing more than to be out of your business, but to do that, we need to know that you're in control of things. We're not doing our job as parents if you aren't taking care of yourself and we don't step in. Show us that you can stay away from drugs and manage your schoolwork and we'll gladly back off.'"

Mary tried this approach and called me again in July to let me know how the latest problems had played out. Jeanie finished school with decent grades but tested positive for marijuana and also MDMA (ecstasy) in June. The family forfeited their university deposit and, despite serious opposition from Jeanie, insisted that she stay home to work in the family business instead of leaving for college in the autumn. Jeanie would use the year to pay back the lost deposit, enroll in a rigorous drug treatment program, and demonstrate that she could be trusted to look after herself. I commended Mary for taking a difficult stance that kept her daughter's college options open. There was no doubt in my mind that this was a much better outcome than sending Jeanie off to university before she was ready to take ownership of the work of caring for herself.

Conclusion

As I'm sure you've figured out, the title of this book has more than one meaning. Most obviously, we've taken adolescent development—the snarl of friction and emotion that parents warn one another about—and organized it into seven strands. We've made plain what girls have to do to become adults and gained insight into their sometimes confusing and frustrating behavior. Just appreciating how *many* transitions are involved in moving from childhood to adulthood gives us new respect for what our daughters are going through and clarifies why the teenage years can be taxing for everyone involved.

Less obviously, but perhaps more important, I'm hopeful that this book will help parents untangle themselves from the emotional knots we get caught in with our teenage daughters. We all have intense reactions as our girls move through adolescence, and when they treat us like dirt, make home life chaotic, fight about rules, and do the stupid thing we *just told them* not to do, it's easy to take their behavior personally. Given that so much about being a teenager involves pulling parents in and pushing them away, I understand why we sometimes talk about adolescence as though it is punishment girls inflict upon their parents, when really it's a stressful developmental phase that girls are trying to navigate.

In other words, adolescence isn't about us. Well, except for the part about crazy spots, which is *totally* about us. But even there, even when we need to own our shortcomings as people and parents, we do so in the service of pointing our daughters away from us and into the world. We claim our crazy spots to say, "Yes, I'm not everything you are hoping I'll be, but don't let that stop you or even slow you down. There's a world out there for you to tackle; try not to let my faults get in your way."

When we're not taking our daughters' teenage behavior personally and we help them to stop taking us so personally, we're better parents. We can admire our daughters' successes as evidence of their terrific growth (not our goodness), and we can see their trials as proof that they are working to master the developmental strands we now know well. Untangled, separate but completely present, we have a better feel for when we should let our daughters struggle along and when we owe it to them to offer help.

Raising a young woman will be one of the most vexing, delightful, exhausting, and fulfilling things you will ever do. Sometimes all on the same day. The job is hard enough even under the best conditions, and anyone doing a hard job deserves support. When we get that support, when we understand the developmental tour de force that is adolescence, we can truly enjoy and empower our girls.

Acknowledgments

I'M THE MOST FORTUNATE PERSON I KNOW, SUPPORTED ON MORE sides than I can number. A full accounting of those to whom I am indebted would fill a book of its own; here's the short list.

Forget the convention among writers of describing one's team in hyperbolic terms and trust me when I tell you that Gail Ross, my agent, and Susanna Porter, my editor, are twin literary goddesses. I still do not understand how I have been lucky enough to work with professionals of their caliber in my first foray into writing for a broad audience.

This book and the thinking behind it have also benefited from feedback provided by wise readers at every step of the way: Kate Gjaja, Mark Joseph, Sarah McKenzie, Traci Onders, Emily Patton, Davida Pines, Barbara Richter, Diana Simeon, Lisa Spengler, Kim Thompson, Amy Weisser, and Sarah Wilson. And this project would not have been possible without the ingenious research assistance provided by Amanda Block.

I am grateful every working hour for the incredible training opportunities provided to me at the Yale Child Study Center, the University of Michigan Department of Psychology, and the Hanna Perkins Center. I hope to repay my extraordinary teachers by sharing with others some part of what they so masterfully taught me.

In the day-to-day, I enjoy the boundless support of professional colleagues who are also my dear friends—Tori Cordiano, Maureen Kreick, Debby Paris, and Terry Tobias—and the unparalleled faculty and staff at Laurel School, led by our inspired Head of School, Ann V. Klotz. I credit the best of my thinking and writing to Anne Curzan, my closest friend. I would not be where I am without the steady support of my incredible parents and D, my true partner, and E and C, our girls—I could not love you more.

This book communicates my own ideas and also summarizes excellent work done by others in my field. I have aimed to acknowledge every scholar whose work has developed or shaped my understanding of adolescent girls; any errors or omissions in this book are mine alone.

I'm not the first psychologist to observe that to do our work is the closest a person can come to experiencing multiple lives in a single lifetime. I reserve my deepest gratitude for the girls and families who have so enriched my days by courageously sharing some of the most personal parts of their lives with me.

Notes

Epigraph

vii **While an adolescent remains inconsistent:** Freud, A. (1958). Adolescence. *The Psychoanalytic Study of the Child* 13, 255–78, p. 276.

Introduction

xiv **tend to be most salient:** For example, see Arnett, J. J. (1999). Adolescent storm and stress, reconsidered. *American Psychologist* 54 (5), 317–26. Dr. Arnett discusses research on p. 319, noting, "Different elements of storm and stress have different peaks—conflict with parents in early adolescence (Paikoff & Brooks-Gunn, 1991), mood disruptions in mid-adolescence (Petersen et al., 1993), and risk behavior in late adolescence and emerging adulthood (Arnett, 1992, 1999)."

xv **The concept of developmental strands:** Freud, A. (1965). *Normality and Pathology in Childhood: Assessments of development.* New York: International Universities Press. Ms. Freud referred to her strands as "developmental lines."

xv **Erik Erikson articulated a developmental model:** Erikson, E. H. (1950). *Childhood and Society.* New York: Norton.

Chapter One: Parting with Childhood

6 **Anna Freud noted that the typical:** Freud, A. (1958). Adolescence. *The Psychoanalytic Study of the Child* 13, 255–78, p. 269.

10 **research study that examined how much:** Hawk, S. T., Hale, W. W., Raaijmakers, Q. A. W., and Meeus, W. (2008). Adolescents' perceptions of privacy invasion and reaction to parental solicitation and control. *Journal of Early Adolescence* 28 (4), 583–608.

12 **You've probably heard about research:** While some experts suggest that family dinner may not be the silver bullet it has been trumped up to be, the balance of research shows that it's good for girls when their parents find regular times to be with them. See Musick, K., and Meier, A. (2012). Assessing causality and persistence in associations between family dinner and adolescent well-being. *Journal of Marriage and Family* 74 (3), 476–93.

13 **they *still* found that eating together:** Luthar, S. S., and Latendresse, S. J. (2005). Children of the affluent: Challenges to well-being. *Current Directions in Psychological Science* 14 (1), 49–53.

18 **the words of my wise colleague:** R. Spencer, personal communication, October 24, 2013.

26 **move from having you:** Furman, E. (1992). *Toddlers and Their Mothers*. Madison, CT: International Universities Press.

29 **an all-too-public mutiny:** Freud, S. (1917, 1966). Some thoughts on development and regression—aetiology. *Introductory Lectures in Psychoanalysis*. New York: W. W. Norton & Company, Inc., 423–24.

32 **By age seven, breast buds appear:** Biro, F. M., Galvez, M. P., Greenspan, L. C., et al. (2010). Pubertal assessment method and baseline characteristics in a mixed longitudinal study of girls. *Pediatrics* 126 (3), e583–90.

32 **girls first start menstruating:** Bellis, M. A., Downing, J., and Ashton, J. R. (2006). Trends in puberty and their public health consequences. *Journal of Epidemiological and Community Health* 60 (11), 910–11. African-American girls go through puberty roughly a year before Caucasian girls: Walvoord, E. C. (2010). The timing of puberty: Is it changing? Does it matter? *Journal of Adolescent Health* 47 (5), 433–39.

32 **fascinating book *The New Puberty*:** Greenspan, L., and Deardorff, J. (2014). *The New Puberty*. New York: Rodale.

36 **Girls also use online environments:** Davis, K. (2013). Young people's digital lives: The impact of interpersonal relationships and digital media use on adolescents' sense of identity. *Computers in Human Behavior* 29 (6), 2281–93.

40 **"happy families are all alike":** Tolstoy, L. (1876, 1981). *Anna Karenina.* (J. Carmichael, trans.). New York: Bantam, p. 1.

41 **trouble with relationships, substances:** Allen, J. P., Schad, M. M., Oudekerk, B., and Chango, J. (2014). What ever happened to the "cool" kids? Long-term sequelae of early adolescent pseudomature behavior. *Child Development* 85 (5), 1866–80.

41 **lack a close relationship:** Lammers, C., Ireland, M., Resnick, M., and Blum, R. (2000). Influences on adolescents' decision to postpone onset of sexual intercourse: A survival analysis of virginity among youths aged 13 to 18 years. *Journal of Adolescent Health* 26 (1), 42–48; Tucker, J. S., Orlando, M., and Ellickson, P. L. (2003). Patterns and correlates of binge drinking trajectories from early adolescence to young adulthood. *Health Psychology* 22 (1), 79–87; Schinke, S. P., Fang, L., and Cole, K. C. A. (2008). Substance use among early adolescent girls: Risk and protective factors. *Journal of Adolescent Health* 43 (2), 191–94.

43 **parent-child relationship can be strained:** See, for example, Dodge, K. A., Pettit, G. S., and Bates, J. E. (1994). Socilization mediators of the relation between socioeconomic status and child conduct problems. *Child Development* 65 (2), 649–65.

43 **Suniya Luthar, the prolific psychologist:** Luthar, S. S., and Latendresse, S. J. (2005). Comparable "risks" at the socioeconomic status extremes: Preadolescents' perceptions of parenting. *Development and Psychopathology* 17 (1), 207–30, p. 207.

43 **parental absence seems to contribute:** Luthar, S. S., and D'Avanzo, K. (1999). Contextual factors in substance use: A study of suburban and inner-city adolescents. *Developmental Psychopathology* 11 (4), 845–67.

43 **Psychologist Monique Ward:** Ward, M. L., and Friedman, K. (2006). Using TV as a guide: Associations between television viewing and adolescents' sexual attitudes and behavior. *Journal of Research on Adolescence* 16 (1), 133–56.

Chapter Two: Joining a New Tribe

51 **two different kinds of peer popularity:** Cillessen, A. H. N., and Rose, A. J. (2005). Understanding popularity in the peer system. *Current Directions in Psychological Science* 14 (2), 102–5.

51 **girls are described by their classmates:** Cillessen, A. H. N., and Mayeux, L. (2004). Sociometric status and peer group behavior: Previous findings and current directions. In J. B. Kupersmidt and K. A. Dodge (eds.), *Children's Peer Relations*. Washington, DC: American Psychological Association, 3–36.

51 **They are amiable and faithful:** Parkhurst, J. T., and Hopmeyer, A. (1998). Sociometric popularity and peer-perceived popularity: Two distinct dimensions of peer status. *The Journal of Early Adolescence* 18 (2), 125–44.

52 **girls are more likely to use potent:** Rose, A. J., Swenson, L. P., and Waller, E. M. (2004). Overt and relational aggression and perceived popularity: Developmental differences in concurrent and prospective relations. *Developmental Psychology* 40 (3), 378–87.

52 **girls who continue to be nasty:** de Bruyn, E. H., and Cillessen, A. H. N. (2006). Popularity in early adolescence: Prosocial and antisocial subtypes. *Journal of Adolescent Research* 21 (6), 1–21.

52 **old *New Yorker* cartoon:** Mankoff, R. (November 16, 1992). One politician talking to another. *The New Yorker*.

53 **having a single terrific friend:** Waldrip, A. M., Malcolm, K. T., and Jensen-Campbell, L. A. (2008). With a little help from your friends: The importance of high-quality friendships on early adolescent development. *Social Development* 17 (4), 832–52. The research on this topic is complex, and there is certainly evidence that having a large social network improves the likelihood of having strong dyadic (one-on-one) friendships (see, for example, Nangle, D. W., Erdley, C. A., Newman, J. E., et al. [2003]. Popularity, friendship quantity, and friendship quality: Interactive influences on children's loneliness and depression. *Journal of Clinical Child and Adolescent Psychology* 32 [4], 546–55). However, Waldrip et al. (2008), p. 847, found that "an adolescent who has at least one friend who offers support, protection, and intimacy is less likely to display problems after controlling for other important relationships as

well as the number of friends. Based on these findings, it appears that friendship quality is indeed a unique predictor of an adolescent's adjustment."

53 **what cultural anthropologists call "sustainable routines":** Weisner, T. S. (1998). Human development, child well-being, and the cultural project of development. In D. Sharma and K. Fisher (eds.), *Socioemotional Development Across Cultures. New Directions in Child Development*, vol. 81. San Francisco: Jossey-Bass, 69–85.

58 **slang as "the people's poetry":** Adams, M. (2009). *Slang: The People's Poetry.* New York: Oxford University Press.

61 **phenomenon in a research lab:** Gardner, M., and Steinberg, L. (2005). Peer influence on risk taking, risk preference, and risky decision making in adolescence and adulthood: An experimental study. *Developmental Psychology* 41 (4), 625–35.

62 **throw caution to the wind:** Studies like Gardner and Steinberg's help explain the success of graduated driver licensing laws in reducing fatal car accidents among young adolescents. See, for example, Masten, S. V., Foss, R. D., and Marshall, S. W. (2011). Graduated driver licensing and fatal crashes involving sixteen- to nineteen-year-old drivers. *Journal of the American Medical Association* 306 (10), 1098–103.

62 **experience social acceptance as highly rewarding:** Steinberg, L. (2008). A social neuroscience perspective on adolescent risk-taking. *Developmental Review* 28 (1), 78–106.

62 **"more may also be riskier":** Steinberg (2008), p. 92.

68 **we developed a successful program:** Damour, L. K., Cordiano, T. S., and Anderson-Fye, E. P. (2014). My sister's keeper: Identifying eating pathology through peer networks. *Eating Disorders* 23 (1), 76–88.

70 **"They're addicted to each other":** Costanza, K. (March 11, 2014). "Teens and Social Media? 'It's Complicated.'" Retrieved from http://remakelearning .org/blog/2014/03/11/teens-and-social-media-its-complicated/

71 **reflects what happens in real life:** Selfhout, M. H. W., Branje, S. J. T., Delsing, M., et al. (2009). Different types of Internet use, depression, and social anxiety: The role of perceived friendship quality. *Journal of Adolescence* 32 (4), 819–33.

71 **also have trouble getting along online:** Valkenburg, P. M., and Peter, J. (2011). Online communication among adolescents: An integrated

model of its attraction, opportunities, and risks. *Journal of Adolescent Health* 48 (2), 121–27.

72 **healthy, face-to-face relationships:** Pea, R., Nass, C., Meheula, L., et al. (2012). Media use, face-to-face communication, media multitasking, and social well-being among 8- to 12-year-old girls. *Developmental Psychology* 48 (2), 327–36.

75 **harm of being socially isolated:** Hall-Lande, J. A., Eisenberg, M. E., Christenson, S. L., and Neumark-Sztainer, D. (2007). Social isolation, psychological health, and protective factors in adolescence. *Adolescence* 42 (166), 265–86.

75 **individuals best equipped to prevent it:** Black, S. (2003). An ongoing evaluation of the bullying prevention program in Philadelphia schools: Student survey and student observation data. Paper presented at Centers for Disease Control's Safety in Numbers Conference, Atlanta, GA.

75 **ignore or avoid their isolated peers:** Evans, C., and Eder, D. (1993). "No exit": Processes of social isolation in the middle school. *Journal of Contemporary Ethnography* 22 (2), 139–70.

78 **clear picture of some bullying situations:** Fekkes, M., Pijpers, F. I. M., and Verloove-Vanhorick, S. P. (2004). Bullying: Who does what, when, and where? Involvement of children, teachers and parents in bullying. *Health Education Research* 20 (1), 81–91; Wang, J., Iannotti, R. J., and Nansel, T. R. (2009). School bullying among US adolescents: Physical, verbal, relational, and cyber. *Journal of Adolescent Health* 45 (4), 386–75.

78 **brain's left and right hemispheres:** Copeland, W. E., Wolke, D., Angold, A., and Costello, E. J. (2013). Adult psychiatric outcomes of bullying and being bullied by peers in childhood and adolescence. *JAMA Psychiatry* 70 (4), 419–26; Teicher, M. H., Samson, J. A., Sheu, Y., et al. (2010). Hurtful Words: Exposure to peer verbal aggression is associated with elevated psychiatric symptom scores and corpus callosum abnormalities. *American Journal of Psychiatry* 167 (12), 1464–71.

80 **Experts on bullying counsel against:** Olweus, D. (1993). *Bullying at School: What we know and what we can do.* Boston, MA: Blackwell.

80 **"when they are on the outside":** T. Tobias, personal communication, July 2009.

81 **alleviate boredom in their group:** Merrell, K. W., Buchanan, R., and Tran, O. K. (2006). Relational aggression in children and adolescents:

A review with implications for school settings. *Psychology in the Schools* 43 (3), 345–60, p. 348.

81 **drug abuse, and antisocial behavior:** See, for example, Copeland, W. E., Wolke, D., Angold, A., and Costello, E. J. (2013). Adult psychiatric outcomes of bullying and being bullied by peers in childhood and adolescence. *JAMA Psychiatry* 70 (4), 419–26.

Chapter Three: Harnessing Emotions

83 **"that's just a normal teenager":** A helpful description of high rates of adolescent false positives on the Rorschach Schizophrenia Index can be found in Smith, S. R., Baity, M. R., Knowles, E. S., and Hilsenroth, M. J. (2001). Assessment of disordered thinking in children and adolescents: The Rorschach Perceptual-Thinking Index. *Journal of Personality Assessment* 77 (3), 447–63.

83 **came across this account of adolescence:** Freud, A. (1958). Adolescence. *The Psychoanalytic Study of the Child* 13, 255–78, p. 276. Italics added.

84 **brain remodels dramatically:** Wenar, C., and Kerig, P. (2006). *Developmental Psychopathology.* 5th ed. Boston, MA: McGraw-Hill.

85 **Updates to the limbic system:** Casey, B. J., Jones, R. M., and Hare. T. A. (2008). The adolescent brain. *Annals of the New York Academy of Sciences* 1124 (1), 111–26.

85 **functional magnetic resonance imaging:** Hare, T. A., Tottenham, N., Galvan, A., et al. (2008). Biological substrates of emotional reactivity and regulation in adolescence during an emotional go-nogo task. *Biological Psychiatry* 63 (10), 927–34.

85 **new period of emotional upheaval:** Siegal, D. J. (2013). *Brainstorm: The power and purpose of the teenage brain.* New York: Penguin Group.

85 **studies find that hormones respond:** Steinberg, L., and Morris, A. S. (2001). Adolescent development. *Annual Review of Psychology* 53, 83–110; Brooks-Gunn, J., Graber, J. A., and Paikoff, R. L. (1994). Studying links between hormones and negative affect: Models and measures. *Journal of Research on Adolescence* 4 (4), 469–86. Interestingly, a recent study (Marceau, K., Dorn, L. D., and Susman, E. J. [2012]. Stress and puberty-related hormone reactivity, negative emotionality, and parent-

adolescent relationships. *Psychoneuronendocrinology* 37 [8], 1286–98) found that increases in hormonal reactivity to stress lead to "negative emotionality and family problems during early adolescence in boys *but not girls*" (italics added). Even here the evidence suggests that hormonal reactivity (a spike in pubertal hormones in response to stress) might be shaped by early environmental stressors (such as traumatic events). In other words, the relationships among pubertal hormones, adolescent moodiness, early life events, and contemporaneous events are highly complex and not easily boiled down to "hormones acting up," despite popular perception.

86 **"You must work with the assumption":** D. Barrett, personal communication, September 2002.

87 **great neurologist Oliver Sacks:** Sacks, O. (1998). *The Man Who Mistook His Wife for a Hat.* New York: Touchstone.

89 **harmless and creative research studies:** Baumeister, R. F., Bratslavsky, E., Muraven, M., and Tice, D. M. (1998). Ego depletion: Is the active self a limited resource? *Journal of Personality and Social Psychology* 74 (5), 1252–65.

102 **girls discuss while boys distract:** Hampel, P., and Petermann, F. (2006). Perceived stress, coping, and adjustment in adolescents. *Journal of Adolescent Health* 38 (4), 409–15.

103 **Rumination can lead to depression:** Rood, L., Roelofs, J., Bogels, S. M., and Nolen-Hoeksema, S. (2009). The influence of emotion-focused rumination and distraction on depressive symptoms in non-clinical youth: A meta-analytic review. *Clinical Psychology Review* 29 (7), 607–16; Tompkins, T. L., Hockett, A. R., Abraibesh, N., and Witt, J. L. (2011). A closer look at co-rumination: Gender, coping, peer functioning and internalizing/externalizing problems. *Journal of Adolescence* 34 (5), 801–11.

103 **scholars who study boys:** There's a spirited scholarly debate about the emotional lives of boys. To oversimplify, some scholars (e.g., psychologist William Pollack) argue that boys learn to follow an emotion-blind "boy code" and thus, per psychologists Dan Kindlon and Michael Thompson, become "emotionally illiterate" (Kindlon, D., and Thompson, M. [2000]. *Raising Cain: Protecting the emotional lives of boys.* New York: Ballantine Books, 197) while others (e.g., psychologists Niobe Way and Margarita Azmitia) argue that boys are as emotionally attuned as girls through early and middle adolescence and don't become

"less emotionally articulate" until late adolescence (Way, N. [2011]. *Deep Secrets: Boys' friendships and the crisis of connection.* Cambridge, MA: Harvard University Press, 18). Agreement exists that boys are given less cultural support for talking about their feelings than girls are, and that boys come to equate emotionality with homosexuality or femininity, but not in a good way.

103 **psychologists Dan Kindlon and Michael Thompson:** Kindlon and Thompson (2000).

105 **Rumination isn't the only emotional challenge:** Rose, A. J., and Rudolph, K. D. (2006). A review of the sex differences in peer relationship processes: Potential trade-offs for the emotional and behavioral development of boys and girls. *Psychological Bulletin* 132 (1), 98–131.

111 **too much time on their hands:** Hinduja, S., and Patchin, J. W. (2008). Cyberbullying: An exploratory analysis of factors related to offending and victimization. *Deviant Behavior* 28 (2), 129–56.

115 **more likely to occur in girls:** Thapar, A., Collishaw, S., Pine, D. S., and Thapar, A. K. (2012). Depression in adolescence. *Lancet* 379 (9820), 1056–67.

116 **Bipolar disorders—mood disorders that involve:** Blader, J. C., and Carlson, G. A. (2007). Increased rates of bipolar disorder diagnoses among U.S. child, adolescent, and adult inpatients, 1996–2004. *Biological Psychiatry* 62 (2), 107–14.

117 **teenagers may suffer from full-blown anxiety:** Costello, E. J., Mustillo, S., Erkanli, A., et al. (2003). Prevalence and development of psychiatric disorders in childhood and adolescence. *Archives of General Psychiatry* 60 (8), 837–44.

117 **moods are grounds for concern:** Freud, A. (1965). *Normality and Pathology in Childhood: Assessments of development.* New York: International Universities Press, 124.

Chapter Four: Contending with Adult Authority

121 **Jean Piaget, a towering figure:** Inhelder, B., and Piaget, J. (1958). *The Growth of Logical Thinking from Childhood to Adolescence: An essay on the construction of formal operational structures.* New York: Basic Books.

123 **When your daughter was a toddler:** A brilliant, detailed description of this dynamic can be found at Fraiberg, S. H. (1959). *The Magic Years.* New York: Charles Scribner's Sons, 64–65.

128 **one of my clinical colleagues commented:** T. Barrett, personal communication, November 2001.

128 **research has long established that teens:** Lamborn, S. D., Mounts, N. S., Steinberg, L., and Dornbusch, S. M. (1991). Patterns of competence and adjustment among adolescents from authoritative, authoritarian, indulgent, and neglectful families. *Child Development* 62 (5), 1049–65.

131 **Statistically, people take more risks:** Steinberg, L., Albert, D., Cauffman, E., et al. (2008). Age differences in sensation seeking and impulsivity as indexed by behavior and self-report: Evidence for a dual systems model. *Developmental Psychology* 44 (6), 1764–78.

131 **Yet contrary to popular belief:** Steinberg, L. (2007). Risk taking in adolescence: New perspectives from brain and behavioral science. *Current Directions in Psychological Science* 16 (2), 55–59.

131 **can't calculate risks:** For a summary of the cognitive processes that influence adolescent judgment in risky situations, see Albert, D., and Steinberg, L. (2011). Judgment and decision making in adolescence. *Journal of Research on Adolescence* 21 (1), 211–24.

135 **A long-standing area of study:** Steinberg, L. (2001). We know some things: Adolescent-parent relationships in retrospect and prospect. *Journal of Research on Adolescence* 11 (1), 1–19.

136 **Dr. Fonagy and his research team:** Fonagy and his team use the term *mentalizing,* not *emotional intelligence,* to describe their area of study. I've gone with *emotional intelligence* because I feel it's a more accessible term for a lay audience. The sprawling work done by Fonagy's team is summarized elegantly in the book *Affect Regulation, Mentalization, and the Development of the Self* (Fonagy, P., Gergely, G., Jurist, E. L., and Target, M. [2002]. New York: Other Press).

136 **"seeing ourselves from the outside":** Asen, E., and Fonagy, P. (2012). Mentalization-based therapeutic interventions for families. *Journal of Family Therapy* 34 (4), 347–70, p. 347.

136 **Almost everyone comes wired:** I say "almost" here because disorders on the autism spectrum are characterized, in part, by what seems to be the innate absence of emotional intelligence.

136 **Research demonstrates that emotional intelligence:** Gallagher, H. L., and Frith, C. D. (2003). Functional imaging of "theory of mind." *Trends in Cognitive Science* 7 (2), 77–82; Fine, C., Lumsden, J., and Blair, R. J. (2001). Dissociation between "theory of mind" and executive functions in a patient with early left amygdala damage. *Brain* 124 (2), 287–98.

138 **we build emotional intelligence in teens:** See, for example, Sharp, C., Ha, C., Carbone, C., et al. (2013). Hypermentalizing in adolescent inpatients: Treatment effects and association with borderline traits. *Journal of Personality Disorders* 27 (1), 3–18.

140 **in the context of loving relationships:** I'm referring here to the activation of the attachment system, which has been demonstrated, empirically, to calm negative emotions. (See Sroufe, L. A. [1996]. *Emotional development: The organization of emotional life in the early years.* New York: Cambridge University Press.) Also relevant is Fonagy's highly plausible conjecture that people who have marked difficulties with mentalization as adolescents or adults may arrive at that place as a function of early childhood trauma that overwhelmed the child and precluded the possibility of reflecting on internal mental states.

154 **yelling at teenagers actually exacerbates:** Wang, M. T., and Kenny, S. (2014). Longitudinal links between fathers' and mothers' harsh verbal discipline and adolescents' conduct problems and depressive symptoms. *Child Development* 85 (3), 908–23.

158 **Research has long demonstrated that boys:** Zahn-Waxler, C., Crick, N. R., Shirtcliff, E. A., and Woods, K. E. (2006). The origins and development of psychopathology in females and males. In D. Cicchetti and D. J. Cohen (eds.), *Developmental Psychopathology, Volume 1: Theory and Method.* Hoboken, NJ: John Wiley & Sons, Inc., 76–138.

159 **Brett Laursen and W. Andrew Collins:** Laursen, B., and Collins, W. A. (2009). Parent-child relationships during adolescence. In R. Lerner and L. Steinberg (eds.), *Handbook of Adolescent Psychology.* 3rd ed., vol. 2. New York: Wiley, 3–42, p. 21.

160 **most teenagers get along:** See, for example, Steinberg (2001).

159 **A fascinating longitudinal research study:** Jacobs, J. E., Chin, C. S., and Shaver, K. (2005). Longitudinal links between perceptions of adolescence and the social beliefs of adolescents: Are parents' stereotypes

related to beliefs held about and by their children? *Journal of Youth and Adolescence* 34 (2), 61–72.

160 **a disheartening line of research:** Burke, J. D., Hipwell, A. E., and Loeber, R. (2010). Dimensions of oppositional defiant disorder as predictors of depression and conduct disorder in preadolescent girls. *Journal of the American Academy of Child and Adolescent Psychiatry* 49 (5), 484–92; Loeber, R., Burke, J. D., Lahey, B. B., et al. (2000). Oppositional defiant and conduct disorder: A review of the past 10 years, part 1. *Journal of the American Academy of Child and Adolescent Psychiatry* 39 (12), 1468–84.

161 **storm and stress:** The phrase *storm and stress* was coined to describe adolescence by G. Stanley Hall, one of the founding fathers of the field of psychology. See Hall, G. S. (1904). *Adolescence: Its psychology and its relation to physiology, anthropology, sociology, sex, crime, religion, and education.* Vols. 1 and 2. Englewood Cliffs, NJ: Prentice Hall. It is worth noting that psychologist Jeffrey Arnett has documented that, as discussed throughout this book, adolescence involves an increase in "conflict with parents, mood disruptions, and risk behavior," yet he notes that "research also indicates that there are substantial individual differences in these difficulties and that storm and stress is by no means universal and inevitable." Arnett, J. J. (1999). Adolescent storm and stress, reconsidered. *American Psychologist* 54 (5), 317–26, p. 323.

Chapter Five: Planning for the Future

165 **Research consistently finds that girls:** Klettke, B., Hallford, D. J., and Mellor, D. J. (2014). Sexting prevalence and correlates: A systematic literature review. *Clinical Psychology Review* 43 (1), 44–53.

169 **They get better grades than boys:** Freeman, C. E. (2004). *Trends in Educational Equity of Girls and Women: 2004* (NCES 2005-16). U.S. Department of Education, National Center for Education Statistics. Washington, DC: U.S. Government Printing Office; Kena, G., Aud, S., Johnson, F., et al. (2014). *The Condition of Education 2014* (NCES 2014-083). U.S. Department of Education, National Center for Education Statistics. Washington, DC: U.S. Government Printing Office; Cornwell, C.,

Mustard, D. B., and Van Parys, J. (2013). Noncognitive skills and the gender disparities in test scores and teacher assessments: Evidence from primary school. *Journal of Human Resources* 48 (1), 236–64.

170 **develop more rapidly in girls:** Else-Quest, N. M., Hyde, J. S., Goldsmith, H. H., and Van Hulle, C. A. (2006). Gender differences in temperament: A meta-analysis. *Psychological Bulletin* 132 (1), 33–72.

172 *The Princess Bride:* Reiner, R. (1987). *The Princess Bride.* Twentieth Century Fox Film Corp.

180 **Girls, more than boys, feel threatened:** Cassady, J. C., and Johnson, R. E. (2002). Cognitive test anxiety and academic performance. *Contemporary Educational Psychology* 27 (2), 270–95; Chapell, M. S., Blanding, Z., Silverstein, M. E., et al. (2005). Test anxiety and academic performance in undergraduate and graduate students. *Journal of Educational Psychology* 97 (2), 268–74.

181 **moderate levels of anxiety:** See, for example, Keeley, J., Zayac, R., and Correia, C. (2008). Curvilinear relationships between statistics anxiety and performance among undergraduate students: Evidence for optimal anxiety. *Statistics Education Research Journal* 7 (1), 4–15.

181 **research finds that highlighting:** Dunlosky, J., Rawson, K. A., Marsh, E. J., et al. (2013). Improving students' learning with effective learning techniques: Promising directions from cognitive and educational psychology. *Psychological Science in the Public Interest* 14 (1), 4–58.

182 **they learn the material more thoroughly:** See, for example, Larsen, D. P., Butler, A. C., and Roediger, H. L. (2013). Comparative effects of test-enhanced learning and self-explanation on long-term retention. *Medical Education* 47 (7), 674–82.

182 **the phenomenon of *stereotype threat*:** Steele, C. M., and Aronson, J. (1995). Stereotype threat and the intellectual test performance of African Americans. *Journal of Personality and Social Psychology* 69 (5), 797–811.

182 **girls *most* eager to disprove:** Schmader, T. (2002). Gender identification moderates stereotype threat effects on women's math performance. *Journal of Experimental Social Psychology* 38 (2), 194–201.

183 **mere mention of a gendered pattern:** Spencer, S. J., Steele, C. M., and Quinn, D. M. (1999). Stereotype threat and women's math performance. *Journal of Experimental Psychology* 35 (1), 4–28.

184 **Examples of tough but kind girls:** Bancroft, T., and Cook, B. (1998). *Mulan.* Buena Vista Pictures; Ross, G. (2012). *The Hunger Games.* Lionsgate.

190 **derailed by disappointment:** Beyer, S., and Bowden, E. M. (1997). Gender differences in self-perceptions: Convergent evidence from three measures of accuracy and bias. *Personality and Social Psychology Bulletin* 23 (2), 157–72.

191 **Her research clearly demonstrates:** Henderson, V., and Dweck, C. S. (1990). Adolescence and achievement. In S. S. Feldman and G. R. Elliott (eds.) (1991). *At the Threshold: The developing adolescent.* Cambridge, MA: Harvard University Press, 197–216.

193 **terrific new research on** *grit:* Duckworth, A. L., Peterson, C., Matthews, M. D. et al. (2007). Grit: Perseverance and passion for long-term goals. *Journal of Personality and Social Psychology* 92 (6), 1087–101.

194 **As Anna Freud noted:** Freud, A. (1966). *The Ego and Mechanisms of Defense.* Madison, CT: International Universities Press, Inc., p. 168.

194 **one of my psychological colleagues:** M. McConville, personal communication, January 2001.

195 **experience school as intensely stressful:** Undheim, A. M., and Sund, A. M. (2005). School factors and the emergence of depressive symptoms among young Norwegian adolescents. *European Child and Adolescent Psychiatry* 14 (8), 446–53; Verboom, C. E., Sijtsema, J. J., Verhulst, F. C., et al. (2014). Longitudinal associations between depressive problems, academic performance, and social functioning in adolescent boys and girls. *Developmental Psychology* 50 (1), 247–57; Wiklund, M., Malmgren-Olsson, E., Ohman, A., et al. (2012). Subjective health complaints in older adolescents are related to perceived stress, anxiety and gender—a cross-sectional school study in Northern Sweden. *BMC Public Health* 12 (993), 1–13.

Chapter Six: Entering the Romantic World

201 **Nationally, 3 percent of girls:** Kann, L., Kinchen, S., and Shanklin, S., et al. (2014). Youth Risk Behavior Surveillance—United States, 2013. *MMWR Surveillance Summaries* 63 (4), 1–178.

201 **Psychologists Michelle Fine:** See, for example, Fine, M., and McClelland, S. I. (2006). Sexuality education and desire: Still missing after all these years. *Harvard Educational Review* 76 (3), 297–338.

203 **twenty years of research documents:** Eder, D. (1993). "Go get ya a French!": Romantic and sexual teasing among adolescent girls. In D. Tannen (ed.), *Gender and conversational interaction. Oxford studies in sociolinguistics,* 17–31. New York: Oxford University Press.

203 **psychologists Jennifer Connolly and Adele Goldberg:** Connolly, J. A., and Goldberg, A. (1999). Romantic relationships in adolescence: The role of friends and peers in their emergence and development. In W. Furman, B. B. Brown, and C. Feiring (eds.), *The development of romantic relationships in adolescence.* New York: Cambridge University Press, 266–90.

207 **Music, television, and movie industry executives:** See, for example, Lawrence, J. (2013, August 2). One Direction Could Be the First Boy Band Worth \$1 Billion. *Business Insider.* Retrieved from businessinsider.com/one-direction-worth-1-billion-2013-8 on January 30, 2015.

209 **Some of the best minds:** I refer here to the excellent work of Lyn Mikel Brown, Lisa Diamond, Michelle Fine, Carol Gilligan, Sharon Lamb, Sara McClelland, Deborah Tolman, and others.

210 **Research finds that the more sexist:** Ward, M. L. (2003). Understanding the role of entertainment media in the sexual socialization of American youth: A review of empirical research. *Developmental Review* 23 (3), 347–88.

210 **compared to girls who question chauvinism:** Impett, E. A., Schooler, D., and Tolman, D. L. (2006). To be seen and not heard: Feminist ideology and adolescent girls' sexual health. *Archives of Sexual Behavior* 35 (2), 131–44; Zurbriggen, E. L., Collins, R. L., Lamb, S., et al. (2007). *Report on the APA Task Force on the Sexualization of Girls, Executive Summary.* Washington, DC: American Psychological Association.

210 **psychologists at the University of Michigan:** Fredrickson, B. L., Roberts, T. A., Noll, S. M., et al. (1998). That swimsuit becomes you: Sex differences in self-objectification, restrained eating, and math performance. *Journal of Personality and Social Psychology* 75 (1), 269–84.

212 **author Marybeth Hicks:** M. Hicks, personal communication, October 2009. Marybeth's politics couldn't be more different than mine (I'm

about as liberal as she is conservative), but I agree with her fully on this point.

212 **statistically boys, more than girls:** Peter, J., and Valkenburg, P. M. (2006). Adolescents' exposure to sexually explicit material on the internet. *Communication Research* 33 (2), 178–204.

212 **wide availability of highly explicit:** Zillmann, D. (2000). Influence of unrestrained access to erotica on adolescents' and young adults' dispositions toward sexuality. *Journal of Adolescent Health* 27 (2), 41–44.

213 **Research finds that by fourteen:** Brown, J. D., and L'Engle, K. L. (2009). X-Rated: Sexual attitudes and behaviors associated with U.S. early adolescents' exposure to sexually explicit material. *Communication Research* 36 (1), 129–51.

213 **studies tell us that teens:** Häggström-Nordin, E. (2005). Association between pornography consumption and sexual practices among adolescents in Sweden. *International Journal of STD and AIDS* 16 (2), 102–7.

213 **linked to an increased likelihood:** Brown and L'Engle (2009); Braun-Courville, D. K., and Rojas, M. (2009). Exposure to sexually explicit web sites and adolescent sexual attitudes and behaviors. *Journal of Adolescent Health* 45 (2), 156–62.

214 **repeated requests for nude photos:** Barter, C., and Stanley, N. (2015). *Safeguarding Teenage Intimate Relationships.* Bristol: University of Bristol. Retrieved from www.bristol.ac.uk/news/2015/february/stir-study.html on March 5, 2015.

221 **Reports of the death:** This is, obviously, a play on a famous Mark Twain misquotation: "Reports of my death have been greatly exaggerated."

221 **sexually active outside of ongoing relationships:** Kreagar, D. A., and Staff, J. (2009). The sexual double standard and adolescent peer acceptance. *Social Psychology Quarterly* 72 (2), 143–64; Dunn, H. K., Gjelsvik, A., Pearlman, D. N., and Clark, M. A. (2014). Association between sexual behaviors, bullying victimization and suicidal ideation in a national sample of high school students: Implications of the sexual double standard. *Women's Health Issues* 24 (5), 567–74.

222 **Indeed, studies find that girls:** See, for example, Cornell, J. L., and Halpern-Felsher, B. L. (2006). Adolescents tell us why teens have oral sex. *Journal of Adolescent Health* 38 (3), 299–301; Bay-Cheng, L. Y., and

Fava, N. M. (2011). Young women's experiences and perceptions of cunnilingus during adolescence. *Journal of Sex Research* 48 (6), 531–42.

222 **feel used after having oral sex:** Brady, S. S., and Halpern-Felsher, B. L. (2007). Adolescents' reported consequences of having oral sex versus vaginal sex. *Pediatrics* 119 (2), 229–36. The finding described in the text applies both to oral and vaginal sex.

222 **Research suggests that by having:** Halpern-Felsher, B. L., Cornell, J. L., Kropp, R. Y., and Tschann, J. M. (2005). Oral versus vaginal sex among adolescents: Perceptions, attitudes, and behavior. *Pediatrics* 115 (4), 845–51.

224 **one especially wise mother:** K. Gjaja, personal communication, August 2014.

224 **sometimes establish their in-group status:** See, for example, Tarrant, M., North, A. C., Edridge, M. D., et al. (2001). Social identity in adolescence. *Journal of Adolescence* 24 (5), 597–609.

225 **research finds that people:** Weinstein, N., Ryan, W. S., DeHann, C. R., et al. (2012). Parental autonomy support and discrepancies between implicit and explicit sexual identities: Dynamics of self-acceptance and defense. *Journal of Personality and Social Psychology* 102 (4), 815–32.

225 **research finds that LGBTQ teens:** Legate, N., Ryan, R. M., and Weinstein, N. (2012). Is coming out always a "good thing"? Exploring the relations of autonomy support, outness, and wellness for lesbian, gay, and bisexual individuals. *Social Psychological and Personality Science* 3 (2), 145–52.

226 **teenagers with stronger ties:** Waldner, L. K., and Magruder, B. (1999). Coming out to parents: Perceptions of family relations, perceived resources, and identity expression as predictors of identity disclosure for gay and lesbian adolescents. *Journal of Homosexuality* 37 (2), 83–100.

226 **bullying occurs when a person:** Olweus, D. (1993). *Bullying at School: What we know and what we can do.* Boston, MA: Blackwell.

227 **Half of the LGBTQ adolescents:** Padilla, Y. C., Crisp, C., and Rew, D. L. (2010). Parental acceptance and illegal drug use among gay, lesbian, and bisexual adolescents: Results from a national survey. *Social Work* 55 (3), 265–75.

227 **elevated alcohol and drug use among LGBTQ:** See, for example, Marshal, M. P., Friedman, M. S., Stall, R., et al. (2008). Sexual orientation

and adolescent substance use: A meta-analysis and methodological review. *Addiction* 103 (4), 546–56.

227 **research also finds that parental acceptance:** Padilla et al. (2010); Ryan, C., Russell, S. T., Huebner, D., et al. (2010). Family acceptance in adolescence and the health of LGBTQ young adults. *Journal of Child and Adolescent Psychiatric Nursing* 23 (4), 205–13.

233 **research consistently shows that girls:** See, for example, Walsh, J. L., Ward, L. M., Caruthers, A., and Merriwether, A. (2011). Awkward or amazing: Gender and age trends in first intercourse experiences. *Psychology of Women Quarterly* 35 (1), 59–71.

234 **People feel good about themselves:** This wisdom comes from Jim Hansell, one of the critical mentors in my life and career, who made this point while supervising my psychotherapeutic work with a young woman who had robbed herself of every available source of self-esteem and was, not surprisingly, very depressed.

236 **girls, on average, hit puberty:** Tanner, J. M. (1981). Growth and maturation in adolescence. *Nutrition Reviews* (39) 2, 43–55.

236 **dating older guys increases the chances:** For an excellent summary of the findings on this topic, see Haydon, A. A., and Halpern, C. T. (2010). Older romantic partners and depressive symptoms during adolescence. *Journal of Youth and Adolescence* 39 (10), 1240–51.

Chapter Seven: Caring for Herself

238 **Anna Freud described:** Freud, A. (1965). *Normality and Pathology in Childhood: Assessments of development.* New York: International Universities Press, pp. 75–76. The developmental strand of learning to care for oneself extends upon the developmental line "From Irresponsibility to Responsibility in Body Management" articulated by Ms. Freud. She felt less optimistic than I do about teenagers' capacity to take over the work of looking after themselves, stating, "Children will be remarkably uncompromising and obstructive in health matters. According to their mothers' frequent complaints, they behave as if they claimed it as their right to endanger their health while they left it to their mothers to protect and restore it, an attitude which lasts often until the end of

adolescence and may represent the last residue of the original symbiosis between child and mother," p. 77.

242 **a group of Harvard researchers:** Becker, A. E., Burwell, R. A., Herzog, D. B., et al. (2002). Eating behaviours and attitudes following prolonged exposure to television among ethnic Fijian adolescent girls. *British Journal of Psychiatry* 180 (6), 509–14.

242 **Yet during research interviews:** Becker et al. (2002), p. 513.

242 **The more girls are exposed:** Stice, E., and Shaw, H. E. (1994). Adverse effects of the media portrayed thin-ideal on women and linkages to bulimic symptomatology. *Journal of Social and Clinical Psychology* 13 (3), 288–308.

242 **the effects of visual media:** Baker, D., Sivyer, R., and Towell. T. (1998). Body image dissatisfaction and eating attitudes in visually impaired women. *International Journal of Eating Disorders* 24 (3), 319–22.

243 **are more likely to feel dissatisfied:** Shroff, H., and Thompson, J. K., (2006). Peer influences, body-image dissatisfaction, eating dysfunction and self-esteem in adolescent girls. *Journal of Health Psychology* 11 (4), 533–51.

243 **study with one of my favorite:** Kelly, A. M., Wall, M., Eisenberg, M. E., et al. (2005). Adolescent girls with high body satisfaction: Who are they and what can they teach us? *Journal of Adolescent Health* 37 (5), 391–96.

247 **recent research evidence finds that:** Neumark-Sztainer, D., Croll, J., Story, M., et al. (2002). Ethnic/racial differences in weight-related concerns and behaviors among adolescent girls and boys: Findings from Project EAT. *Journal of Psychosomatic Research* 53 (5), 963–74.

248 **teenagers need about *nine* hours:** Roberts, R. E., Roberts, C. R., and Duong, H. T. (2009). Sleepless in adolescence: Prospective data on sleep deprivation, health and functioning. *Journal of Adolescence* 32 (5), 1045–57; Johnson, E. O., Roth, T., Schultz, L., and Breslau, N. (2006). Epidemiology of DSM-IV insomnia in adolescence: Lifetime prevalence, chronicity, and an emergent gender difference. *Pediatrics* 117 (2), 247–56.

249 **body stops recognizing the bed:** LeBourgeois, M. K., Giannotti, F., Cortesi, F., et al. (2005). The relationship between reported sleep quality and sleep hygiene in Italian and American adolescents. *Pediatrics* 115 (1), 257–65.

249 **research indicates that the blue-spectrum:** Higuchi, S., Motohashi, Y., Liu, Y., et al. (2003). Effects of VDT tasks with a bright display at night

on melatonin, core temperature, heart rate, and sleepiness. *Journal of Applied Physiology* 94 (5), 1773–76; Kozaki, T., Koga, S., Toda, N., et al. (2008). Effects of short wavelength control in polychromatic light sources on nocturnal melatonin secretion. *Neuroscience Letters* 439 (3), 256–59.

252 **roughly 80 percent of adolescents:** Swendsen, J., Burstein, M., Case, B., et al. (2012). Use and abuse of alcohol and illicit drugs in US adolescents. *Archives of General Psychiatry* 69 (4), 390–98.

252 **White teens are significantly more likely:** Blum, R. W., Beuhring, T., Shew, M. L., et al. (2000). The effects of race/ethnicity, income, and family structure on adolescent risk behaviors. *American Journal of Public Health* 90 (12), 1897–84.

252 **more likely to drink if their friends do:** Osgood, D. W., Ragan, D. T., Wallace, L., et al. (2013). Peers and the emergence of alcohol use: Influence and selection processes in adolescent friendship networks. *Journal of Research on Adolescence* 23 (3), 500–512.

253 **structures associated with feelings of reward:** Pascual, M., Boix, J., Felipo, V., and Guerri, C. (2009). Repeated alcohol administration during adolescence causes changes in the mesolimbic dopaminergic and glutamatergic systems and promotes alcohol intake in the adult rat. *Journal of Neurochemistry* 108 (4), 920–31.

254 **harms the developing brain:** Silveri, M. M. (2012). Adolescent brain development and underage drinking in the United States: Identifying risks of alcohol use in college populations. *Harvard Review of Psychiatry* 20 (4), 189–200.

255 **heavy drinking can damage:** See, for example, Brown, S. A., Tapert, S. F., Granholm, E., and Delis, D. C. (2000). Neurocognitive functioning of adolescents: Effects of protracted alcohol use. *Alcoholism: Clinical and Experimental Research* 24 (2), 164–71.

255 **impaired driving or drinking to the point of death:** Kann, L., Kinchen, S., and Shanklin, S., et al. (2014). Youth Risk Behavior Surveillance—United States, 2013. *MMWR Surveillance Summaries* 63 (4), 1–178.

262 **Recent large-scale surveys:** Johnston, L. D., O'Malley, P. M., Bachman, J. G., et al. (2014). *Monitoring the Future: National survey results on drug use, 1975–2013. Volume I, Secondary school students.* Ann Arbor: Institute for Social Research, The University of Michigan.

262 **marijuana causes much less societal harm:** Nutt, D. J., King, L. A., and

Philips, L. D. (2010). Drug harms in the UK: A multicriteria decision analysis. *The Lancet* 376 (9752), 1558–65.

262 **toxic to the maturing adolescent brain:** See, for example, Gruber, S. A., Sagar, K. A., Dahlgren, M. K., et al. (2012). Age of onset of marijuana use and executive function. *Psychology of Addictive Behaviors* 26 (3), 496–506.

262 **An extraordinary research program:** Meier, M. H., Caspi, A., Ambler, A., et al. (2012). Persistent cannabis users show neuropsychological decline from childhood to midlife. *Proceedings of the National Academy of Sciences* 109 (40), E2657–64.

263 **using pot regularly as a teenager:** Jacobus, J., Bava, S., Cohen-Zion, M., et al. (2009). Functional consequences of marijuana use in adolescents. *Pharmacology Biochemistry and Behavior* 92 (4), 559–65.

263 **you might find yourself thinking:** Rates for marijuana use in the 1980s and 1990s hovered, like today's rates, around 40 percent: Johnston, L. D., O'Malley, P. M., and Bachman, J. G. (2000). *Monitoring the Future: National Results on Adolescent Drug Use: Overview of Key Findings, 1999.* U.S. Department of Health and Human Services, National Institute on Drug Abuse.

263 *seven* **times more potent:** It's not entirely clear why marijuana has become so much more potent since the 1970s, but current hypotheses point to shifts in where the cannabis supply comes from (from foreign to domestic) and/or increasingly sophisticated cultivation techniques. Sevigny, E. L. (2013). Is today's marijuana more potent simply because it's fresher? *Drug Testing and Analysis* 5 (1), 62–67.

263 **concentrated marijuana known as "wax":** See, for example, Schneberk, T., Sterling, G. P., Valenzuela, R., and Mallon, W. K. (2014). 390 "A little dab will do ya": An emergency department case series related to a new form of "high-potency" marijuana known as "wax." *Annals of Emergency Medicine* 64 (4), S139.

264 **the effects of the substance:** See, for example, Zawilska, J. B., and Wojcieszak, J. (2014). Spice/K2 drugs—More than innocent substitutes for marijuana. *International Journal of Neuropsychopharmacology* 17 (3), 509–25; Bauman, J. L., and DiDomenico, R. J. (2002). Cocaine-induced channelopathies: Emerging evidence on the multiple mechanisms of sudden death. *Journal of Cardiovascular Pharmacology and Therapeutics* 7

(3), 195–202; Verheyden, S. L., Hadfield, J., Calin, T., and Curran, H. V. (2002). Sub-acute effects of MDMA (+3,4-methylenedioxymethamphetamine, "ecstasy") on mood: Evidence of gender differences. *Psychopharmacology* 161 (1), 23–31.

264 **hijack the brain's pleasure centers:** See, for example, Robinson, T. E., and Berridge, K. C. (1993). The neural basis of drug craving: An incentive-sensitization theory of addiction. *Brain Research Reviews* 18 (3), 247–91.

265 **nearly four times more likely:** Edwards, E., Bunting, W., and Garcia, L. (2013). *The War on Marijuana in Black and White*. New York: American Civil Liberties Union.

265 **Taking unprescribed stimulants:** Pilkinton, M., and Cannatella, A. (2012). Nonmedical use of prescription stimulants: Age, race, gender, and educational attainment patterns. *Journal of Human Behavior in the Social Environment* 22 (4), 409–20.

265 **stimulant medication has been associated:** Morton, W. A., and Stockton, G. G. (2000). Methylphenidate abuse and psychiatric side effects. *Primary Care Companion to the Journal of Clinical Psychiatry* 2 (5), 159–64.

265 **increase the risk of cardiac complications:** Kaye, S., and Darke, S. (2012). The diversion and misuse of pharmaceutical stimulants: What do we know and why should we care? *Addiction* 107 (3), 467–77.

269 **most compelling and inventive research studies:** Kearney, M. S., and Levine, P. B. (2014). Media Influences on Social Outcomes: The Impact of MTV's *16 and Pregnant* on Teen Childbearing. Presented at the NBER Working Paper Series, National Bureau of Economic Research.

270 *16 and Pregnant* **first aired:** *16 and Pregnant*. MTV, June 11, 2009.

270 **tweets included in the research report:** Kearney and Levine (2014), appendix B.

271 **research shows that teens care:** See, for example, Blake, S. M., Simkin, L., Ledsky, R., et al. (2001). Effects of a parent-child communications intervention on young adolescents' risk for early onset of sexual intercourse. *Family Planning Perspectives* 33 (2), 52–61.

271 **research consistently suggests that the older:** Mitchell, K., and Wellings, K. (1998). First sexual intercourse: Anticipation and communication. *Journal of Adolescence* 21 (6), 717–26.

273 **one nationally representative survey:** Albert, B. (2010). *With One Voice 2010: America's Adults and Teens Sound Off About Teen Pregnancy.* Washington, DC: The National Campaign to Prevent Teen and Unplanned Pregnancy.

274 **a third of people who develop an eating disorder:** Keel, P. K., and Brown, T. A. (2010). Update on course and outcome in eating disorders. *International Journal of Eating Disorders* 43 (3), 195–204.

274 **For roughly every twenty people:** Smink, F. R. E., van Hoeken, D., and Hoek, H. W. (2012). Epidemiology of eating disorders: Incidence, prevalence, and mortality rates. *Current Psychiatric Reports* 14 (4), 406–14.

Recommended Resources

Chapter One: Parting with Childhood

Harris, R. H., and Emberley, M. (2009). *It's Perfectly Normal: Growing bodies, growing up, sex, and sexual health*. Somerville, MA: Candlewick Press.

Lamb, S., and Brown, L. M. (2006). *Packaging Girlhood: Rescuing our daughters from marketers' schemes*. New York: St. Martin's Press.

Natterson, C., and Masse, J. (2013). *The Care and Keeping of You 2: The body book for older girls*. Rev. ed. Middleton, WI: American Girl Publishing.

Schaefer, V., and Masse, J. (2012). *The Care and Keeping of You: The body book for younger girls*. Rev. ed. Middleton, WI: American Girl Publishing.

Chapter Two: Joining a New Tribe

Boyd, D. (2015). *It's Complicated: The social lives of networked teens*. New Haven, CT: Yale University Press.

Simmons, R. (2011). *Odd Girl Out, Revised and Updated: The hidden culture of aggression in girls*. New York: First Mariner Books.

Thompson, M., Grace, C. O., and Cohen, L. J. (2002). *Best Friends, Worst Enemies: Understanding the social lives of children*. New York: Ballantine Books.

Wiseman, R. (2009). *Queen Bees and Wannabes: Helping your daughter survive cliques, gossip, boyfriends, and the new realities of girl world.* New York: Three Rivers Press.

Chapter Three: Harnessing Emotions

Foa, E. B., and Andrews, L. W. (2006). *If Your Adolescent Has an Anxiety Disorder: An essential resource for parents.* New York: Oxford University Press.

Hollander, M. (2008). *Helping Teens Who Cut: Understanding and ending self-injury.* New York: The Guilford Press.

Machoian, L. (2006). *The Disappearing Girl: Learning the language of teenage depression.* New York: Dutton.

Siegel, D. J. (2014). *Brainstorm: The power and purpose of the teenage brain.* New York: Jeremy P. Tarcher.

Chapter Four: Contending with Adult Authority

Barkley, R. A., Robin, A. L., and Benton, C. M. (2013). *Your Defiant Teen, Second Edition: 10 steps to resolve conflict and rebuild your relationship.* New York: The Guilford Press.

Brown, L. M., and Gilligan, C. (1993). *Meeting at the Crossroads: Women's psychology and girls' development.* New York: Ballantine Books.

Simmons, R. (2010). *The Curse of the Good Girl: Raising authentic girls with courage and confidence.* New York: The Penguin Press.

Chapter Five: Planning for the Future

Cooper-Kahn, J., and Dietzel, L. (2008). *Late, Lost, and Unprepared: A parents' guide to helping children with executive functioning.* Bethesda, MD: Woodbine House.

Dweck, C. S. (2006). *Mindset: The new psychology of success.* New York: Ballantine Books.

Silver, L. B. (2006). *The Misunderstood Child, Fourth Edition: Understanding and coping with your child's learning disabilities.* New York: Three Rivers Press.

Chapter Six: Entering the Romantic World

Durham, M. G. (2008). *The Lolita Effect: The media sexualization of young girls and what we can do about it.* New York: The Overlook Press.

Levin, D. E., and Kilbourne, J. (2009). *So Sexy, So Soon: The new sexualized childhood and what parents can do to protect their kids.* New York: Ballantine Books.

Orenstein, P. (2011). *Cinderella Ate My Daughter.* New York: Harper.

Tolman, D. L. (2005). *Dilemmas of Desire: Teenage girls talk about sexuality.* Cambridge, MA: Harvard University Press.

Chapter Seven: Caring for Herself

Jensen, F. E., and Nutt, A. E. (2015). *The Teenage Brain: A neuroscientist's guide to raising adolescents and young adults.* New York: Harper.

Kuhn, C., Swartzwelder, S., and Wilson, W. (2002). *Just Say Know: Talking with kids about drugs and alcohol.* New York: W. W. Norton & Co.

Lock, J., and Le Grange, D. (2015). *Help Your Teenager Beat an Eating Disorder, Second Edition.* New York: The Guilford Press.

Pipher, M. (2005). *Reviving Ophelia: Saving the selves of adolescent girls.* New York: Riverhead Books.

Index

About the Author

Lisa Damour, Ph.D., directs Laurel School's Center for Research on Girls, maintains a private psychotherapy practice where she specializes in working with teenage girls, and consults and speaks internationally. Dr. Damour is also a faculty associate of the Schubert Center for Child Studies and a clinical instructor in the Department of Psychological Sciences at Case Western Reserve University. She lives with her husband and two daughters in Shaker Heights, Ohio.

drlisadamour.com